SIMON FRASER UNIVERSITY LIBRARY

Unless recalled, all materials
due on last date stamped

Solving Business Problems with MRP II

Solving Business Problems with MRP II

A L A N   D .   L U B E R

Digital Press • Bedford, Massachusetts

Printed in the United States of America.

9   8   7   6   5   4   3   2   1

Order number EY-F582E-DP

The Digital logo is a trademark of Digital Equipment Corporation. Other trademarks and trademarked products mentioned in this book include: IDMS, a trademark of Cullinet division of Computer Associates; DATACOM/DB, a trademark of Applied Data Research, Inc.; and IMS, a trademark of International Business Machines Corporation.

Views expressed in this book are those of the author, not of the publisher. Digital Equipment Corporation is not responsible for any errors that may appear in this book.

Design: Sandra Calef
Production: Editorial Services of New England, Inc.
Composition: Editorial Services of New England, using Ventura Publisher®
Printer: Hamilton Printing Company

Library of Congress Cataloging-in-Publication Data:

Luber, Alan, 1951–
    Solving business problems with MRP II / by Alan Luber.
        p.   cm.
    Includes bibliographical references (p.) and index.
    ISBN 1-55558-058-0 :
        1. Business—Data processing.   I. Title.
HF5548.2.L78   1990
658'.05—dc20   90-46063
                                                                              CIP

This book is dedicated to my wife, Eleanor, and my children, Michelle, Jessica, and Mallory, who gave me the time and space to complete this project.

Contents

Foreword

In the past decade manufacturing companies have searched frantically for tools to gain better control of their businesses. Since their businesses appeared complex, they looked for complex solutions. Many companies mistakenly assumed that complex meant computerized. They bought a computer, bought software, and bought disappointment. Next, they bought new software, a larger computer, and even more frustration! And, of course, the blame was pinned squarely on the computer and the software.

The focus was on "installation." Manufacturers did not take time to sit down and look at how they ran their businesses, their management problems, and the solutions they needed to solve the problems. They simply tried to install solutions. In short, they saw computers and software as the solution, rather than as tools.

In reality, software and computers are part of the solution but not the whole solution.

Fortunately, other companies have taken a different approach. They have used the computer's capability to calculate and communicate at the speed of light to their advantage. They realized that the only constant in the world of manufacturing is change—in forecasts, customer orders, bills of material and so forth. The issue is not whether things will change, it's how to profitably manage change. Computer horsepower provides the capability to digest changes, make new plans and communicate them quickly. The advent of Manufacturing Resource Planning (MRP II) has brought an organized approach to managing change. In the words of Dr. Edward Deming, "We can now reduce the variation and bring the process under control." In this case, the variation is not in product quality, but in schedules, inventory records, profits, and so on.

Companies that effectively harness the computer's power have realized that the key is more than having a computer. Valid data, policies for managing their master schedules, and a valid simulation of what is really needed and when are essential.

This book is an excellent tool for helping companies bridge the gap between what computers and software can do and the job that good managers must do. It provides the reader clear direction on how to use the information generated by a good MRP II system and how to make the enhancements necessary to make the system more effective. This is an invaluable handbook for applying the power of MRP II to the bottom line, while vaulting your company out in front in the competitive race.

Dave Garwood
Atlanta, Georgia

Preface

A few years ago, as a manufacturing consultant for a well-known applications software company, my job was to turn prospects into actual customers by extolling the many virtues of our Manufacturing Resource Planning (MRP II) system. One of my less interesting and less productive responsibilities was to respond to requests for proposals (RFPs) received from companies that were evaluating MRP II packages. Invariably, each RFP would require that the software vendor respond to a list of hundreds of features. The company would weigh and rate the responses and, presumably, use the results to narrow the field down to a few software vendors. The vendors that made the short list would be given further consideration.

One day while I was responding to a particularly long laundry list of features, a number of questions occurred to me:

- How many of the features on this list will the customer actually use?

- Of these features, which ones are really required to help the customer solve critical business problems?

- Are there other features not on the list that the customer needs to solve business problems?

- How many times has my company been eliminated from an evaluation based on our response to the RFP, even though we might have had the best solution for the business problems?

I contacted our salesman and suggested that we would have a better chance of winning the business if we refused to respond to the RFP.

"Are you out of your mind!" he yelled. "The customer is going to eliminate us from the evaluation if we don't respond by next Thursday."

"If we respond to the RFP, the customer is going to eliminate us anyway," I explained. "There are too many features that the customer has asked for that we don't have. We're never going to make the short list based on our response."

"Then what do you suggest?" the salesman asked.

"Tell the customer that we have a number of questions regarding the RFP, and that we would like to spend a day with them to learn more about their business issues in order to do a better job of responding to the RFP."

A visit was arranged, and I was able to interview a number of key managers to determine what business problems the customer was trying to solve. When I responded to the RFP, instead of responding negatively to a number of questions, I was able to write:

"We do not have this feature, but we can address your business problem of material shortages in the following way. . ."

Or,

"We do not have this feature, but this feature is not required to address your material shortage or customer service problem, which you indicated were your two critical business problems."

Or,

"We have this feature, but you will probably not use it to solve your business problems." (This type of response always enhanced our credibility.)

Or,

"Here are some additional features that we have that you did not ask about, but which we feel are critical to help you solve your customer service problem . . ."

We won the business, but more importantly, this experience gave me the idea to write this book.

Experiences with other companies that were either evaluating manufacturing software or attempting to implement our MRP II system convinced me that most companies simply don't understand how to apply the capabilities of an MRP II software package to solve their business problems. In fact, most companies don't take the time (or seek the help) to understand what is causing their problems. It's impossible to have a vision of a solution unless the cause is clear.

The fact that most companies don't know how to use MRP II software to help solve their business problems is not surprising when you consider the following:

MRP II software packages have thousands of features that can easily confuse the user. Most companies need to use only a small percentage of these features to solve their business problems. But a company can easily be overwhelmed by the functionality in an MRP II package and not understand how to selectively use the package's capabilities.

Many MRP II software vendors sell features instead of benefits. They don't take the time to understand what the customer really needs, and they may spend hours discussing and demonstrating features that are unimportant to the customer. (My favorite story—and it is absolutely true—is that of a consultant who was demonstrating a software package to a prospect. "You're not a hospital," he said, "but if you were, you would really like this feature." He went on for ten minutes to describe a feature that he had just admitted had no relevance to the customer. If the customer was confused *before* the presentation, you can imagine how he felt *after* the presentation.)

There is no MRP II literature available that shows companies how to use the capabilities of an MRP II package to solve their business problems. On the one hand, there are excellent textbooks such as *Manufacturing Planning and Control Systems* by Vollmann, Berry, and Whybark. Such books do an outstanding job of explaining the mechanics of MRP II systems, but they lack practical advice on how to use specific features to solve specific business problems.

On the other hand, there are some very good "how to" books such as *The Right Choice: A Complete Guide to Evaluating and Installing MRP II Software* by Christopher Gray. But even the available "how to" books don't show companies how to solve their business problems.

Gray makes some excellent points about the importance of going beyond the checklist approach described earlier to make certain that the underlying logic of the system works properly. He points out that a vendor might answer "yes" to a question, but further investigation might determine that the feature was not designed properly. He also notes that some vendors will answer "yes" to almost every item on a checklist to avoid being eliminated early in the evaluation, and hope to explain the discrepancies and misunderstandings later in the sales cycle. To avoid this situation, Gray advocates that customers obtain a complete copy of the vendor's system documentation (under a nondisclosure agreement) and answer their own checklist.

Gray discusses other important issues that should be considered in a software evaluation, such as the financial stability of the software vendor, the ease with which modifications can be made, and the quality of the vendor's support. He also explains how to go about negotiating a software contract.

All this is good practical advice, but the "how to" advice stops short of how to identify and apply the features needed to solve business problems.

I decided to write this book to fill the MRP II literature void. This book is based on my experience as a user of manufacturing software, my knowledge of MRP II software packages, and my experience as a manufacturing consultant. Throughout the book I present scenarios to show how some common business problems arise. To avoid using the clumsy construction he/she I have often used the male pronoun, although I am aware of the increasing number of women involved in manufacturing management and do not mean to exclude them in any way. I hope that this book will put the emphasis back where it should have always been—on solving business problems.

A.L.
August 1990

Abbreviations

ANSI	American National Standards Institute
ATP	Available-to-promise
BOM	Bill of materials
CAPP	Computer aided process planning
CEO	Chief executive officer
CFO	Chief financial officer
CIM	Computer integrated manufacturing
EDI	Electronic data interchange
FIFO	First-in/first-out
ID	Identification
JIT	Just-in-time
MIS	Management information systems
MRP	Material requirements planning
MRP II	Manufacturing resource planning
MPS	Master production schedule
OEM	Original equipment manufacturer
PO	Purchase order
RCCP	Rough cut capacity planning
RFP	Request for proposal
RFQ	Request for quote
SPC	Statistical process control

Introduction

W*e don't have an MRP II system, but we would like to know how an MRP II software package might help us solve our business problems."*

"We are currently evaluating MRP II software packages, and we want to know what features we should look for to help us solve our business problems. We would also like to know how to determine if the features that we need have been designed properly by the software vendor."

"We recently implemented an MRP II software package. Frankly, the results have been less than spectacular. We still have material shortages, and our inventory turns are still far higher than the average for our industry. We know that we purchased a good system, and although we followed the vendor's instructions for a successful implementation, we can't seem to get the benefits we expected."

If one of the above statements applies to your company, then you will benefit from this book.

This book is intended for all manufacturing company managers who are responsible for solving such business problems as material shortages, high inventory, poor customer service, low productivity, rising material costs, and poor quality. The following business managers are included:

- Chief Executive Officer (CEO)
- Chief Financial Officer (CFO)
- Manager of Manufacturing
- Manager of Shop Operations
- Manager of Materials
- Manager of Inventory Control
- Manager of Material Control
- Manager of Purchasing

- Manager of Marketing
- Manager of Customer Service
- Manager of Quality Control
- Manager of Information Systems

(Some organizations may use different job titles to refer to these positions. For example, some companies might have a Vice President of Manufacturing or a Production Manager instead of a Manager of Manufacturing.)

This book is also intended for manufacturing consultants who want to better advise their clients on how to use the capabilities of an MRP II package to help solve their business problems.

Prerequisites

A basic knowledge of the principles of MRP II will be helpful, but it is not necessary for you to be an MRP II expert to understand and apply the solutions presented in this book. For those of you who want to understand the mechanics of MRP II systems, a bibliography that includes MRP II textbooks appears in Appendix F.

This book assumes the following:

- You understand the basic functions of the modules of an MRP II system.
- You have a good understanding of the roles of each organization in a manufacturing company.
- You are familiar with manufacturing terminology. Terms that you may not be familiar with are defined the first time they are used.

Problem Ownership and Integration

Each manager in a manufacturing company "owns" or is responsible for solving certain business problems. For example, the material shortages problem is typically the responsibility of the Manager of Materials and his direct reports, the Manager of Material Control, and the Manager of Purchasing. However, the business problems of manufacturers are highly integrated. This means that one manager's business problem is often the cause of another manager's problem. For example, the Manager of Manufacturing and the Manager of Customer Service are concerned about material shortages because they can result in missed shipments and poor customer service. The Manager of Quality Control is concerned about material shortages because they can result in the improper and unauthorized substitution of components, which can cause a quality problem.

You are probably familiar with a diagram that is commonly used to show the relationship between assemblies and components on a bill of materials (BOM). This diagram, called a **Product Structure Diagram,** is shown in Figure 1.1. A similar diagram can be used to show the relationship between business problems in the company. I call it a **Problem Structure Diagram** (Figure 1.2). To carry the analogy further, an assembly on a product structure diagram may be comprised of other assemblies and purchased components. Similarly, a business problem may be comprised of (caused by) other business problems and root (component) causes of the problem. *It should be clear from the problem structure diagram that the key to solving the business problems is to find solutions for all the root causes.*

I do not intend to imply that an MRP II system can provide solutions for all root causes. An MRP II system will not solve problems that are caused by poor procedures, invalid business measurements, or bad management. At one company where I worked, the manager of the printed circuit-board manufacturing

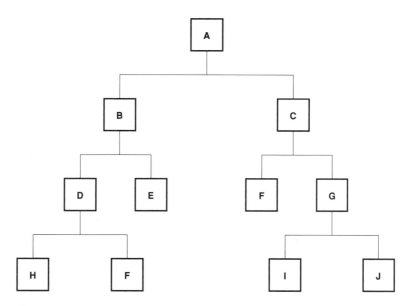

Figure 1.1
Product Structure Diagram

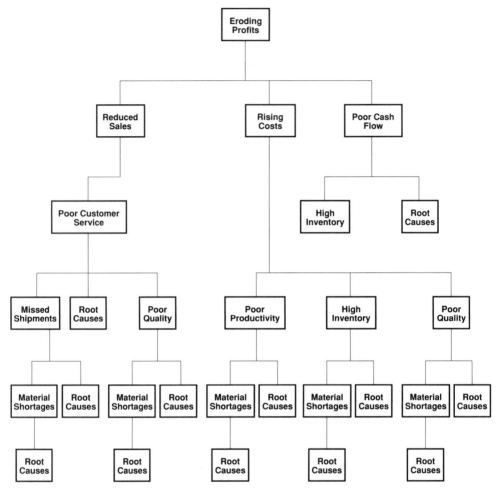

Figure 1.2
Problem Structure Diagram

operation was evaluated on the number of boards produced per week. The manager met his production quota by producing the boards that were easiest to make. By producing what was easy to make instead of what was required, the manager caused a material shortage problem, an inventory problem, and a customer service problem. The manager's actions were driven by an invalid business measurement.

This book will focus on the root causes of business problems that *can* be addressed by MRP II.

How This Book Is Organized

This book explains how to use the capabilities of an MRP II system to help solve the following business problems:

- Material shortages

- High inventory

- Poor quality

- Poor customer service

- Poor productivity

- Poor cash management

A separate chapter is devoted to each of these problems. Each chapter defines a problem, identifies some of the major root causes, and presents solutions (problem-solving features) found in most MRP II packages.

Certain features apply to more than one business problem. For example, the Planner Action Report (see Chapter 2) can help solve both the material shortages problem and the inventory problem. The first time a feature is presented in this book, it is explained in detail. If the feature is referred to again in subsequent chapters, only the application of the feature is discussed; you are referred to an earlier chapter for the explanation of the feature. In many cases, caveats are provided to help you determine if the feature has been properly designed by the software vendor, or to advise you about certain limitations found in MRP II packages.

The problems are discussed in order from the bottom to the top of the problem structure diagram. In this way, the problems discussed in earlier chapters help build a solution foundation for the problems discussed in later chapters.

The solutions presented are found in the various software modules that comprise an MRP II system (Figure 1.3). While some purists might argue that two of the modules shown in Figure 1.3 (the Electronic Data Interchange and the Management Reporting System) are not part of an MRP II system, they are such an integral part of an MRP II system that they must be included in any discussion of solutions. Most MRP II software packages include a Management Reporting System and on-line query tools that allow end users to query the database and write reports that help them solve their business problems. An increasing number of MRP II software vendors are also offering an Electronic Data Interchange module that enables companies to integrate their MRP II systems with their vendors' and customers' MRP II systems.

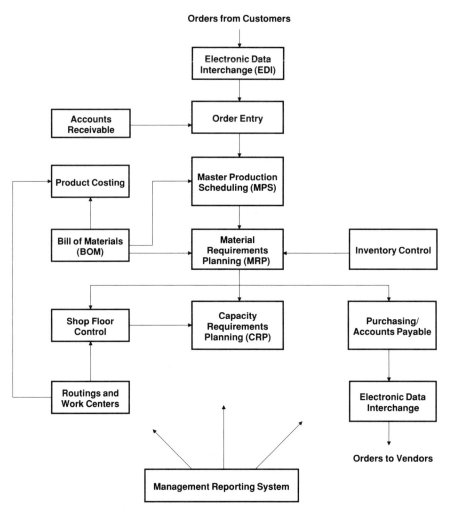

Figure 1.3
Manufacturing Resource Planning (MRP) II
System Diagram

MRP II Packages and Homegrown Computer Systems

Frequent comparisons appear throughout this book between MRP II software packages and "homegrown" computer systems (systems that are developed in-house). My intent in this book is not to denigrate all homegrown systems with these comparisons. Some companies have developed systems that match or surpass the functionality, quality, and ease of use of MRP II software packages. Such companies would have little to gain by replacing their systems with a commercial MRP II software package. However, the vast majority of homegrown systems do not seem to compare favorably to MRP II software packages for the following reasons.

Homegrown systems often lack realtime functionality. Most homegrown systems are ten to twenty years old and were not developed using realtime technology. They do not provide users with timely information needed to make business decisions.

Homegrown systems are often poorly documented. The systems have been modified significantly over a period of years, and the documentation has not been updated to reflect changes.

Homegrown systems are often difficult to maintain. Many of the parameters that control the system processing logic of MRP II packages are stored in tables external to the application programs. This enables end users to make many changes without the support of a skilled programmer. In homegrown systems, the parameters that control system logic are often "buried" in the application programs, making it difficult to modify the system to meet changing business needs.

Homegrown systems are also difficult to maintain because they tend to be poorly documented, and the original developers of the system may have left the company. Once, when I worked for GE, I asked Management Information Systems (MIS) to add a new user ID to our purchasing system. Normally, MIS responded to this type of request in less than a day. This time, however, it took MIS three weeks to complete the request. The programmer who normally performed this task had left the company, leaving no documentation behind on how to add new user IDs to the system.

Homegrown systems are often poorly integrated. Most homegrown systems are developed over a period of many years. The resulting system is a hodgepodge of modules that were developed in different programming languages, on different operating systems, and using different hardware. Such systems are very difficult to integrate.

Homegrown systems often have redundant databases. Because the systems are not integrated, data has to be stored and maintained redundantly in several systems. For example, it is not unusual to find multiple item master files and bill of materials files in homegrown systems.

Homegrown systems are often incomplete. Some modules may be missing due to long development cycles.

Homegrown systems are often difficult to use. The lack of up-to-date user documentation makes it difficult for new employees to learn how to use the system.

Homegrown systems may also be difficult to use because complex layers of logic have been added to the system over the years (often to correct deficiencies in the original design). Over time, the systems have become so complex that the users can no longer understand how they work. In one company I worked for, the system logic was so complicated that the master scheduler needed a master's degree to use the master scheduling system.

Homegrown systems often contain serious design flaws. Many homegrown systems aren't developed from a functional specification and design specification; they merely evolve over time. Such systems often have fundamental flaws that have a negative impact on the business for years.

The following list summarizes the problems associated with many homegrown systems. Comparisons in this book between MRP II packages and homegrown systems apply only to systems that have most of these characteristics.

1. Lack of realtime functionality

2. Poor documentation

3. Difficult maintenance

4. Lack of integration

5. Redundant databases or files

6. One or more modules missing

7. Difficult operation

8. Fundamental design flaws

MRP II and Just-in-Time (JIT)

The Goal of JIT

Simply stated, the goal of JIT is to eliminate waste, where waste is broadly defined as "anything that adds unnecessary expense to the product." A JIT management philosophy views inventory as waste, because inventory carrying costs add unnecessary expense to the product. A JIT approach to manufacturing attempts to reduce inventory by purchasing and producing only *what* is needed *when* it is needed. However, JIT is much more than a zero inventory program. Some of the major causes of waste that a JIT management philosophy tries to eliminate are

1. Expediting

2. Incoming inspection

3. Materials handling

4. Manufacturing setup costs

5. Scrap and rework

6. Excessive inventory

7. Excessive overhead costs in such functions as design engineering, manufacturing engineering, purchasing, accounts payable, order entry, and information systems

The Groundless Conflict

Some people believe that an inherent conflict exists between an MRP II system and a just-in-time management philosophy. They have been led to this incorrect conclusion by

- JIT consultants who do not understand MRP II

- MRP II consultants who do not understand JIT

- Software vendors who are trying to make money by repackaging existing features of an MRP II system into a JIT module

JIT consultants who do not understand MRP II. Some JIT consultants don't understand the philosophy behind MRP II. They incorrectly describe MRP II systems as "just-in-case" material control systems that cause manufacturers to buy and make more than what is needed, thereby adding unnecessary expense to the product.

Ironically, MRP II systems were specifically developed to enable companies to purchase and produce what is needed when it is needed. Prior to MRP, most companies operated with order-point material control systems. Order-point systems truly are just-in-case systems because they ignore the concept of dependent demand. By treating each item as if its demand were independent of the demand for other items, order-point systems frequently resulted in excessive inventory.

MRP II systems operate on the principle of dependent demand. They use a time-phased order-point approach that enables a company to schedule material to be delivered just-in-time.[1]

MRP II consultants who do not understand JIT. Some MRP II consultants view JIT as an inventory reduction system intended to shift inventory back onto the suppliers.

JIT is not an inventory reduction system. Rather it is a management philosophy that focuses on eliminating anything that does not add value to the product. JIT programs are not designed to force the burden of inventory carrying costs back onto suppliers. In fact, JIT works best when a company's suppliers and customers are also committed to the JIT management philosophy.

Software vendors who develop JIT software modules. Some software vendors have added to the confusion surrounding MRP II and JIT by "developing" JIT software modules.[2] If MRP II really works, one wonders, why would MRP II software vendors need to develop another system to help companies implement JIT?

The plain truth is that some MRP II software vendors are trying to cash in on the popularity of JIT by repackaging standard features (features that have been available for years in the better MRP II software packages) into a separate module and charging customers extra for these features. Some of these features are

1. Backflushing
2. Lead time offset
3. Phantom assemblies
4. Production schedules
5. Gateway reporting
6. Point of usage code
7. Floorstock replenishment
8. Concurrent and overlapping operations scheduling
9. Multiple ship schedules
10. Automatic routing of receipts to the production line

1. A few older MRP II systems are only capable of scheduling weekly deliveries of material. Such systems conflict with the JIT management philosophy. Today, most MRP II systems are capable of scheduling daily deliveries.

2. Some MRP II vendors use the term **repetitive manufacturing** instead of JIT, because one of the objectives of JIT is to streamline the manufacturing process to achieve the efficiencies of repetitive manufacturing.

A brief explanation of these features and their relationship to JIT follows. Many of these features are explained in more detail later in this book under the discussion of specific business problems.

Backflushing. Backflushing is the ability to automatically report labor and inventory consumption based on reported production quantities. This eliminates the indirect labor required to post inventory issues.

Lead time offset. Lead time offset is a feature that allows components (on a single-level bill of materials) that are not needed at the beginning of the assembly cycle to be scheduled for later delivery. This reduces inventory by scheduling just-in-time delivery of parts.

Phantom assemblies. This feature allows companies to structure "flatter" bills of materials, i.e., bills that have fewer levels of stocked assemblies. A phantom assembly is an assembly that is manufactured and immediately consumed (used) in the production process. The use of phantom assemblies helps companies reduce inventory, reduce cycle times, and reduce material handling by eliminating the need to produce and stock subassemblies.

Production scheduling. This feature allows manufacturing to be controlled by production schedules instead of by individual work orders. This eliminates much of the paperwork and indirect labor associated with a work order system.

Gateway reporting. Gateway reporting simplifies the labor and material reporting process by allowing the establishment of key operations, known as **gateways** or **checkpoints**, where production will be reported and inventory will be backflushed.

Point of usage code. This is a code on the component record of the bill of materials that specifies where a component should be delivered along an assembly line. The delivery location may be a specific operation number or a physical location on an assembly line. This facilitates just-in-time delivery of parts to the assembly line.

Floorstock replenishment. The floorstock replenishment feature provides reports that facilitate just-in-time delivery of material to the assembly line based on production schedule requirements, floorstock inventories, lead time offsets, and point of usage codes.

Concurrent and overlapping operations scheduling. This capability allows operations to be scheduled to occur at the same time or to overlap for a certain period of time. This reduces work-in-process inventory by allowing manufacturing cycle times to be compressed.

Multiple ship schedules. This feature facilitates just-in-time delivery by enabling the buyer to schedule multiple shipments against an individual line item on a purchase order.

Automatic routing of receipts to the production line. This feature allows material to bypass incoming inspection and be automatically routed to a predefined stocking location, which is usually a point on an assembly line.

From the above discussion, it should be apparent that there is no inherent conflict between MRP II and JIT. Nothing inherent in an MRP II system causes waste. MRP II does not cause a company to buy or make more than is needed. Nor does an MRP II system cause a company to have long setup times, scrap and rework, or require incoming inspection. *In fact, MRP II is one of the most important tools that a company has at its disposal for implementing JIT.*

This book explains how MRP II can help companies reduce inventory (Chapter 3), reduce scrap and rework (Chapter 4), and improve productivity (Chapter 6), all of which are goals of JIT.

The Impact of JIT on MRP II

The JIT management philosophy has had a definite impact on how MRP II systems are used. A prime example of this is a feature found in MRP II systems that allows the user to specify scrap and yield factors on components and assemblies on a bill of materials. In effect, this feature allows an MRP II system to plan for more material than is needed to compensate for anticipated losses during the manufacturing process. This feature seems to say, "It's okay to have scrap. In fact, let's plan on it!" This is totally contrary to the JIT management philosophy, which plans for zero scrap. The JIT philosophy is to force production problems to the surface so that they can be solved instead of hiding production problems behind excess inventory.

MRP II consultants who advocate the continued use of such features may be in conflict with JIT. However, no MRP II software package forces a company to use a feature that conflicts with the JIT management philosophy.

Also, some MRP II software vendors have added features that facilitate the implementation of JIT. One of the problems that companies encounter in implementing JIT is that frequent deliveries of material result in higher transaction processing costs. For example, a company that used to receive one shipment a month may receive daily shipments of material after JIT is implemented. The effort required to perform more receiving transactions detracts from the benefits of JIT. To solve this problem, some MRP II vendors are adding a Kanban master file to their database to define every standard container of parts in use in the factory. The Kanban master file cross-references the container number with the corresponding part number, purchase order number, vendor, and standard container quantity. When a standard container is received, the receiving clerk can "swipe" the bar code label on the container. The system then automatically records the part number, purchase order number, and quantity received by referencing the Kanban master file. Receiving transactions that used to take minutes require about a second to perform. The normal receiving transactions can still be used for non-Kanban receipts.

As companies make progress implementing JIT, certain features of an MRP II system will take on less importance and others will take on more importance. The impact of JIT on MRP II is addressed throughout this book.

MRP II and Computer-Integrated Manufacturing (CIM)

Application Solutions for Manufacturers

Although the primary focus of this book is on using MRP II to solve business problems, it is not intended to depict MRP II as a panacea for all that ails manufacturing. An MRP II system is just one of many tools that a company may need to achieve a total CIM solution. Table 1.1 lists application solutions for manufacturers.

MRP II: Foundation for CIM

Many companies and industry experts view MRP II as the foundation for CIM for the following reasons:

- Many of the applications listed in Table 1.1 overlap and extend the functionality of an MRP II system. For example, a distributed shop floor control system provides priority planning and quality management features that are not available in an MRP II shop floor control module. Similarly, a quality management system provides incoming inspection features that are not available in an MRP II purchasing module.

- MRP II either drives (provides inputs to) or is driven by (receives inputs from) many of the applications in Table 1.1. Table 1.2 shows the relationship between MRP II and other applications that may be required to implement CIM.

Table 1.1
Applications Solutions for Manufacturers

Manufacturing Management
MRP II (includes the following modules):
   Order Entry
   Accounts Receivable
   Master Production Scheduling
   Bill of Materials
   Routings and Work Centers
   Inventory Control
   Material Requirements Planning
   Purchasing
   Accounts Payable
   Shop Floor Control
   Capacity Requirements Planning
   Product Costing
   Manufacturing Accounting
   Electronic Data Interchange
   Management Reporting

Distributed Shop Floor Management System
Maintenance Management
Tool Management
Rapid Modeling Systems

Design Engineering
Computer Aided Design (CAD)
Finite Element Analysis (FEA)
Engineering Document Control
Engineering Change Control

Manufacturing Engineering
Computer Aided Manufacturing (CAM)
Computer Aided Process Planning (CAPP)
Shop Floor Graphics

Supervisory Control
Cell Control

Data Collection
Factory Data Collection (FDC)

Quality
Quality Management
Statistical Process Control
Data Analysis
Automated Testing

Material Handling
Automated Storage/Retrieval Systems (ASRS)

Business Support
Office Automation
Technical Publishing

Sales and Marketing
Sales Forecasting
Sales Force Management
Sales Analysis

Personnel
Human Resources
Payroll/Personnel
Time and Attendance

- MRP II systems provide more solutions and benefits to a company than any other single application listed in Table 1.1. This is because an MRP II system contains modules that help almost every organization in the company.

- The MRP II engineering database is viewed by most companies as the foundation for other applications such as CAD, distributed shop floor management, and computer aided process planning.

Summary

The problems of material shortages, high inventory, poor quality, poor customer service, poor productivity, and poor cash management are highly integrated. The key to solving these business problems is to identify and eliminate the root causes of each problem.

This book identifies the root causes that can be addressed by MRP II. It explains how to apply specific features of an MRP II system to eliminate these causes. This book does not address problems caused by poor procedures, invalid measurements, or bad management.

This book also explains how to evaluate these problem-solving features to determine if they have been properly designed, and it discusses the limitations of MRP II packages.

MRP II software packages often succeed in solving business problems where homegrown computer systems fail. This is because many homegrown systems are difficult to use, are difficult to maintain, and fail to provide users with timely, accurate information.

Table 1.2
Relationship between MRP II and Other CIM Applications

Application	Data Input (from MRP II)	Data Output (to MRP II)
Shop Floor Management System	Production schedules or released orders	Work-in-process status
Maintenance Management	Preventive maintenance schedules	Changes in capacity
Automated Storage/ Retrieval Systems	Picklists	Inventory status
Computer Aided Design	Part masters, bills of materials	Updated bills of materials
Engineering Change Control	Where-used bills of materials	Approved engineering changes
Computer Aided Process Planning	Bills of materials	Routings
Cell Control	Production schedules or released orders	Work-in-process status
Quality Management	Vendor master file	Supplier ratings and inspection status
Sales Forecasting		Sales forecast to master schedule

MRP II is one of the most important tools that a company has at its disposal for implementing JIT. MRP II features such as backflushing, leadtime offset, phantom assemblies, and schedule-driven production help companies reduce inventory and indirect labor. Some MRP II software vendors have repackaged these and other features into a JIT module.

MRP II is not a panacea for all that ails manufacturing. However, MRP II systems provide more solutions and benefits to a company than any other single application solution for manufacturers. This is because MRP II contains modules that help nearly every organization in the company. Many companies and industry consultants consider MRP II to be the foundation for implementing computer-integrated manufacturing.

The Material Shortages Problem

*T*he Manager of Manufacturing was furious. For the third consecutive month, material shortages had caused him to miss his factory output quota. The CEO was making his life miserable. Angry customers were ringing his phone off the hook. Determined to get to the bottom of the problem, he walked out to the factory floor and pulled a shortage list off a job in final assembly. He walked over to the Manager of Materials' office and threw the list on his desk.

"There are ten shortages on this job. I want you and your material systems specialist to investigate these shortages and tell me the cause of every shortage on this list. I don't care how long it takes. We've got to get to the bottom of this problem!"

A five-day paper chase ensued. After tracking down each of the shortages, the Manager of Materials reported the following results to his boss:

- Two of the shortages had been caused by lost shop orders. Microfilm records proved conclusively that the orders had been printed, but they had been lost somewhere between the computer room and the shop floor.

- One of the parts on the shortage list had never been ordered because it wasn't listed on the bill of materials. The factory worker knew that the part was needed, but the materials ordering system didn't.

- Two of the shortages had occurred because purchase orders had not been rescheduled. The master production schedule had been changed, but the purchase orders had not been changed to reflect the new schedule.

- Three of the parts on the shortage list had been "stolen" by production control to fill shortages on other, more critical jobs.

- Two of the shortages were caused by shortages at a lower level of assembly.

The Manager of Manufacturing shook his head in dismay. "I had hoped that your investigation would help solve this problem. I know now what caused these specific shortages to occur, but I don't know how to prevent the same thing from happening again next month!"

Introduction

Many companies spend more time and money identifying and expediting material shortages than on any other business problem. The material shortages problem is the most logical place to begin an analysis of how to solve business problems, because material shortages directly impact other business problems, such as high inventory, poor customer service, poor quality, low productivity, and rising material costs. By solving the material shortages problem, a company makes significant progress toward solving the other problems.

The shortages problem is the responsibility of the Manager of Materials and his direct reports, the Manager of Material Control, and the Manager of Purchasing. However, because of the impact that material shortages has on other business problems, the shortages problem is also of concern to the Manager of Manufacturing, the Manager of Customer Service, the Manager of Quality Control, and the Chief Financial Officer (CFO). Indeed, even the Chief Operating Officer (CEO) of the company may become involved in expediting material if a shortage holds up a shipment to an important customer.

Some of the major causes of material shortages are listed below. These causes and their solutions are discussed in detail in the sections that follow.

1. Inability to determine when or how much material to order

2. Inability to reschedule orders

3. Overstated open orders

4. Inability to differentiate between usable and unusable inventory

5. Lack of visibility into on-hand inventory

6. Late shipments from vendors

7. Inability to execute the Material Requirements Plan

8. Inability to identify material substitutes

9. Incomplete bills of materials

10. Long internal lead times

11. Abnormal delays in ordering materials

12. Lost orders

13. Lack of timely, accurate information

14. Inability to allocate receipts to fill shortages

Inability to Determine When or How Much Material to Order

The material planner needs to know when and how much material to order to prevent material shortages. Many companies have home-grown computer systems to aid the material planner in making these decisions. Some homegrown systems have serious deficiencies that can cause material shortages.

A typical homegrown inventory planning system produces a report that, for purposes of this discussion, is called the Part Activity Report (Figure 2.1). This report provides the material planner with the following information about each part:

- Total quantity

- Total quantity on order

- Total requirements by week or by month

●●

```
                    Part Activity Report

07/01/91

Item Number: ADL071951      Planner: 01      Buyer: 01

Description: Rotary Switch

Quantity on Hand:   200    Quantity on Order:  500

Requirements by Month:

Jul      Aug      Sep      Oct      Nov      Dec
100      250      150      100       50        0


Jan      Feb      Mar      Apr      May      Jun
  0        0        0        0        0        0
```

●●

Figure 2.1
Part Activity Report

For purposes of this discussion, the requirements are shown by month. By analyzing this information, the material planner can determine how much material is needed to satisfy future requirements.

Unfortunately, the Part Activity Report may have deficiencies that can cause material shortages.

The data on the Part Activity Report may be insufficient for the planner to make informed decisions. For example, the Part Activity Report may show how much material is on order, but it may not show when the material is scheduled to arrive. This is because the inventory planning system that produced the report may not be integrated with the execution systems. The planning system can keep track of how much material has been ordered, but the execution systems (e.g., the purchasing system) keep track of when material is scheduled to arrive. If these systems are not integrated, the planner cannot determine if orders are scheduled to arrive in time to meet future needs. An incorrect assumption can result in a shortage.

In Figure 2.1, it appears that there is enough material on hand and on order to satisfy all future requirements:

Supply	*Demand*
On Hand + On Order = 700	Future Requirements = 650

Because the material planner cannot determine from the Part Activity Report when the 500 pieces on order are scheduled to arrive, he is unable to forecast that there will be a shortage of 100 pieces in October. There is enough material on order to cover all future requirements, but the orders are not scheduled properly. Table 2.1 illustrates how the distribution of scheduled purchase order receipts will result in a material shortage.

The Part Activity Report may also lack sufficient data about material requirements. Because the requirements are grouped into monthly time periods (also called **buckets**), the planner cannot accurately determine when the material is really needed. If the planner assumes that all requirements for a month are needed at the beginning of the month, he may create an inventory problem by scheduling material to arrive before it is needed (see Chapter 3 for a discussion of the inventory problem). Lacking better information, the planner may assume that requirements are evenly distributed throughout the month. If, in fact, the requirements distribution is skewed toward the beginning of the month, the planner may cause a shortage problem by scheduling material to arrive after it is needed. This is illustrated in Table 2.2. By assuming that requirements are

Table 2.1
Material Shortages Caused by Insufficient Data about
Scheduled Receipts

Actual Distribution of Scheduled Receipts

ORDER 1 QTY 100 DUE IN JUL
ORDER 2 QTY 200 DUE IN AUG
ORDER 3 QTY 200 DUE IN NOV

Impact on Material Shortages

Beginning On-Hand Balance: 200

	Jul	Aug	Sep	Oct	Nov
Requirements	100	250	150	100	50
Receipts	100	200	0	0	200
Ending Balance	200	150	0	−100	50

Note: A negative ending balance indicates a material shortage.

Table 2.2
Material Shortages Caused by Insufficient Data about
Requirements

Distribution Requirements	Week 1	Week 2	Week 3	Week 4
What planner sees on Part Activity Report	Monthly requirement of 400			
What planner assumes (even weekly distribution)	100	100	100	100
Actual distribution of requirements (unknown to planner)	200	150	50	0
How planner schedules receipts	200	0	200	0
End-of-week balance	0	−150	0	0

evenly distributed throughout the month, the planner has scheduled receipts in a manner that will cause a shortage of 150 pieces during the second week of the month.

The Part Activity Report does not allow the planner to manage by exception. Many homegrown computer systems produce a Part Activity Report for every part on a weekly basis. The planner must review every part and take the appropriate action. Studies indicate that only 10 to 20 percent of the parts require some type of action. *This means that the planner wastes up to 90 percent of his time reviewing parts that require no action.*

A material planner is typically responsible for hundreds of parts. In theory, the planner is supposed to review each part weekly. But in practice, the planner may have so many parts to manage that he may only be able to review each part monthly. This means that a need-to-order situation may go unnoticed and unresolved for up to a month. Because of this, orders may be placed with insufficient lead time, resulting in material shortages.

Solution

Use Material Requirements Planning (MRP) and the Planner Action Report.

The heart of an MRP II system is the Material Requirements Planning (MRP) module. The primary output from the MRP module is a report known as the Planner Action Report (Figure 2.2). Like the Part Activity Report, it provides the material planner with information about how much material is on hand, how much is on order, and future requirements. But the similarity between the two reports (and the systems that generated them) ends there.

There are some significant differences between the Part Activity Report produced by some homegrown systems and the Planner Action Report produced by an MRP II system. First and foremost, like many reports produced by an MRP II system, the Planner Action Report is an exception report. The MRP module has a batch processing computer program known as the **planning program**. The planning program uses the master production schedule and bills of materials to calculate the demand for each part, and it uses the on-hand balance and open orders (referred to as **scheduled receipts** or **replenishment orders** in the Planner Action Report) to calculate supply. It analyzes this information to determine if any action is required to balance supply and demand. Possible actions include:

- Placing new orders
- Canceling orders that are no longer needed

Date: 01/21/91   Planner Action Report

Part Number	Description	U/M	Plnr Code	Buyr Code	MRP Avail Quantity	Lead Time	Dock-to-Stock Lead Time	Paperwork Lead Time	Standard Cost Per
ADL2938	Microswitch	EA	01	04	1000	10	0	0	3.23 Each

Safety Stock Policy Code	Safety Stock	Order Policy	Fixed Ord Quantity	Min Ord Quantity	Max Ord Quantity	Mult Ord Quantity
F			1000	1000		1000

	Past Due	01/21	01/28	02/04	02/11	02/18	02/25	03/04	03/11
Requirements		525	850	1030	512		490		
Scheduled Receipts			1000						
Planned Receipts				1000			1000		
Available	1000	475	625	595	83		593		
Planned Orders					1000				1000

	03/18	03/25	04/01	04/08	04/15	04/22	04/29	05/06	05/13
Requirements	265	495		200					
Scheduled Receipts									
Planned Receipts		1000							
Available	328	833	633						
Planned Orders									

Exception Messages:

Release Planned Order Qty 1000 Due Date 02/08/91

Pegged Requirements Detail

Quantity	Due Date	Needed for
100	01/21/91	MBL203902
300	01/22/91	JSL204934
125	01/24/91	BJL203034
240	01/28/91	MBL203902
125	01/29/91	MAL304934
485	02/02/91	JSL204934

Scheduled Receipts Detail

Order	Quantity	Due Date
1S390490	1000	02/02/91

Figure 2.2
Planner Action Report

- Rescheduling orders to an earlier delivery date
- Rescheduling orders to a later delivery date

Only those parts requiring action (typically 10 to 20 percent of the total number of parts) are reported on the Planner Action Report. This enables the planner to review exceptions on a weekly basis and take timely action to prevent material shortages.

The Planner Action Report also takes the guesswork out of determining when material is needed and when orders are scheduled to arrive. The MRP II database stores detailed, permanent records of the quantity and need date of every requirement, as well as the quantity and due date of every scheduled receipt (Table 2.3). These details may be optionally printed on the bottom of the Planner Action Report. For convenience, this data is summarized into weekly time buckets on the Planner Action Report. However, the MRP planning program actually uses the detailed, "unbucketed" data to perform the supply/demand analysis.

For this reason, MRP II systems are often described as **bucketless** planning systems. It might be more accurate to say that modern MRP II systems store detailed data in daily time buckets, whereas many homegrown systems store only summarized data in weekly or monthly time buckets. The MRP planning program analyzes the detailed data to determine when and how much material is needed.

Table 2.3
Detailed Requirement and Replenishment Records
Stored in the MRP II Database

Part Number: MAL101078

Requirements		Replenishments	
Quantity	Need Date	Quantity	Due Date
100	07/01/90	300	07/01/90
200	07/05/90		
50	07/12/90	300	07/12/90
150	07/14/90		
50	07/17/90		
200	07/25/90	300	07/25/90
100	08/01/90		
100	08/03/90	300	08/03/90
200	08/12/90		
50	08/15/90		
200	08/22/90	300	08/22/90

Table 2.4
How MRP Uses Lead Time Offsetting to Recommend
New Orders to the Material Planner

Lead Time: 3 Weeks
Fixed Order Quantity: 20
On Hand: 0
Current Date: 10/07/91

	Periods						
	1	*2*	*3*	*4*	*5*	*6*	*7*
Gross Requirements	10	20	10	10	20	0	20
Scheduled Receipts	20	20					
Projected Balance	10	10	0	10	10		10
Planned Receipt				20	20		20
Planned Release	20	20		20			

Exception Messages:

Release Order   Qty 20   Due Date 10/28/91

A third major difference between the two reports is that the Part Activity Report is usually a passive report, whereas the Planner Action Report is, as the name implies, an active report. The Part Activity Report must be carefully analyzed by the planner to determine if some action is required to balance supply and demand. If the planner analyzes the data incorrectly, he may order too much or too little material, causing inventory or material shortage problems. The MRP planning program automatically analyzes the data and recommends actions to balance supply and demand. These recommendations are presented to the planner in the form of exception messages printed on the Planner Action Report. This analysis is done in the following manner.

The lead time (the time required to replenish the inventory supply) for each part is stored on the part master record in the MRP II database. The MRP planning program offsets (subtracts) the part lead time from the part need date to determine when an order should be placed (i.e., the need-to-order date):

Need-to-Order Date = Part Need Date – Part Lead Time

When the need-to-order date is the current date, an exception message is printed on the Planner Action Report advising the material planner to place an order. Table 2.4 illustrates lead time offsetting. MRP has planned a receipt in period 4 on 10/28. The part lead time is three weeks. The planner receives an exception message on 10/07 to release an order for 20 pieces with a due date of 10/28.

Some MRP II systems allow the planner to define a paperwork lead time. This is the amount of time required for the planner to review the exception messages and take action. This time is added to the part lead time to force exception messages out a few days earlier. This helps to prevent material shortages by giving the planner time to review the Planner Action Report and release an order.

Caveat

Some older MRP II software packages store data in weekly time buckets. This is a throwback to the days when computers were not fast enough to do the tremendous amount of number crunching required in a bucketless planning system. With today's technology, there is no longer any justifiable reason for a bucketed planning system. If you are presently evaluating MRP II packages, my recommendation is that you should eliminate any bucketed systems from your evaluation.

Inability to Reschedule Orders

For some companies, the inability to reschedule orders is a primary cause of material shortages. Changes in the master production schedule may require some orders to be rescheduled to arrive at an earlier date. If these orders are not rescheduled, the company will experience material shortages.

Part of the difficulty in rescheduling may stem from ordering material too soon. Some companies have systems that automatically order material as soon as a requirement is known, regardless of the need date or the lead time. For example, a part that has a five-week lead time may be ordered twelve weeks prior to the need date, even though the order did not need to be placed for another seven weeks. Once the order is placed, it is more difficult to reschedule because a change order notice must be generated and sent to the vendor or, if the part is manufactured, to the shop floor.

Companies often do not do an effective job rescheduling orders because their systems do not alert the material planner of the need to reschedule. The Part Activity Report, discussed earlier in this chapter, may not provide the planner with enough information to make informed decisions about rescheduling.

Solutions   *Provide the ability to delay placing orders.*

MRP II systems are delayed-action systems. The MRP module does not advise the material planner to place an order until the part lead time has been reached. Until then, orders remain in the system as planned orders. When the master production schedule changes, fewer orders need to be rescheduled because fewer orders have been placed!

Some people find it difficult to accept the idea that it is best to delay placing orders for as long as possible. They feel that it is best to put material on order as soon as possible. However, placing orders early takes away a company's ability to change plans. Truly this is a case of "less is more"—less material on order means more flexibility.

Provide a method of notifying the material planner when an open shop order or purchase order needs to be rescheduled to an earlier date.

The Planner Action Report, discussed earlier, is more than just a vehicle for determining when and how much material to order. The Planner Action Report also identifies orders (scheduled receipts) that need to be rescheduled to balance supply and demand. When the planning program determines that an order needs to be rescheduled to an earlier date, an exception message is printed that shows the order number and the new need date. The planner can then take the appropriate action (i.e., issue a change request to Purchasing or to the shop) to reschedule the order.

Table 2.5 summarizes the differences between the typical Part Actvity Report and the MRP II Planner Action Report.

Overstated Open Orders

Some companies fail to order enough material because they have an inflated view of how much material is on order. Usually a vendor will ship the exact quantity of material that was ordered. However, a vendor may occasionally ship less than the purchase order quantity and consider the order complete. For example, if an order is placed for 100 pieces and the vendor only has 98 pieces in stock, the vendor may ship 98 pieces and consider the order complete. The vendor has no intention of shipping the remaining two pieces, but unless the

Table 2.5
Summary of Differences between the Typical Part Activity Report and the MRP II Planner Action Report

Typical Part Activity Report	MRP II Planner Action Report
Printed for every part	Exception report
Data is stored in weekly or monthly time buckets. No details available	Bucketless system; detailed data is available and is used to perform supply/demand analysis
Passive report; no action messages	Active report; analyzes data and prints exception messages
No lead time offsetting	Lead time offsetting lets planner know when to order

purchase order is closed, it will appear as if there are still two pieces on order.

A similar situation may occur in the shop. If a manufacturing order is released for 100 pieces and two pieces are scrapped during production, only 98 pieces will be delivered to the stockroom. Unless the manufacturing order is closed, it will appear as if there are still two pieces on order.

These errors will accumulate over time, and the material planner will see an overstated quantity-on-order number on the Part Activity Report. The planner will not order enough material to satisfy future requirements (believing that the material is already on order) and material shortages will occur.

Solution   *Provide the ability to close orders automatically.*

Some MRP II systems provide the option of closing orders automatically when the cumulative receipts are within a specified percentage of the order quantity. For example, if the automatic close percentage is 95 percent, an order for 200 pieces will be closed automatically when 190 pieces have been received. Most packages allow the automatic close percentage to be set on the part master record and on individual manufacturing orders and purchase orders. The automatic close option will be used most often on low-to-medium-value parts that are purchased in large quantities.

Impact of JIT on Short Shipments and Manufacturing Yield

One of the goals of a JIT program is to establish long-term relationships with suppliers who will deliver the exact quantity required, with zero defects, on the exact day required. Another goal of JIT is 100 percent yield (zero scrap) in the manufacturing process. If a company achieved both these goals, there would be no need for an automatic close percentage option, because every order would be received 100 percent. However, few (if any) companies have achieved this state of perfection. The use of this feature may diminish as companies establish JIT relationships with more vendors and improve their control of the production process, but the automatic close option will continue to be an important feature for most companies for many years to come.

Inability to Differentiate between Usable and Unusable Inventory

Some companies fail to order enough material because their computer systems are unable to differentiate between usable and unusable inventory, as illustrated in the following example.

A part has an on-hand inventory of 1000, an on-order quantity of 100, and total or gross requirement of 1500. The net requirement is calculated as follows:

Net Requirement

$$= \text{Gross Requirements} - (\text{On-Hand} + \text{On-Order})$$

$$= 1500 - (1000 + 100) = 400$$

A problem arises because of the implicit assumption that all 1000 pieces of on-hand inventory are usable inventory. This may not be the case. Some inventory may be material that has failed inspection and is awaiting final disposition. Some inventory may no longer be usable because its shelf life has expired. Unusable material is often referred to as **nonnettable inventory,** since the system should not net (subtract) this inventory against (from) the gross requirement when computing the net requirement. Failure to exclude nonnettable inventory from the net requirement calculation will result in material shortages, because the net requirement will be underspecified.

```
Next Transaction: ___                                    Date: 08/01/91
This Transaction: IDI                                    Time: 11:30
                            Inventory Detail Inquiry            ✳

Part Number: ADL30543           Qty Available to Be Allocated:    140
                                Qty Unavailable for Manufacturing: 280
                                Qty Available for MRP Planning:    310
                                Qty Unavailable for MRP Planning:  180


Lot          Quantity Quantity  MRP   Inv Reason Date     Shelf   Order   Lot
Nbr Location on Hand Allocated Avail? Stat Code   Received ExpDate Number  Trc


001 RM120       100        0     N    RJ Reject  04/14/91         1S229328
002 SB127        50        0     Y    AM          05/01/91        1S209348
003 SB132       100       70     Y    AM          05/15/91        1W333842
004 SB132        60        0     Y    AM          06/02/91        1S236493
005 RM120        80        0     N    RJ Reject  07/15/91         1R334993
006 IN127       100        0     Y    II Ininsp   08/01/91        1W530402
```

Figure 2.3
Inventory Detail Inquiry Screen

Solution

Provide the ability to identify and exclude unusable inventory from netting calculations.

The Inventory Control module in most MRP II packages allows nonnettable inventory to be identified and excluded from the planning process. This is done by providing a code in the inventory detail record to indicate whether or not a lot of inventory is available for MRP planning.

Figure 2.3 illustrates how inventory is identified as nettable or nonnettable. Nettable inventory lots have an MRP AVAILABLE code of Y and are included in the netting calculation. Nonnettable inventory lots have an MRP AVAILABLE code of N and are ignored by the MRP planning program. There are six inventory lots in Figure 2.3. Lots 001 and 005 are not available for MRP planning. The reason code indicates that the lots have been rejected.

Lack of Visibility into On-Hand Inventory

Material shortages may be caused by a lack of visibility into on-hand inventory. Companies that cannot check inventory availability from a terminal must pick material needed for manufacturing orders to determine if there is sufficient material on hand to release orders to the shop floor. Partially picked orders (orders that have one or more shortages) are held in inventory until the shortages have been filled. These partially picked manufacturing orders are referred to as **kits, accumulations,** or **staged orders.** They are stored in a separate area of the stockroom known as the **accumulation** or **staging area.**

The kitting process, which is intended to identify and eliminate material shortages, actually aggravates the shortage problem, because inventory in the staging area cannot be used to fill other orders. The net effect is a vicious cycle—material shortages result in more staged orders, which in turn result in more shortages.

Table 2.6 illustrates how the kitting process causes materials shortages. All three orders in Table 2.6 were picked at different times on the same day, and all three orders are being held in the staging area due to shortages. The shortages on Orders 2 and 3 could be filled from inventory that has been kitted for Order 1. This would leave Order 1 with three shortages, but Orders 2 and 3 could be released immediately. But because all three orders are in the staging area, the staged inventory for Order 1 is not available to complete Order 2 and Order 3.

For one company, the vicious cycle was so severe that the company developed a special inventory system to keep track of staged inventory and to facilitate swapping material from one staged order to another to fill shortages. Even with this sophisticated system, the company periodically breaks down some staged orders and returns material to inventory to make the inventory more accessible.

Solution   *Provide the ability to simulate the picking function.*

MRP II packages eliminate the need to kit orders to identify material shortages. In the Inventory Control module most MRP II packages provide the capability to simulate the picking function on-line. This simulation allows the material planner to check inventory availability without actually picking material. The planner can make the best use of available inventory by picking only those orders that can be picked complete and released to the shop floor.

The material planner initiates the simulation process for a specific manufacturing order. The system nets the requirements for each

Table 2.6

Effect of Kitting on Material Shortages

| Order #1 | Assembly: JWL100940 | | |
| Date Picked: 08/01 | Time Picked: 8:30 | Due Date: 08/15 | |

Components	Quantity Required	Quantity Picked	Quantity Short	
ADL071951	10	10	0	
MAL101078	5	0	5	(Shortage)
JSL022583	2	2	0	
MBL070784	8	8	0	

| Order #2 | Assembly: JPM062042 | | |
| Date Picked: 08/01 | Time Picked: 9:00 | Due Date: 08/15 | |

Components	Quantity Required	Quantity Picked	Quantity Short	
ADL071951	10	5	5	(Shortage)
REL051023	5	5	0	
JSL022582	3	3	0	
MBL070784	1	1	0	

| Order #3 | Assembly: GH022543 | | |
| Date Picked: 08/01 | Time Picked: 9:30 | Due Date: 08/15 | |

Components	Quantity Required	Quantity Picked	Quantity Short	
PL020948	8	8	0	
REL051023	3	3	0	
JSL022582	3	3	0	
MBL070784	1	1	1	(Shortage)
BJL081023	6	6	0	

component against available inventory and displays a list of components that do not have sufficient inventory (Figure 2.4). If there are no shortages, the planner instructs the system to produce a picklist. The inventory is immediately allocated (reserved) for the order, so that it is not available when the picking simulation function is performed for other manufacturing orders.

For the simulation function to work properly, the system must be able to distinguish between inventory that is available for manufacturing and inventory that is not available. **Unavailable inventory** is inventory that is not available to be picked and released to the shop floor. Nonnettable inventory is one type of unavailable inventory, but there may also be some nettable inventory that is unavailable to be picked. An example of nettable, unavailable inventory is material that is awaiting inspection. MRP should not ignore this material in the planning process, because it is presumably good material. However, the Inventory Control module *should* ignore this material when the picking function is simulated because the material is not available to be picked.

Most MRP II packages provide an inventory status code on the inventory detail record to distinguish between available and unavailable inventory. A status code of AM means that the inventory is available for manufacturing. Any other status code is considered to be unavailable inventory by the system. Table 2.7 lists some typical inventory status codes.

Figure 2.5 illustrates how inventory detail records are identified with an inventory status code. Note that lot 006 is available for MRP planning but is unavailable for manufacturing because it is in inspection.

```
Next Transaction: ___                                    Date: 08/01/91
This Transaction: PSI                                    Time: 11:30
                          Picking Simulation Inquiry

Order Number:  18273   Part Number:  GH022543   Quantity:  10

The Following Components May Have Shortages If This Order Is Picked:

                Quantity   Quantity   Potential   Due Date of Next
Part Number     Required   Available  Short Qty   Scheduled Receipt

PL020948          80         62          18         08/17/91
REL051023         30          0          30         08/20/91

Do You Want to Pick This Order? _ (Y = Yes, N = No)
```

Figure 2.4
Picking Simulation Inquiry Screen

Table 2.7
Inventory Status Codes

Code	Description
AM	Available for manufacturing
RJ	Rejected material
AI	Awaiting inspection
II	In inspection
EX	Expired material
SP	Service parts
IT	In-transit inventory
FG	Finished goods inventory

```
Next Transaction: ___                                    Date: 08/01/91
This Transaction: IDI                                    Time: 11:30
                          Inventory Detail Inquiry

Part Number: ADL30543          Qty Available to Be Allocated:     140
                               Qty Unavailable for Manufacturing: 280
                               Qty Available for MRP Planning:    310
                               Qty Unavailable for MRP Planning:  180
```

Lot Nbr	Location	Quantity on Hand	Quantity Allocated	MRP Avail?	Inv Stat	Reason Code	Date Received	Shelf ExpDate	Order Number	Lot Trc
001	RM120	100	0	N	RJ	Reject	04/14/91		1S229328	
002	SB127	50	0	Y	AM		05/01/91		1S209348	
003	SB132	100	70	Y	AM		05/15/91		1W333842	
004	SB132	60	0	Y	AM		06/02/91		1S236493	
005	RM120	80	0	N	RJ	Reject	07/15/91		1R334993	
006	IN127	100	0	Y	II	Ininsp	08/01/91		1W530402	

Figure 2.5
Inventory Data Inquiry Screen

Some MRP II packages allow the user to define a default inventory status code for each inventory location. Thus, if certain inventory locations are normally used to store inventory that is awaiting inspection, a default status code of AI can be assigned to these locations. Whenever a lot of inventory is received into one of these locations, it will automatically be assigned a status code of AI. (The user can override the status code for a specific lot.) This feature helps to ensure that the proper status code is assigned to inventory lots.

Late Shipments from Vendors

Three dates are of particular importance in preventing late shipments from vendors: the material wanted date, the due-on-dock date, and the required ship date. The **material wanted date** (also known as the **material needed date**) is the date that the material is needed for production. The **due-on-dock date** is the date the material should be received at the receiving dock. The **required ship date** is the date that the vendor should ship the material. These dates are related in the following way:

Due-on-Dock Date
   = Material Wanted Date – Dock-to-Stock Lead Time

where the **dock-to-stock lead time** is the number of days required to receive, inspect, and put away material in the stockroom. This time may vary from part to part depending on inspection requirements.

Required Ship Date = Due-on-Dock Date – Transit Time

where the **transit time** is the number of days the shipment is in transit from the vendor to the receiving dock.

Many companies have systems that cannot calculate required ship dates. Instead, the material wanted date is printed on the purchase order. This is a formula for failure, because vendors normally interpret dates on purchase orders as required ship dates. When the vendor ships material on the material wanted date, it will be overdue by the in-transit time plus the dock-to-stock lead time.

Solution

Provide vendors with the required ship date.

The key to preventing late shipments is to provide vendors with the correct date on purchase orders, that is, the required ship date.

Some MRP II packages allow the material planner to specify the dock-to-stock lead time on the part master record. The Material Requirements Planning module subtracts the dock-to-stock lead time from the material wanted date and passes the due-on-dock date to the Purchasing module.

The Purchasing module in some MRP II packages allows the buyer to specify the in-transit time on the vendor master file (Figure 2.6). This allows vendors that are located far away to be allowed longer in-transit times than local vendors. When a purchase order is created, the Purchasing module subtracts the in-transit time from the due-on-dock date and prints the required ship date on the purchase order.

Caveats

Some MRP II packages calculate due-on-dock dates but stop short of calculating required ship dates. To compensate for this deficiency, the planner can increase the dock-to-stock lead time to allow for some in-transit time.

```
Next Transaction: ___                                    Date: 08/01/91
This Transaction: VMI                                    Time: 11:30
                        Vendor Master File Inquiry

Vendor Code: 19283   Group Code:      Name: Industrial Control Corp.

Street: 3040 Golden Hind Rd.   City:  Roanoke        State: VA
Zip: 24018-1923      Country: USA   Attn: Jim Martin

Acknowledgment Required?     Y           Small Business? N
Transit Days                 05          Minority Vendor? N
EDI Business Partner?        Y
```

	Year to Date	1990	1989
Dollars Purchased	$87,898.23	$128,283.43	$104,239.08
Dollars Early Shipments	2,983.18	5,093.12	3,209.20
Number of Late Shipments	2	6	6
Number of On-Time Shipments	35	75	70
Total Number of Shipments	45	91	86
Dollars Overshipments	3,123.24	4,232.26	3,232.28
Percent On-Time Shipments	77.8	82.4	81.4
Percent Overshipments	8.9	6.6	9.8

Figure 2.6
Vendor Master File Inquiry Screen

Table 2.8
*In-Transit Times Based on Distance
to Ship-to Locations*

Vendor:	Blair Fabricating
Address:	6391 Kristy Lane
	Roanoke, VA 24018

Ship-to Locations	In-Transit Days
Roanoke, VA	0
Columbia, SC	3
New York, NY	5
San Jose, CA	10

Some companies have centralized purchasing organizations that buy materials for different manufacturing locations. In this case, the in-transit time should be based on the "ship-to" location (Table 2.8). Unfortunately, most MRP II packages do not provide the ability to specify different in-transit times for vendors based on ship-to locations.

Inability to Execute the Material Requirements Plan

Some companies do an adequate job of planning when and how much material to order but fail to execute according to the Material Requirements Plan. Often this is because the organizations responsible for executing the plan don't have exception reports comparable to the Planner Action Report to help them execute the plan. Purchasing needs exception reports to help predict and prevent late deliveries from vendors. Shop management needs exception reports that assign priorities to manufacturing orders.

Solution   *Provide buyers and shop managers with exception reports that help them execute the Material Requirements Plan.*

The Purchasing module in some MRP II packages produces an exception report called the Vendor Action Report (Figure 2.7). The Vendor Action Report is really four separate reports that follow the life cycle of a purchase order:

1. Late Acknowledgment Report

2. Potential Late Shipments Report

Vendor Action Report

(Sorted by Buyer / Vendor / Message Type / PO Number)
Page Break on: Vendor

Buyer: 01

Vendor: 28474   Name: Blair Fabricating   Contact: Joe Brown   Phone: 703-989-0711

Exception Message	PO Number	Item	Part Number	Quantity Ordered	PO Issue Date	Due-on-Dock Date	Required Ship Date	Ship Promise Date
Late Acknowledgment	1S394834	01	ADL071951	100	07/15/91	11/12/91	11/04/91	
Late Acknowledgment	1S443244	01	MBL070784	50	07/17/91	10/11/91	10/04/91	
Late Acknowledgment	1S546571	01	JSL022583	25	07/18/91	12/18/91	12/11/91	
Potential Late Shipment	1S308572	01	ADL071951	2	06/28/91	09/12/91	09/05/91	10/01/91
Potential Late Shipment	1S354345	01	MBL070784	50	06/28/91	09/23/91	09/16/91	10/12/91
Pending Shipment	1S234839	01	ADL071951	100	05/15/91	08/10/91	08/03/91	08/03/91
Pending Shipment	1S435249	04	BJL081023	35	06/17/91	08/12/91	08/05/91	08/05/91
Pending Shipment	1S542341	01	JSL022583	200	06/18/91	08/12/91	08/05/91	08/05/91
Overdue Shipment	1S336546	01	EL011253	200	05/18/91	07/28/91	07/21/91	07/21/91
Overdue Shipment	1S457569	02	SBL090574	10	05/20/91	07/23/91	07/16/91	07/16/91

Figure 2.7
Vendor Action Report

3. Pending Shipments Report

4. Overdue Shipments Report

These reports are combined into a single report and sorted by vendor (within buyer) to give the buyer one convenient report to work from when contacting vendors. Some companies send a copy of the Vendor Action Report to the vendor, either electronically or by facsimile (fax) transmission, so that both the buyer and the vendor can work from the same report.

These reports key off three date fields in the purchase order file:

1. Required ship date

2. Ship promise date

3. Due-on-dock date

The required ship date and due-on-dock date are defined earlier in this chapter. The **ship promise date** field is used to record the date the vendor has promised shipment. When the purchase order is created, the ship promise date field is left blank. The vendor enters the ship promise date on the acknowledgment copy of the purchase order. This date is entered on the purchase order file when the acknowledgment is received from the vendor.

The selection criteria for purchase orders appearing on the Vendor Action Report are shown below:

- *Late Acknowledgments*

   Exception Message: LATE ACKNOWLEDGMENT

   Selection Criteria: Orders that have not been acknowledged within a specified number of days (usually two weeks) after the purchase orders were issued.

- *Potential Late Shipments*

   Exception Message: POTENTIAL LATE SHIPMENT

   Selection Criteria: Orders that have ship promise dates later than the required ship dates by more than a specified number of days. (This keeps orders that are only a day or two late from showing on the report.)

- *Pending Shipments*

   Exception Message: PENDING SHIPMENT

   Selection Criteria: Orders that have ship promise dates that fall within the next five days.

- *Overdue Shipments*

  Exception Message: OVERDUE SHIPMENT

  Selection Criteria: Orders that have not been received within a specified number of days after the due-on-dock dates. (This keeps orders that are only a day or two late from showing on the report.)

Caveat   When evaluating MRP II software packages, make certain that the Purchasing module provides data fields for the following dates:

- Due-on-dock date

- Required ship date

- Ship promise date

Even if the software package does not provide a standard Vendor Action Report, as long as these dates are stored in the database for each scheduled shipment, it is relatively easy to use the Management Reporting System to produce such a report.

```
Next Transaction: ___                              Date: 07/22/91
This Transaction: MOI                              Time: 11:30
                  Manufacturing Order Operations Detail Inquiry

Order Number:  18273   Part Number:  GH022543   Quantity:  10  Due Date: 07/26/91

Status: Released
```

Oper No	Work Cntr	Operation Description	Scheduled Start	Scheduled Complete	Actual Start	Actual Complete	Quantity Complete
0010	A978	ASSEMBLE PARTS	07/21/91	07/22/91	07/21/91	07/22/91	10
0020	A978	SOLDER	07/22/91	07/23/91	07/22/91		
0030	B832	LABEL	07/23/91	07/23/91			
0040	I723	INSPECT	07/23/91	07/24/91			
0050	T938	TEST	07/24/91	07/25/91			
0060	P298	PACK	07/25/91	07/26/91			

Figure 2.8
Manufacturing Order Operations Detail Inquiry Screen

Shop Exception Reports

The Shop Floor Control module of an MRP II system uses shop routings to backschedule orders from their due dates to determine the start and due dates for each operation on an order (Figure 2.8). The Shop Floor Control module also tracks the status of work in process by means of transactions that allow employees to report actual start and completion dates for each operation. The scheduled and actual start and completion dates are used to produce a number of reports that help shop floor personnel execute the manufacturing plan. The most significant of these reports are as follows:

- Dispatch List Inquiry
- Work Center Load Inquiry
- Work Center Detail Report
- Work Center Input/Output Inquiry

Of these, the Dispatch List Inquiry, Work Center Load Inquiry, and Work Center Input/Output Inquiry are usually available in both on-line and hardcopy output. The Work Center Detail Report is usually a long report that is only available in hardcopy output. These reports are described in more detail in the following subsections.

Dispatch List Inquiry   The Dispatch List Inquiry (Figure 2.9) helps the shop dispatcher set priorities for orders at a work center.

MRP II systems use a priority calculation known as the **critical ratio**. This is the ratio of the amount of time available to complete the order to the amount of work remaining on the order:

$$\text{Critical Ratio} = \frac{\text{Time Available}}{\text{Work Remaining}}$$

$$\text{Critical Ratio} = \frac{\text{Order Due Date} - \text{Today's Date}}{\text{Order Due Date} - \text{Operation Schedule Start Date}}$$

A critical ratio of 1.0 indicates that the order is on schedule. A ratio of more than 1.0 indicates that the order is ahead of schedule. A ratio of less than 1.0 indicates that the order is behind schedule.

The critical ratio is computed for every shop order at a work center and is shown on the Dispatch List Inquiry. The critical ratio calculation is meaningless for overdue orders. Once an order is overdue, the Dispatch List Inquiry displays the number of days the order is overdue instead of the critical ratio.

```
Next Transaction: ___                                    Date: 07/22/91
This Transaction: DLI                                    Time: 11:30
                          Dispatch List Inquiry
                        (Sorted by Critical Ratio)

For Work Center: A878    Description: Assembly    Daily Capacity:  8 Hours

                              Critical  Scheduled  Scheduled
Part Number   Order No. Oper  Ratio     Start      Complete   Status

MBL198273     M01288    0080  Overdue   07/18/91   07/20/91   Running
ADL071956     M02837    0020      .23   07/20/91   07/22/91   Running
MBL039046     M03537    0030      .31   07/20/91   07/22/91   Running
ADL071956     M04641    0020      .43   07/20/91   07/22/91   Running
JSL981956     M04734    0060      .50   07/20/91   07/22/91
EL907193      M05147    0020     1.00   07/22/91   07/23/91
BJL071956     M05237    0050     1.02   07/22/91   07/23/91
MBL039046     M05337    0030     1.10   07/23/91   07/24/91
```

Figure 2.9
Dispatch List Inquiry Screen

On the Dispatch Inquiry, overdue orders are listed first; all other orders are sorted by critical ratio. Orders with the lowest critical ratio receive the highest priority (after overdue orders).

Caveats

For the Dispatch List Inquiry to be meaningful, the orders on the report should be sorted by critical ratio, so that the highest priority orders appear near the top of the report (overdue orders should be listed first). One MRP II package has an on-line Dispatch Inquiry that is sorted by part number. This makes the on-line report virtually useless.

MRP II systems have a limited priority planning capability. The critical ratio calculation used by MRP II systems to determine priorities considers only the current status of the order (on schedule, ahead of schedule, or behind schedule). MRP II systems do not consider other factors that might affect priorities, such as the following:

- Orders on quality hold

- Status of work stations further along the route
- Current equipment setup
- Equipment maintenance status
- Required skill code to perform the operation
- Operator availability
- Manually designated priority codes

A number of application software vendors (including some MRP II software vendors) have recently developed shop floor management systems that extend the capabilities of an MRP II Shop Floor Control module. Shop floor management systems excel in the area of priority planning, taking all the above factors into consideration to produce a more useful dispatch report. For example, a shop floor management system will not assign a high priority to an order that will have to wait at the next work center because a machine is down. Conversely, a shop floor management system will assign a high priority to an order if the next operation occurs at a bottleneck work center that is temporarily idle.

Shop floor management systems also consider the number of orders in the input queue at a work center that can use the current equipment setup. Within specified limits, orders that can use the current setup can be given a higher priority than other lots in the input queue.

Shop floor management systems allow different priority rules to be established for each work center. For example, if a work center has a long setup time, the current equipment setup will play an important role in determining what order to process next.

An MRP II system is an adequate priority planning solution for some companies, but other companies may need priority planning features found only in a shop floor management system.

Work Center Load Inquiry   The Work Center Load Inquiry (Figure 2.10) indicates the capacity utilization of each work center by week. Overloaded work centers (those loaded to more than 100 percent capacity) will cause material shortages. This report helps the Manager of Shop Operations determine what work centers are potential bottlenecks so that corrective action can be taken in time to solve the problem and prevent shortages. Possible corrective actions include:

```
Next Transaction: ___                                  Date: 08/01/91
This Transaction: WCL                                  Time: 11:30
                        Work Center Load Inquiry

Work Center: A982     Description: Assembly

        Period     Period    Effective  Scheduled   Load
Per     Start      End       Capacity    Load       Percent       Message

1       08/15/91   08/21/91    240.0     184.6        77
2       08/22/91   08/28/91    240.0     180.0        75
3       08/29/91   09/04/91    192.0     212.0       110        Overloaded
4       09/05/91   09/12/91    240.0     130.0        54        Underloaded
5       09/13/91   09/19/91    240.0     290.4       121        Overloaded
6       09/20/91   09/26/91    240.0     190.6        79
```

Figure 2.10
Work Center Load Inquiry Screen

- Scheduling overtime during overloaded weeks
- Shifting work to an alternate work center that has available capacity
- Rescheduling work into earlier, underloaded weeks

In Figure 2.10, weeks three and five are overloaded by 10 percent and 21 percent, respectively. The shop manager may need to see a detailed breakdown of the orders that are scheduled for weeks three and five to decide which orders to shift to an alternate work center or to reschedule to an earlier week.

The Work Center Detail Report (Figure 2.11) provides a detailed list of orders that comprise the work center load.

Work Center Input/Output Inquiry   The Work Center Input/Output Inquiry (Figure 2.12) provides the Manager of Shop Operations with data on planned versus actual production goals. The user inputs planned hours of input and output for a work center each week, and the system compares actual input and output to planned input and output.

Significant differences between planned and actual production goals might indicate a production problem that needs attention. Timely detection and correction of such problems help achieve the Material Requirements Plan.

In Figure 2.12, the load at work center A982 has been escalating over the last four weeks. Actual input has exceeded planned input

```
Date: 08/15/91                                            Page: 01
                      Work Center Detail Report
           (Sorted by Work Center Number / Scheduled Start Date)
                  Page Break on: Work Center Number

Work Center Number: A982      Description:  Assembly

Order                     Scheduled     Oper    Load Hours
Number    Part Number     Start Date     No    Set Up    Run

39489     ADL39093        08/15/91      0010              14.3
29093     MBL33113        08/15/91      0020              18.6
78201     REL051023       08/16/91      0010              15.0
91823     BJL39807        08/17/91      0035              20.5
17283     EL29093         08/17/91      0010              15.5
19202     ADL201092       08/17/91      0030              25.0
28452     ADL356234       08/18/91      0010              10.6
17873     MBL33676        08/18/91      0020              24.0
23043     ADL236023       08/19/91      0010              14.4
11832     BJL39807        08/19/91      0035              10.7
12353     EL29093         08/20/91      0010              16.0
                      **** Period Totals:               184.6


39449     ADL39093        08/22/91      0020              14.7
24493     MBL33433        08/22/91      0010              18.2
72301     ADL234023       08/22/91      0015              14.1
91813     BJL43807        08/24/91      0025              21.0
27383     EL29093         08/24/91      0010              15.0
13272     BJL934092       08/24/91      0015              21.9
28752     ADL353434       08/25/91      0020              10.0
17763     MBL32376        08/25/91      0005              23.0
63042     REL34542        08/26/91      0016              15.0
18832     MAL34323        08/26/91      0025              11.1
12878     JSL022582       08/28/91      0010              16.0
                      **** Period Totals:               180.0
```

Figure 2.11
Work Center Detail Report

```
Next Transaction: ___                                    Date: 08/10/91
This Transaction: IOI                                    Time: 11:30
                      Work Center Input/Output Inquiry

Work Center: A982     Description: Assembly

              Week     Week    Planned  Actual          Planned  Actual
Week          Start    End      Input   Input Deviatn   Output   Output  Deviatn

1             08/01/91 08/06/91  100.0   105.0  +  5.0   115.0   110.0   - 10.0
2             08/07/91 08/13/91  100.0   105.0  +  5.0   110.0   100.0   - 10.0
3             08/14/91 08/20/91  100.0   110.0  + 10.0   115.0   110.0   -  5.0
4             08/21/91 08/27/91  100.0   105.0  +  5.0   110.0   100.0   - 10.0
Week to Date  08/28/91 09/02/91  100.0    65.0  - 35.0   110.0    70.0   - 40.0
Next Week     09/03/91 09/09/91  100.0                   105.0

Cumulative Deviation: Last Four Weeks            + 25.0                   -35.0

Cumulative Deviation: Year to Date:              +105.0                  -135.0
```

Figure 2.12
Work Center Input/Output Inquiry Screen

by 25 hours, and actual output has been 35 hours less than the planned output, resulting in a net change in load of 60 hours.

Inability to Identify Material Substitutes

When a material shortage occurs, it may be possible to fill the shortage immediately if an acceptable substitute can be found. However, some companies do not have systems that help them identify and use substitutes.

Solution   *Provide features that help companies identify and use substitutes.*

MRP II packages provide the ability to define substitutes and to modify manufacturing orders to replace a part with a substitute. To use this capability, the material planner performs the following steps:

1. Simulates the picking function to identify a component that has an inventory shortage. (The picking simulation function is discussed earlier in this chapter.)

2. Performs a part master inquiry to find the substitute part number. (In most MRP II packages, substitutes can be specified on the part master record.)

3. Performs an inventory inquiry to determine if the substitute is available.

4. Modifies the manufacturing order to replace the shortage part with the substitute.

Caveats

MRP II systems typically provide only the ability to define global substitutes. If part X is defined as a substitute for part Y, the assumption is that part X can always be used as a substitute for part Y. However, this may not be a valid assumption. Part X might be an acceptable substitute for part Y in one product structure, but might *not* be an acceptable substitute in another product structure. For example, if parts X and Y are printed circuit board components, there may be space limitations or circuit parameters that preclude using part X as a substitute for part Y on some circuit boards. Cost and quality factors may also limit the use of a part as a substitute.

If a part can only be used as a substitute on a limited basis, the best place to store part substitute information is in the product structure file. Most MRP II packages provide the ability to associate text with a product structure record. Figure 2.13 illustrates how product structure text can be used to store information about substitutes.

Incomplete Bills of Materials

Material shortages are often caused by incomplete bills of materials (BOMs). The system cannot calculate material requirements for parts that are left off a BOM, and therefore the planner does not order material that is needed. Some companies have incomplete BOMs because too much effort is required to maintain complete BOMs. "Insignificant" parts such as hardware may be left off a BOM, but these insignificant parts become very significant when they show up on the shortage list!

```
Next Transaction: ___                              Date: 08/12/91
This Transaction: PST                              Time: 10:15
                        Add Product Structure Text


Part Number: ADL29384


Product Structure Text:

The Following Substitutes May Be Used on This Product Structure Record:

       Component                     Acceptable Substitutes
    Line    Part Number      Part Number    Part Number    Part Number

    0010    EL29382          EL93847        EL34898
    0050    ADL39489         ADL39404       ADL30490       ADL39090
                             ADL30940
    0070    REL93092         REL39808
```

Figure 2.13
Add Product Structure Text Screen

Solution   *Reduce the effort required to create bills of materials.*

The Bill of Materials module of an MRP II system reduces the effort required to create complete BOMs. An important feature in the Bill of Materials module is the "copy-same-as-except" capability. This feature enables an engineer to create a new BOM by copying an existing, similar BOM (Figure 2.14). By adding and deleting components to the copied bill, the engineer can complete the process of creating the bill in a fraction of the time that would otherwise be required.

Long Internal Lead Times

Internal lead times can contribute to the material shortages problem by adding several weeks to the replenishment cycle. **Internal lead time** is defined as the amount of time that elapses from the time a purchase requisition is generated to the time the vendor receives a purchase order.

To understand why some companies have long internal lead times, consider the typical ordering cycle. Many companies use an internal document known as a **traveling order card** to order production material. The material planner enters the quantity required and the need date on the travel card and sends it to the buyer. This may take from one to five days, depending on whether the planner and the buyer are at the same location. The buyer then selects a vendor, obtains the current price, and places a purchase order. This may take from one to five days, depending on the buyer's backlog of open requisitions. After the purchase order is printed, a clerk puts it in an envelope and mails it to the vendor. This adds from three to five days to the internal lead time, depending on the clerk's backlog and the location of the vendor. In total, the internal lead times in this operating environment range from one to three weeks. In some cases, the order is not received by the vendor until after the need date!

```
Next Transaction: ___                              Date: 08/12/91
This Transaction: CPS                              Time: 10:15
                          Copy Product Structure


New Product Structure:            ADL394893              Model:Eng

Copy from Product Structure:      ADL394892              Model:Eng
```

Figure 2.14
Copy Product Structure Screen

Solutions   *Reduce the time required to forward a requisition to Purchasing.*

MRP II packages provide an electronic link between the MRP module and the Purchasing module. This enables the material planner to forward requisitions to the buyer instantaneously. The requisitions are automatically received into the buyer's work queue or electronic in-basket. This eliminates the time required to forward a traveling order card to the buyer. It also eliminates material shortages that result when traveling order cards are occasionally lost or misplaced.

Reduce the time required to place purchase orders.

Some MRP II packages provide the ability to generate purchase orders from requisitions automatically. To use this feature, the buyer first establishes a valid quote and preferred vendor for a part in the purchasing database. The buyer then sets an indicator on the part master record to activate automatic purchase order generation. When a requisition is passed to the Purchasing module, a purchase order is created immediately without any manual intervention. This eliminates the time required for the buyer to review requisitions and place purchase orders.

Reduce the time required to mail orders to vendors.

Some MRP II systems have an Electronic Data Interchange (EDI) module that allows purchase orders to be transmitted electronically to vendors. EDI provides application-to-application communications, so that a company's purchase orders can be input directly to a vendor's order entry system.

The American National Standards Institute (ANSI) has established standard communication formats for such business documents as purchase orders and invoices. The EDI module prepares purchase orders for electronic transmission by converting them to the standard ANSI format. The vendor receives purchase orders in the standard format, then converts them into the input format for the vendors' order entry system. This eliminates the time (and expense) required to mail purchase orders to vendors.

Figure 2.15 summarizes the reduction in lead time that can be achieved from the electronic link between the material planner and the buyer, automatic purchase order generation, and electronic data interchange.

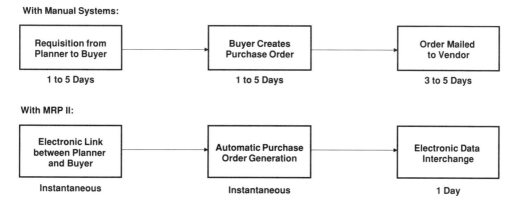

Figure 2.15
Internal Lead Time Reductions

Abnormal Delays in Ordering Materials

Material shortages are often caused by abnormal delays in placing orders. **Abnormal delays** are defined as delays unrelated to the internal lead time normally required to place an order. Such delays may be caused by:

- Failure to verify the existence of part master records in the database before requirements are generated

- Deletion of active components from the part master file

- Failure to explode an assembly and generate requirements at lower levels in the bill of materials

Failure to Verify Part Master Records

Whenever a bill of materials is created (or components are added to an existing bill of materials), it should be reviewed to verify that a part master record exists for each component. Orders cannot be generated for a part until a part master record has been established. The part master record contains information that is essential for the planning and ordering process. This information includes:

- *Material planner code.* This tells the system which material planner to notify when requirements are generated.

- *The make/buy code.* This tells the planner whether a manufacturing order or purchase order should be placed to satisfy the requirement.

- *Part order policies.* This tells the planner what lot sizing rules to apply when placing an order. For example, a purchased part may have a minimum order quantity, and a manufactured part may have a standard lot size.

Some homegrown systems do not automatically verify the existence of part master records when a bill of materials is created or modified. The alternative—having the design engineer or a clerk manually verify every part—is expensive and impractical. Even if every part were manually verified, keypunching errors might introduce invalid part numbers to the product structure file.

Invalid part numbers on a bill of materials may not be discovered until requirements are generated. At this point, the system is unable to process the requirements, since there is no part master record. These requirements are called **mismatch requirements**, because the part number on the product structure file has no corresponding match on the part master file.

Figure 2.16 illustrates a procedure used by some companies to clear mismatch requirements. When a mismatch occurs, a mismatch requirement document is printed and sent to the Process Planning or Industrial Engineering department. The document has all the pertinent information (part number, quantity required, need date, and parent assembly) needed to reenter the requirement into the system. The process planner acts to eliminate the condition which caused the mismatch. Possible actions include:

- Adding a new part master record to the database
- Correcting an error in the product structure file
- Obtaining agreement from engineering to modify the bill of materials to use an existing part number

After the mismatch condition has been corrected, the process planner reenters the requirement into the system for processing.

This routine typically adds one to three weeks of abnormal lead time to the planning and ordering cycle. Furthermore, the mismatch requirements documents are not tracked by the system. If they are lost, material may not be ordered until the shortage is discovered on the shop floor!

Solution   *Validate part numbers on-line.*

MRP II systems totally eliminate mismatch requirements. Bills of materials are maintained on-line, and the system performs realtime validation to ensure that a part master record exists for every part

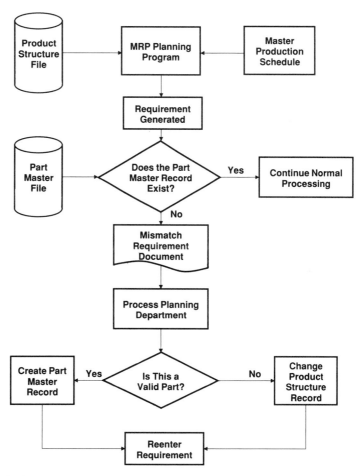

Figure 2.16
Mismatch Requirements Procedure

on the bill of materials. Problems are immediately detected and must be corrected before the part number can be used on a product structure record. Abnormal delays caused by mismatch requirements are thus eliminated.

Deletion of Active Components from the Part Master File

Periodically, inactive and obsolete parts are deleted from the part master file. Most homegrown systems perform no tests before a part number is deleted from the database. If an active component is mistakenly deleted from the part master file, new requirements will mismatch, causing abnormal delays in ordering.

Solution   *Prevent active components from being deleted.*

MRP II systems do not allow a part master record to be deleted from the database if any of the following conditions exist:

- The part number is used on a product structure record.
- Requirements or orders exist for the part number.
- The part has on-hand inventory.
- The part has a routing.

These factors eliminate the possibility that mismatch requirements will be generated after the part number is deleted.

Failure to Explode an Assembly

Requirements are generated by exploding the bill of materials, level by level, until the lowest level of the BOM has been reached. If this process is stopped prematurely, lower-level requirements will not be generated and shortages will occur.

Figure 2.17 shows a bill of materials consisting of five levels below the top level, which is traditionally called **level 0**. If the system is unable to recognize that Part A is an assembly, the explosion process will stop and no requirements will be generated for any of the parts at levels 2 through 5 of the BOM.

The key to the explosion process is the MRP II system's ability to determine when a part has lower-level components. Some home-grown systems make this determination by keying off a digit in the part number. For example, in many divisions of GE, the presence of a letter G in a certain position of the part number field means that the part is an assembly (i.e., that the explosion process should continue). (The G stands for "group." All assemblies consist of groups of parts.) Thus, part number 68A7035G12 is recognized as an assembly, whereas part number 68A8374P12 is treated as a purchased part. However, if assemblies are coded incorrectly, the system will fail to explode assemblies into their lower-level components.

Solution   *Eliminate significant part numbers.*

MRP II systems do not rely on significant part numbers to drive the explosion process. All MRP II systems provide a separate code

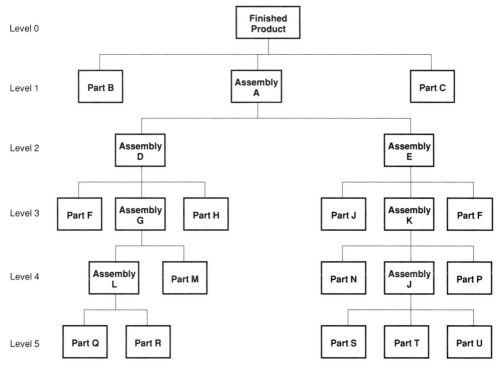

The MRP II system must be able to recognize which parts are assemblies that should be exploded to generate lower-level requirements.

Figure 2.17
Five-Level Bill of Materials

known as the **make/buy code** on the part master record. The code *M* indicates that the part should be exploded.

The make/buy code is a required data-entry field when a new part is added to the database (Figure 2.18). This helps to ensure that all parts are coded correctly to drive the explosion process.

Lost Orders

Many companies have old, poorly integrated batch-processing systems that are prone to data processing errors. These errors can result in lost orders, as illustrated by the following story.

A few years ago, I worked for a company that had old, batch-oriented production and inventory control systems. My position was that of a liaison between the manufacturing and MIS organizations.

```
Next Transaction: ___                                    Date: 08/01/91
This Transaction: APM                                    Time: 11:30
                        Add Part Master Record

Part Number:  MBL070784

Description:  Wiring Module

Make/Buy Code:  M

Commodity Code: 12515010

Material Planner Code:  03

Buyer Code:

Unit of Measure: EA
```

Figure 2.18
Add Part Master Record Screen

A large part of my job was to screen complaints about system problems before submitting them to MIS for resolution. One week, I received an unusual number of complaints of lost orders from the shop. All the jobs that were being released to the shop floor had an unusual number of material shortages, and there were no open purchase orders and manufacturing orders for the missing material. By examining microfiche records of system inputs and outputs, I discovered that three months earlier, data processing had neglected to download the output from the planning system to the execution systems (Shop Floor Control and Purchasing). An entire run of new orders was lost, and no one noticed until the material from the lost orders was overdue. It took the factory several months to recover.

Solution

Provide integrated systems that reduce data processing errors.

MRP II packages reduce the possibility of data processing errors because they are more tightly integrated than outmoded, homegrown systems. More processing is done in realtime, and the batch runs do not require constant intervention from computer operators to load tapes of output from one system into another system.

Lack of Timely, Accurate Information

The lack of timely, accurate information about on-hand inventory often leads to material shortages. If inventory is overstated, the material planner may not order enough material to satisfy future requirements.

Many companies lack timely, accurate inventory information because they have batch inventory systems. When material is issued from inventory or received into inventory, the stockkeeper fills out a data entry form. At the end of the day, these forms are sent to data processing to be keypunched for batch updates to the inventory system. The keypunch cycle may take several days, and keypunch errors are a common occurrence. The result is that inventory records are seldom up to date, and material planners are always basing decisions on old, inaccurate information.

Solution   *Provide the ability to perform realtime updating of inventory information.*

MRP II software packages eliminate the need to batch update inventory information. The Inventory Control module allows realtime updating of inventory records through on-line transactions that allow the following functions:

- Picklist activity reporting
- Receipts of material into inventory
- Issues of material from inventory
- Transfers of material between locations
- Adjustments to inventory balances

The on-line transactions also improve inventory record accuracy by detecting and preventing errors at the time of data entry. For example, if the stockkeeper makes a data entry error that would cause the on-hand balance to go negative, the system will display an error message. The stockkeeper can then correct the error and proceed with the transaction.

Some MRP II packages have an Inventory History Inquiry (Figure 2.19) that provides a time-stamped list of all inventory transactions.

```
Next Transaction: ___                               Date: 08/01/91
This Transaction: IHI                               Time: 11:30
                        Inventory History Inquiry

Part Number   GH022543

Select by: (Leave Blank to Select and Display All Records)

Date:  __/__/__   Transaction Code: ___   From Loc: _____   To Loc: _____
Operator Initials: ____

            Transaction Txn From     To      Rec Adj           Net Avail
Date   Time Description Cde Location Location Nbr Ind Quantity Cde Cde Init

07/14/91 11:10 Receipt     RIN          SB123            10   1  A  DOK
07/15/91 09:23 Issue       OTC SB123                      2      A  DOK
07/23/91 11:29 Receipt     RIN          SB983           100   1  A  ELK
07/23/91 14:02 Pick        PLR SB123                      6         DOP
07/24/91 08:12 Move        MIN SB123    SB893             2   1  A  DOP
07/25/91 13:20 Adjust      CCA          SB893    +        2   1  A  EPL
07/25/91 14:25 Receipt     RIN          SB298          200   1  U  SLP
07/26/91 12:20 Status CHG  STC              001              A  DPL
07/28/91 08:20 Adjust      CCA          SB298    -        1         SPL
```

Figure 2.19
Inventory History Inquiry Screen

This on-line audit trail shows the details of each transaction and the initials of the individual who performed the transaction. This information is extremely useful when investigating and resolving any discrepancies between the on-hand system balance and the actual quantity in a location.

To help narrow down the search for a particular transaction, some MRP II packages allow users to specify selection criteria when performing a history inquiry. For example, a user might be interested in viewing only those transactions entered on a particular day (Figure 2.20), or all transactions performed by a certain operator. The selection criteria can be entered at the top of the screen. If the selection fields are left blank, all history records are displayed.

Inability to Allocate Receipts to Fill Shortages

Even when a company diligently applies the features of an MRP II system to prevent shortages, things do occasionally go wrong and shortages occur. When this happens, the speed with which a shortage is filled using MRP II can lessen the impact that the shortage has on other business problems.

If a substitute cannot be found, the shortage must be filled by an outstanding purchase order or manufacturing order. When the order is received, it should be allocated to any outstanding shortages. However, unless the person entering the receipt is aware that a shortage exists for the part, the receipt will be routed to the stockroom. There it may be stored in inventory for days or weeks, even though manufacturing orders on the shop floor are being delayed due to shortages!

```
Next Transaction: ___                                    Date: 08/01/91
This Transaction: IHI                                    Time: 11:30
                          Inventory History Inquiry

Part Number:  GH022543

Select by: (Leave Blank to Select and Display All Records)

Date:  07/23/91   Transaction Code: ___   From Loc: _____   To Loc: _____
Operator Initials: ____

              Transaction Txn From     To       Rec Adj           Net Avail
Date    Time  Description Cde Location Location Nbr Ind Quantity Cde Cde  Init

07/23/91 11:29 Receipt     RIN         SB983              100 1   A    ELK
07/23/91 14:02 Pick        PLR SB123                        6            DOP
```

Figure 2.20
Inventory History Inquiry Screen for a Particular Day

Solution   *Provide the ability to allocate receipts to shortages.*

Some MRP II systems allow the material planner to flag an open order that is needed to fill shortages. This causes a shortage notification message to be displayed on the terminal when the order is received. The message alerts the receiving clerk to contact the material planner to find out how to allocate and route the quantity received to fill the shortages.

Caveat   This method of allocating receipts to fill shortages is only partially effective, because it relies on the material planner to manually flag orders, and it does not automatically allocate the receipt to fill shortages.

Currently I know of only one MRP II software package that automatically allocates receipts to fill shortages, although this would be relatively easy to do in some MRP II packages. Some MRP II packages keep records of shortages when a manufacturing order is

---

```
Next Transaction: ___                                    Date: 07/26/91
This Transaction: SBO                                    Time: 09:20
                  Shortages by Manufacturing Order Inquiry

Order Number:  14573   Part Number:  ADL22543   Quantity:  10  Due Date: 08/03/91

Order Status: Released

              Quantity        Need         Used on:
Shortages       Short         Date         Oper   Wk Ctr

REL298392          6       07/24/91        0020   A978
BJL394893         10       07/24/91        0020   A978
```

Figure 2.21
Shortages by Manufacturing Order Inquiry Screen

```
Next Transaction: ___                                    Date: 07/26/91
This Transaction: SBP                                    Time: 11:30
                        Shortages by Part Number Inquiry
                          (Sorted by Shortage Need Date)

Part Number: REL298392          Total Quantity Short:   26


Shortage on   Quantity       Need          Used on:
Order Number    Short        Date          Oper   Wk Ctr

14573               6        07/24/91       0020   A978
14652              10        07/26/91       0020   A987
14661              10        07/28/91       0030   A298
```

Figure 2.22
Shortages by Part Number Inquiry Screen

picked short, that is, when an order is picked and one or more parts are not available. The shortage records are stored in the MRP II database in a shortage file. Users can perform inquires against the shortage file to view shortages by order (Figure 2.21) or by part number (Figure 2.22).

The shortage file can be used to allocate receipts to fill shortages automatically by modifying the on-line receiving transaction to check the shortage file. If a shortage exists, a label is printed to route the delivery of the quantity needed to fill the shortage to a specific manufacturing order. If more than one shortage exists, the receipt can be allocated to shortages in priority sequence by need date. A separate routing label is printed for each manufacturing order. Any portion of the receipt not applied to shortages is routed to the stockroom.

Probably, most MRP II vendors have not automated the process of allocating receipts to fill shortages because MRP II packages emphasize shortage prevention and assume that shortages will not occur. Very little functionality is provided to assist users in filling shortages when they *do* occur.

Some MRP II packages don't even track material shortages in the database! If any orders are picked short, the material planner must manually track and resolve shortages. Even if you do not need to allocate receipts to shortages automatically, you should select an MRP II package that tracks shortages in a shortage file. This will eliminate the manual effort required to track shortages.

Summary

Table 2.9 summarizes the causes of and solutions to the material shortages problem that were presented in this chapter. Subsequent chapters show that solving the shortages problem is key to solving other critical business problems.

Table 2.9
Material Shortages: Summary of Causes and Solutions

Causes	Solutions
1. Inability to determine when or how much material to order	The Planner Action Report helps the material planner determine when and how much to order and enables the planner to manage by exception.
2. Inability to reschedule orders	The MRP module delays placing orders until the lead time has been reached. The Planner Action Report prints exception messages when orders need to be rescheduled.
3. Overstated open orders	The automatic close option closes orders when the cumulative receipts are within a specified percentage of order quantity.
4. Inability to differentiate between usable and unusable inventory	The Inventory Control module provides the ability to identify nonnettable inventory. The MRP module ignores nonnettable inventory when calculating the net requirement.
5. Lack of visibility into on-hand inventory	The Inventory Control module provides the picking simulation function. This function considers only inventory that is available for manufacturing.
6. Late shipments from vendors	MRP II systems provide vendors with the required ship date, so that material is shipped in time to arrive by the due-on-dock date.

Table 2.9
Material Shortages: Summary of Causes and Solutions
(continued)

Causes	Solutions
7. Inability to execute the Material Requirements Plan	The Purchasing module provides the Vendor Action Report, which notifies the buyer of late acknowledgments, potential late shipments, pending shipments, and overdue receipts. The Shop Floor Control module provides the Dispatch List Inquiry, Work Center Load Inquiry, Work Center Detail Report, and Work Center Input/Output Inquiry. These reports help the shop manager execute the manufacturing plan.
8. Inability to identify material substitutes	MRP II software packages provide the ability to identify substitutes and modify manufacturing orders to employ these substitutes.
9. Incomplete bills of materials	The Bill of Materials module provides the copy-same-as-except feature, which reduces the effort required to produce complete bills of materials.
10. Long internal lead times	The electronic link between the material planner and buyer, automatic purchase order generation, and electronic data interchange help to reduce internal lead times.
11. Abnormal delays in ordering materials	Automatic verification of part master records prevents mismatch requirements. MRP II packages do not allow active parts to be deleted from database. MRP II packages use the make/buy code instead of significant part numbers to determine if a part should be exploded to calculate lower-level part requirements.
12. Lost orders	The integrated MRP II system reduces manual intervention, which can result in lost orders.
13. Lack of timely, accurate information	All inventory transactions provide on-line, realtime updating of inventory information.
14. Inability to allocate receipts to fill shortages	Open orders can be flagged to cause a shortage notification message to be displayed upon receipt. Some MRP II packages can be modified to perform automatic allocation of receipts to fill shortages.

The Inventory Problem

T*he Manager of Manufacturing was concerned about rising obsolete-inventory costs. This month, the business had written $20,000 of obsolete inventory off the books, bringing the year-to-date total to $80,000. The Manager of Manufacturing summoned the Manager of Materials and Manager of Inventory Control to an emergency inventory task force meeting.*

"Our obsolete inventory situation is getting critical," the Manager of Manufacturing began. "Last year we scrapped $120,000 worth of material. At the present rate, we'll scrap over $200,000 worth of material this year. If we don't solve this problem soon, my replacement will be solving the problem with your replacements."

"Yesterday I went out to the stockroom and made a list." He handed the Manager of Materials and Manager of Inventory Control each a piece of paper. "This is a list of high-value items that have been sitting in the stockroom for at least six months, judging from the amount of dust that has accumulated on them. I've already talked to Purchasing, and I've been assured that we're not buying a six-month supply of material. I'd like you to determine why these items have been in inventory for so long. Let's meet again a week from today. Please have your investigation completed by then."

A week later, the Manager of Materials and Manager of Inventory Control presented their findings to the Manager of Manufacturing.

"The last time you gave me an assignment like this, you handed me a shortage list and asked me to investigate the material shortage problem," the Manager of Materials began. "I followed your instructions to the letter and limited my investigation to the items on the shortage list. I did what you asked, but it didn't really help us solve the shortage problem. This time we went beyond your specific instructions and took a broader view of the inventory problem. Here is what we found."

"The primary cause of obsolete inventory is our inability to phase in engineering changes in a way that permits us to use up on-hand inventory. Most of the items on your list are no longer used on any

bills of materials. That's why they've been sitting in the stockroom long enough to accumulate so much dust."

"Why are we unable to use up on-hand inventory before we implement engineering changes?" asked the Manager of Manufacturing.

"Allow me to explain," said the Manager of Inventory Control. "To put it simply, our computer system permits only one version of the bill of materials to exist at a time. There is no way to phase in changes by assigning effectivity dates to components on bills of materials. This means that all changes to bills of materials take effect immediately."

"I'm not sure I understand the implication of what you're saying," the Manager of Manufacturing interjected. "Can you give me an example of how this causes obsolete inventory?"

"Certainly. One of the parts on your list is ADL200350. This part was replaced by part ADL300400 last November. As soon as the bills of materials were changed, we began using the new part in manufacturing, even though we still had 450 pieces of ADL200350 in inventory."

"Why don't we just delay changing the bills of materials until all the old inventory is used up?" the Manager of Manufacturing asked.

"If we did that, we would continue to order the old part and we would never use up the on-hand inventory. It's a vicious circle."

"I'm beginning to get the picture. How can we solve the problem?"

"The short-term solution is to intervene manually to try to use up existing inventory. I've alerted the stockroom to substitute part ADL200350 on any manufacturing order calling for part ADL300400 until all inventory of ADL200350 is used up. I've also instructed Purchasing to cancel orders for 450 pieces of ADL300400. But with the volume of engineering changes that we have, this solution will be only partially effective, and it will require extra manpower to manage. The long-term solution is to implement systems that enable us to phase in engineering changes in a manner that will allow us to use up on-hand inventory."

"But don't some changes have to be implemented immediately?" asked the Manager of Manufacturing.

"You're absolutely right," the Manager of Materials replied. "Some engineering changes have to be implemented immediately for reasons of safety, liability, or performance, but most changes could be phased in if our systems allowed us to do so without a lot of manual intervention."

Introduction

The inventory problem receives a great deal of attention in most companies because it is easy to quantify the benefits of a successful inventory reduction program. Companies that find ways to reduce inventory without impacting customer service can significantly impact the bottom line. For example, if a company has $50 million in inventory and an annual carrying cost of 20 percent, a 20 percent reduction in inventory will result in a one-time $10 million savings and an annual $2 million savings in inventory carrying costs. For some companies, the potential savings in inventory carrying costs alone is enough to justify all the hardware, software, programming, education, and training costs associated with implementing MRP II.

The inventory problem is the responsibility of the Manager of Materials and the Manager of Inventory Control. However, because of the dramatic impact that inventory has on profits, the CEO and CFO are also very concerned about the problem of high inventory. Some of the major causes of high inventory are listed below. These causes and the solutions found in MRP II systems are discussed in the sections that follow.

1. Material shortages

2. Inability to determine when or how much material to order

3. Inability to deexpedite and cancel orders

4. Excessive obsolete inventory

5. Early shipments and overshipments from vendors

6. Inability to schedule just-in-time delivery of material

7. Inability to schedule deliveries around nonworking days

8. Large economic lot sizes for purchased parts

9. Improper allocation of finished-goods inventory to customer orders

10. Recursivity (looping) on bills of materials

11. Lost inventory

12. Inability to verify the accuracy of inventory records

13. Excessive safety stock

Material Shortages

The material shortages problem and the high inventory problem are interrelated. It is impossible to have a shortage problem without also having an inventory problem, because material shortages prevent products from going out the door. From an inventory perspective, a shortage of a $5 part may be as critical as a shortage of a $500 part, because *any* shortage can prevent many thousands of dollars worth of work-in-process inventory from being completed and shipped. Solutions to the material shortages problem are discussed in Chapter 2.

Inability to Determine When or How Much Material to Order

The inability to determine when or how much material to order can lead to material shortages (see Chapter 2) and high inventory. The typical homegrown inventory planning system produces a Part Activity Report (Figure 3.1) that aids the material planner in deciding when and how much material to order. Chapter 2 discusses the

••

```
                        PART ACTIVITY REPORT

                            07/01/91

Item Number: BJL093100      Planner: 01     Buyer: 01

Description: Microswitch

Quantity on Hand:    100    Quantity on Order:  500

Requirements by Month:

Jul         Aug         Sep         Oct         Nov         Dec
200         200           0           0         200           0


Jan         Feb         Mar         Apr         May         Jun
  0           0           0           0           0           0
```

••

Figure 3.1
Part Activity Report

following deficiencies of the Part Activity Report in relation to material shortages:

- The data on the report may be insufficient for the planner to make informed decisions.
- The report does not allow the planner to manage by exception.

These deficiencies can also lead to high inventory.

Example of inventory problem caused by insufficient data about scheduled receipts. Insufficient data can cause either a material shortages problem or an inventory problem, depending on how the material planner interprets the data on the Part Activity Report. In Figure 3.1, it appears that supply is in perfect balance with demand and that no inventory problem exists:

Supply	Demand
On Hand + On Order = 600	Future Requirements = 600

But because the Part Activity Report does not show when the 500 pieces on order are scheduled to arrive, the material planner is unable to determine that there will be a *surplus* of 100 pieces in August that will not be consumed until November.

Table 3.1 illustrates how the distribution of scheduled purchase order receipts will result in an inventory problem.

Table 3.1
High Inventory Caused by Insufficient Data about Scheduled Receipts

Actual Distribution of Scheduled Receipts

ORDER 1 QTY 100 DUE IN JUL
ORDER 2 QTY 300 DUE IN AUG
ORDER 3 QTY 100 DUE IN NOV

Impact on Inventory

Beginning On-Hand Balance: 100

	Jul	Aug	Sep	Oct	Nov
Requirements	200	200	0	0	200
Receipts	100	300	0	0	100
Ending Balance	0	100	100	100	0

Note: A positive ending balance for more than one time period may indicate an inventory problem, depending on the value of the part.

Table 3.2
*High Inventory Caused by Insufficient Data about
Requirements*

Distribution requirements	Week 1	Week 2	Week 3	Week 4
What planner sees on Part Activity Report	Monthly requirement of 400			
What planner assumes (even weekly distribution)	100	100	100	100
Actual distribution of requirements (unknown to planner)	0	50	150	200
How planner schedules receipts	100	100	100	100
End-of-week balance	100	150	100	0

Example of inventory problem caused by insufficient data about requirements. The Part Activity Report may also lack sufficient data about material requirements. Because the requirements are grouped into monthly time buckets, the material planner cannot accurately determine when the material is really needed. Lacking better information, the planner may assume that requirements are evenly distributed throughout the month. If, in fact, the requirements distribution is skewed toward the end of the month, the planner may cause an inventory problem by scheduling material to arrive before it is needed. This is illustrated in Table 3.2. By assuming that requirements are evenly distributed throughout the month, the planner has scheduled receipts in a manner that will cause an inventory surplus until the last week of the month.

Inability to manage by exception. Because the Part Activity Report is not an exception report, the planner is expected to review every part on a weekly basis and take the appropriate action. This is an impossible task, given that a planner typically is responsible for hundreds of parts. In practice, the planner may be able to review each part only monthly. This means that the planner may fail to notice a potential inventory problem in time to reschedule or cancel orders.

Solution   *Use Material Requirements Planning (MRP) and the Planner Action Report.*

The MRP module and its primary output, the Planner Action Report, helps the material planner determine when and how much material to order. The MRP module and the Planner Action Report are discussed in detail in Chapter 2.

Inability to Deexpedite and Cancel Orders

Changes in the master production schedule may require some orders to be deexpedited (rescheduled to a later delivery date) and some orders to be canceled. For some companies, the inability to deexpedite and cancel orders is a major cause of high inventory.

Part of the difficulty in deexpediting and canceling orders may stem from ordering too soon. Some companies have systems that automatically order material as soon as a requirement is known, regardless of the need date or the lead time. Once the order has been placed, it is more difficult to deexpedite or cancel it because a change order notice must be generated and sent to the vendor or, if the part is manufactured, to the shop floor.

It may be especially difficult to deexpedite or cancel purchase orders. Conventional wisdom among buyers holds that the easiest way to (unintentionally) expedite an order is to try to deexpedite or cancel the order. The typical response from a vendor is, "It's too late, the order has been shipped!" and it certainly *will* be shipped by the end of the day. In some cases, cancellation charges may make it impractical to cancel an order.

Another reason why companies are not effective at deexpediting and canceling orders is that their systems do not alert the material planner to the need to deexpedite or cancel.

Solutions   *Provide the ability to delay placing orders.*

MRP II systems are delayed-action systems. The MRP module does not advise the material planner to place an order until the part lead time has been reached. Until such time, orders remain in the system as planned orders. When the master production schedule changes, fewer orders need to be deexpedited or canceled because fewer orders have been placed!

Provide a method of notifying the material planner when an open manufacturing order or purchase order needs to be deexpedited or canceled.

Chapter 2 discusses how the MRP planning program analyzes detailed information about requirements, replenishments, and on-hand balances to determine if any action is required to balance supply and demand. Possible actions include:

- Placing new orders
- Canceling orders that are no longer needed
- Rescheduling orders to an earlier delivery date
- Rescheduling orders out to a later delivery date

Specific recommendations are presented to the planner in the form of exception messages printed on the Planner Action Report.

Chapter 2 focuses on potential material shortage problems, that is, situations in which demand is greater than supply. Such situations result in exception messages that advise the planner to place new orders or reschedule orders to an earlier delivery date.

The Planner Action Report also highlights potential inventory problems, that is, situations in which supply is greater than demand. Such situations result in exception messages that advise the planner to cancel orders or reschedule orders to a later delivery date.

Additional Benefits of Deexpediting and Canceling Orders

The obvious benefit of deexpediting and canceling orders is reduced inventory. Another, not so obvious benefit is fewer material shortages. Deexpediting and canceling orders makes internal or external (vendor) capacity available for other orders that are being expedited. For example, if a work center or a vendor is loaded to 100 percent capacity, deexpediting some orders may make it possible to expedite other orders successfully. The problem with some homegrown systems is that priorities change only in one direction: Orders are expedited when shortages occur, but orders are never deexpedited or canceled. This makes it even more difficult to expedite successfully.

Excessive Obsolete Inventory

The major causes of obsolete inventory are as follows:

- Inability to phase in global engineering changes

- Inability to prevent obsolete parts from being specified on bills of materials

- Excessive expired inventory

- Inability to identify slow-moving inventory

Inability to Phase in Global Engineering Changes

A **global engineering change** is one in which a part is replaced wherever it is used. Sometimes a global change must be implemented immediately for a specific reason, such as product safety or performance. In such cases, the on-hand inventory of the old part (the part being replaced) is usually scrapped. In most instances, however, global changes should not be implemented until the inventory of the old part has been used up. The inability to phase in global changes to allow inventory to be used up can be a major cause of obsolete inventory.

Many homegrown systems allow only one version of the bill of materials to exist at a time. Because of this limitation, any changes to bills of materials take effect immediately. If part *A* is replaced globally with part *B*, the system immediately begins to allocate part *B* on picklists. The inventory of part *A* is never used up, and it eventually becomes obsolete.

Solution   *Provide the ability to phase in global engineering changes.*

All MRP II packages allow engineering changes to be phased in at a specified date. MRP II software vendors refer to this feature as **engineering change control.**[1]

MRP II systems provide the ability to specify effectivity dates for engineering changes. Effectivity dates allow engineering changes to be phased in so that:

- Inventory of the old part is used up before the change becomes effective, and

- Inventory of the new part is ordered and is available in the required quantities on the date the change becomes effective.

---

1. The term engineering change control is an inappropriate and misleading name for this feature. See Appendix A for an explanation of engineering change control and a discussion of misleading naming conventions used by MRP II software vendors.

Design Approaches to Engineering Change Control

There are two different design approaches used by MRP II software vendors for engineering change control. The first approach stores effectivity dates in an engineering change control record, and cross-references components on bills of materials to an engineering change number. This approach is illustrated in Figures 3.2 and 3.3.

In Figure 3.2, engineering change number 938498 is established with an effectivity date of 11/12/91. In Figure 3.3, line items 030 and 032 on the bill of materials are linked to engineering change number 938498. Line item 030 is assigned a change control code of I to indicate that it will become inactive on 11/12/91 (the date specified in the engineering change record). Line item 032 is assigned a change control code of A to indicate that it will become active on 11/12/91. This will provide time for the inventory of part ADL203940 to be used up before part ADL290489 becomes active.

```
Next Transaction: ___                                      Date: 09/12/91
This Transaction: ECN                                      Time: 14:05
                        Engineering Change Notice

ECN Number: 938498

Reason for Change: Cost Reduction

Created by: John Hammer

Effectivity Dates:    Start: 11/12/91    Stop:
```

Figure 3.2
Engineering Change Notice Screen

```
Next Transaction: ___                                    Date: 09/12/91
This Transaction: BMI                                    Time: 14:08
                    Single Level Bill of Materials Inquiry


Part Number: MBL190200        Model Code: ENG
Description: Module           Make/Buy/Phantom Code: M        Used by MRP?: Y

                                              Make
Line   Oper   Component    Quantity           Buy    LT    ECN       ECN
Nbr    No     Part Number  Per Assy    U/M    Phan   Off   Number    Code

0010          JSL200849    1.000       EA     M
0020          MAL309465    5.000       EA     B
0030          ADL203940    2.000       EA     B            938498    I
0032          ADL290489    2.000       EA     B            938498    A
0040          BJL139332    1.000       EA     M
```

Figure 3.3
Single Level Bill of Materials Inquiry

The second design approach to engineering change control is to incorporate effectivity dates directly into the product structure record. This approach is illustrated in Figure 3.4.

In Figure 3.4, it is clear that line item 030 is in effect on the bill of materials until 11/12/91 and that line item 032 becomes effective (active) on 11/12/91.

Technically, both approaches will work. From an MIS point of view, the first approach is more efficient than the second approach because the effectivity dates are stored only once, in the engineering change number record. This approach was popular years ago when ease of access to data took a back seat to data storage costs. The second approach is more popular today because it allows users to query the database easily to view the bill of materials in effect on any date (past, present, or future). In Figure 3.5, the user has specified a search date of 11/13/91, and the system displays only those components that are in effect on that date.

```
Next Transaction: ___                                    Date: 09/12/91
This Transaction: BMI                                    Time: 14:08
                   Single Level Bill Of Materials Inquiry


Part Number: MBL190200          Effectivity Date Search:       Model Code: ENG
Description: Module             Make/Buy/Phantom Code: M        Used by MRP?: Y

                                            Make
Line   Oper   Component    Quantity         Buy    LT    Start      End
Nbr    No     Part Number  Per Assy   U/M   Phan   Off   Eff Date   Eff Date

0010          JSL200849    1.000      EA    M
0020          MAL309465    5.000      EA    B
0030          ADL203940    2.000      EA    B                       11/11/91
0032          ADL290489    2.000      EA    B             11/12/91
0040          BJL139332    1.000      EA    M
```

Figure 3.4
Single Level Bill of Materials Inquiry

Caveat

The ability to specify effectivity dates for engineering changes is not a perfect solution to the problem of obsolete inventory, as illustrated in the following example.

Say a company decides to do a global replacement of part *A* with part *B*. There are currently 450 pieces of part *A* in inventory. Based on the current requirements for part *A*, the material planner estimates that it will take about 60 days to use up the 450 pieces in inventory. Accordingly, the effectivity date for the global change is set 60 days into the future. After the effectivity date has been entered, new customer orders generate additional requirements for part *A* within the 60-day use-up period. The planner places an order for 1000 pieces (the economic lot size) of part *A* to cover these additional requirements. At the end of the 60-day use-up period, the on-hand inventory of part *A* has actually increased from 450 pieces to 700 pieces!

To guard against this situation, it is wise to change the lot size on the part being replaced to one. If the planner places an order during the use-up period, the order quantity will not exceed actual requirements.

As a further safeguard, some MRP II packages have the ability to print a warning message on the Planner Action Report if a need-to-order exception message is printed for a part that is affected by a global replacement. This enables the planner to reevaluate the situation to determine if the global change can be implemented sooner than expected.

Inability to Prevent Obsolete Parts from Being Added to Bills of Materials

Most companies have an engineering standards organization that is responsible for designating approved, standard parts and for declaring parts obsolete. Some reasons why a part may be declared obsolete are as follows:

- New technology causes the part to be eliminated or replaced.

- The part is replaced by another part that has a better price/performance ratio.

- Product safety.

```
Next Transaction: ___                                    Date: 09/12/91
This Transaction: BMI                                    Time: 14:09
                    Single Level Bill of Materials Inquiry


Part Number: MBL190200        Effectivity Date Search: 11/13/91 Model Code: Eng
Description: Module           Make/Buy/Phantom Code: M        Used by MRP?: Y


                                            Make
Line   Oper   Component    Quantity         Buy    LT      Start      End
Nbr    No     Part Number  Per Assy   U/M   Phan   Off     Eff Date   Eff Date

0010          JSL200849    1.000      EA    M
0020          MAL309465    5.000      EA    B
0032          ADL290489    2.000      EA    B              11/12/91
0040          BJL139332    1.000      EA    M
```

Figure 3.5
Single Level Bill of Materials Inquiry

- Product reliability.
- Environmental concerns.
- Lack of customer acceptance of a product feature.

Declaring a part obsolete is one thing; enforcing the decision is quite another. Some companies have no method of preventing an engineer from using obsolete parts. If the engineer specifies an obsolete part on a bill of materials, a purchase order or manufacturing order will be placed and obsolete inventory will be purchased or manufactured.

Solution

Provide a way to prevent obsolete parts from being used on bills of materials.

Most MRP II systems provide a part status code on the part master file. This code is used to validate bill of material maintenance. Table 3.3 lists typical part status codes.

If an engineer attempts to add anything other than an active part (part status A) to a bill of materials, the system will display an error message (Figure 3.6). The engineer must delete the part or replace it with an active part to complete the transaction. This eliminates

Table 3.3
Part Status Codes and Descriptions

Status Code	Description
A	Active part. The part can be used on any bill of materials.
O	Obsolete part. The part cannot be ordered and cannot be used on any bill of materials. A part can only be assigned this code after it has been deleted from *every* bill of materials.*
P	The part is in the process of being phased out by a global engineering change. The part cannot be added to any bill of materials. This code causes a warning message to appear on the Planner Action Report if a need-to-order exception message is generated during the phase-out period.
S	Service part. The part can be ordered as a service part but cannot be added to any bill of materials. However, the part does not have to be deleted from existing bills of materials.
H	The part is on engineering hold. The part cannot be ordered or used on any bill of materials. This status is valid only for new parts awaiting approval from engineering standards.

*An obsolete part may remain on the product structure record for historical purposes, provided it is no longer effective (active). Refer to the earlier discussion of engineering changes and effectivity dates.

obsolete inventory caused by unauthorized use of obsolete or unapproved parts.

Caveat   Some MRP II packages have a part status code but do not use the code to validate bill of materials maintenance. This code is of little value when it is used for information purposes only.

Excessive Expired Inventory

Most companies have some parts or raw materials that have a limited shelf life. In some industries (such as the food and beverage industry and the chemicals and pharmaceuticals industry), almost all materials have a shelf life. If material is not used by its shelf life expiration date, it automatically becomes obsolete inventory. Expired materials can be a major cause of obsolete inventory for companies that are unable to allocate materials to production based on shelf life expiration dates.

```
Next Transaction: ___                              Date: 10/02/91
This Transaction: BMM                              Time: 11:10
                        Bill of Materials Maintenance


Part Number: REL200423          Model Code: ENG
Description: Pump               Make/Buy/Phantom Code: M        Used by MRP?: Y


Line   Oper   Component      Quantity          LT    Start       End
Nbr    No     Part Number    Per Assy   U/M    Off   Eff Date    Eff Date

0010          MBL100849       1.000     EA
0020          JSL989405       5.000     EA
0030          ADL294569       2.000     EA
0040          BJL134532       1.000     EA
0050          BJL304953       1.000     EA




MSG0203: Part BJL304953 Is Obsolete (Part Status Code = 0). Transaction cannot
be processed until part is deleted or changed.
```

Figure 3.6
Bill of Materials Maintenance Screen

Solution

Provide the ability to allocate inventory by shelf life expiration date.

Some MRP II packages automatically allocate (reserve) inventory when a picklist is requested for a manufacturing or customer order. The allocation process serves two purposes:

1. It supports the picking simulation feature described in Chapter 2.

2. It allocates a specific lot of inventory and instructs the stockkeeper to pick that lot.

It is the second purpose that is of interest here. Some MRP II packages allow a shelf life expiration date to be assigned to each lot of inventory. The shelf life expiration date is stored on the inventory detail record (Figure 3.7).

Some MRP II packages use the shelf life expiration date to allocate inventory. When a picklist is requested, the system allocates inventory in sequence from earliest to latest shelf life expiration date. In Figure 3.7, if 100 pieces of part JSL394042 are required, the system will allocate 30 pieces from lot 002 and 70 pieces from lot 001. The picklist will instruct the stockkeeper to pick 30 pieces from lot 002 in location SB920 and 70 pieces from lot 001 in location SB390. This helps to eliminate obsolete inventory by ensuring that the oldest material is used first.

Caveat

Some MRP II packages do not allocate inventory. A picklist is printed showing the stockkeeper the location of all the inventory lots, but the stockkeeper has to decide manually how to pick the material.

Some MRP II packages provide the ability to allocate inventory on a first-in, first-out (FIFO) basis. FIFO allocation is not quite the same thing as allocation by expiration date. FIFO allocation keys off the receipt date to allocate material instead of the shelf life expiration date. If a part is purchased from only one vendor, the receipt date may relate directly to the shelf life expiration date. However, if a part is purchased from two vendors, the receipt date may not be related to the expiration date.

For example, in Figure 3.7, lot 002 was received two weeks after lot 001 but has an earlier expiration date. This is because lots 001 and 002 were purchased from different vendors. FIFO allocation would allocate material from lot 001 before lot 002 even though lot 002 has an earlier expiration date.

```
Next Transaction: ___                                           Date: 08/01/91
This Transaction: IDI                                           Time: 11:30
                          Inventory Detail Inquiry

Part Number: JSL394042    Qty Available to Be Allocated:         130
                          Qty Unavailable for Manufacturing:       0
                          Qty Available for MRP Planning:        130
                          Qty Unavailable for MRP Planning:        0

Lot           Quantity Quantity  MRP    Inv Reason  Date      Shelf     Order    Lot
Nbr Location  on Hand Allocated Avail?  Stat Code   Received  ExpDate   Number   Trc

001 SB390        100        0    Y      AM          05/07/91  03/12/92  1S229328
002 SB920         30        0    Y      AM          05/21/91  01/13/92  1S209348
```

Figure 3.7
Inventory Detail Inquiry

Some MRP II packages provide the option to calculate the shelf life expiration date automatically based on the receipt date. The useful shelf life (in days) is specified on the part master record. When an order is received, the system automatically adds this number of days to the receipt date to determine the shelf life expiration date. This method of determining shelf life expiration dates is viable only for parts that are manufactured in-house. It is not viable for purchased materials because, as was previously noted, the expiration date cannot be accurately predicted from the receipt date. Expiration dates on purchased materials are specified by suppliers and are usually marked clearly on the package. The expiration date should be entered manually into the system when the lot is received.

Some MRP II packages provide a number of different ways to allocate material but do not support either allocation by expiration date or FIFO allocation. Other allocation methods include:

- *Primary stock location method.* This method allocates inventory from a designated primary stock location first, then randomly from other stock locations.

- *Lowest quantity method.* This method allocates inventory from locations that have the lowest on-hand inventory. This helps to free up storage locations.

- *Entire requirement method.* This method allocates inventory from a location that can satisfy the total quantity required. This improves productivity by reducing the number of locations from which the stockkeeper has to pick to satisfy a requirement.

The above allocation methods are more concerned with the physical location of the material than the physical characteristics (e.g., age) of the material. These allocation methods are useful for parts that do not have a shelf life, but they do nothing to help reduce obsolete inventory.

Inability to Identify Slow-Moving Inventory

Today's slow-moving inventory is tomorrow's obsolete inventory. Unfortunately, the only test some companies have to identify slow-moving inventory is the infamous "white glove test," which checks the amount of dust that has accumulated on inventory in the stockroom.

Solution   *Provide a report that identifies slow-moving parts.*

Many MRP II packages provide a standard report that identifies slow-moving parts (Figure 3.8). The report typically lists all parts that meet the following criteria:

- On-hand balance greater than zero

- Last date of issue greater than *x* days ago, where *x* is an exception reporting parameter set by the user

The report may also calculate the extended value of the inventory at standard or actual cost. Sorting the data by extended value in descending order focuses attention on the exceptions that have the greatest impact on inventory carrying costs.

The Slow-Moving Parts Report can be distributed to Engineering for evaluation. The engineer may try to use up inventory of slow-moving parts by:

```
Date: 08/01/91                                              Page: 01
                         Slow-Moving Parts Report
                 Sorted by Extended Dollar Value (Descending Order)
                    Last Date of Issue Greater Than 100 Days Ago
                          Cutoff: $100 Extended Value


                           Inventory        Last
                 On-Hand    Value at       Date of     Expiration
Part Number      Quantity   Std Cost        Issue         Date

ADL675684          120    $ 4347.63       04/14/91       09/14/91
MBL295674           35      3224.95       11/12/90
JSB453447          130      2050.10       01/23/91
MBL047689           12      1332.00       10/08/90       11/08/91
REL213424          200       930.00       09/12/89
BJL465741         1000       530.00       01/14/90
MJM346584           10       340.00       05/28/91       10/14/91
AEM455654          200       230.00       05/14/91
BJL347891          234       119.34       08/12/90




Total Inventory Value:              $22,749.32
```

Figure 3.8
Slow-Moving Parts Report

- Making a temporary change to a bill of materials.
- Incorporating the part into a design for a customer order. This technique is most applicable in engineer-to-order type businesses.

Early Shipments and Overshipments from Vendors

Many companies lack a viable tool to help them prevent or detect early shipments and overshipments. Without an effective method of monitoring vendor delivery performance, a company may spend an amount equal to 1/2 percent of its annual purchases on inventory carrying costs caused by early shipments and overshipments.

For example, consider a $200 million company that has about $100 million in annual purchases and an annual carrying cost of 20 percent. If material is received an average of one week before the due-on-dock date, the company will incur about $400,000 in additional carrying costs per year. If vendors ship an average of 5 percent over the order quantity, and if the excess material stays in inventory for an average of four weeks, the company will incur about $80,000 in additional carrying costs per year. The combined total of $480,000 is about 1/2 percent of the company's total annual purchasing budget.

Solution

Provide effective methods of monitoring vendor delivery performance.

MRP II software packages provide methods of monitoring vendor delivery performance by means of vendor delivery performance statistics and receiving exception processing.

Vendor Delivery Performance Statistics

Some MRP II systems detect early shipments and overshipments at the time of receipt. The on-line receiving transaction compares the date received to the due-on-dock date. If the date received is *earlier* than the due-on-dock date, and if the dates differ by more than a specified number of days (known as the **early shipment tolerance parameter**), the receipt is classified as an early shipment.

The on-line receiving transaction also compares the quantity received to the quantity ordered. If the quantity received exceeds the quantity ordered by more than a specified percentage (known as the **overshipment tolerance parameter**), the receipt is classified as an overshipment.

Statistics on early shipments and overshipments are stored in the vendor master file and can be viewed on-line (Figure 3.9).[2] These statistics help buyers monitor vendor delivery performance and select vendors that comply with company policies on early shipments and overshipments.

Some MRP II systems also maintain statistics on early shipments and overshipments by buyer. This enables the Manager of

2. Some MRP II packages also compare the date received to the due-on-dock date to calculate statistics on late shipments. Such statistics are of dubious value, because the vendor cannot be faulted for missing the due-on-dock date if the order was placed with insufficient lead time.

A more valid approach to measuring late shipments would be to compare the date received to the ship promise date, allowing for in-transit time. I am not aware of any MRP II package that takes this approach to measuring vendors on late shipments.

```
Next Transaction: ___                              Date: 08/21/91
This Transaction: VPI                              Time: 09:24
                        Vendor Performance Inquiry

Vendor Code: 35673       Group Code:      Name: Robertson Instruments

Street: 1020 Middle St.  City: Milford       State: CT
Zip: 06460-1453          Country: USA        Attn: Eddie Carpman

                                      Year
                           Current    to
                           Quarter    Date    1990    1989    1988

Number of Shipments Inspected    26     145     201     212     186
Number of Shipments Rejected      0       2       5       7      10
** Quality Performance Rating   100    98.6    97.5    96.7    94.6
Total Number of Shipments Received 35   153     245     234     212
Number of Early Shipments         1       3       7      12      12
** Percent Early Shipments      2.9     2.0     2.1     5.1     5.7
Number of Overshipments           2       5       7       8      10
** Percent Overshipments        5.8     3.3     2.9     3.4     4.7
Total Dollars Purchased      12,692  80,302 132,242 132,272 134,669
Total Dollars at Std Cost    13,340  85,203 128,902 123,289 143,203
** Percent under Standard Cost  4.9     5.8    -2.6    -7.3     5.6
```

Figure 3.9
Vendor Performance Inquiry

Purchasing to evaluate how well each buyer is managing vendor delivery performance. Delivery performance statistics by buyer are stored in the buyer record in the MRP II database and can be viewed on-line (Figure 3.10). The performance statistics may be divided into time periods to help the Manager of Purchasing evaluate buyer performance for a specific performance evaluation period.

Early shipment and overshipment policies are implicit in the specification of early shipment and overshipment tolerance parameters. For example, an overshipment tolerance parameter of 5 percent means that vendors are allowed to ship up to 5 percent more than the order quantity.

Some MRP II packages only allow these parameters to be specified globally. This does not make much sense, since an early shipment or overshipment of a $500 part will have more impact on inventory carrying costs than an early shipment or overshipment of a $0.05 part. Because of this, the better MRP II packages allow receiving tolerance parameters to be specified independently for each part (Figure 3.11). High receiving tolerances can be assigned to low-value parts, and low receiving tolerances can be assigned to high-value parts. For example, a part that costs $0.05 might have an early shipment tolerance parameter of 30 days and an overshipment tolerance parameter of 20 percent, whereas a part that costs $500 may have an early shipment tolerance of two days and an overshipment tolerance of 0 percent.

Receiving Exception Processing

Some MRP II systems automatically place early shipments and overshipments on hold status in receiving. These receipts must be reviewed by the buyer for final disposition. Possible dispositions for early shipments are as follows:

- Accept the early shipment.

- Return the shipment to the vendor at the vendor's expense.

```
Next Transaction: ___                                      Date: 08/21/91
This Transaction: BPI                                      Time: 09:24
                            Buyer Performance Inquiry

Buyer Code: 03              Name: Jack Coulter        Phone: 703-384-2834

                                        Year
                           Current       to
                           Quarter      Date      1990      1989      1988

Number of Shipments Inspected   180      745       1201      1212
Number of Shipments Rejected      2        8         14        20
** Quality Performance Rating  98.9     99.1       98.8      98.3

Total Number of Shipments       235      953       1545      1634
Number of Early Shipments        11       33         87        92
** Percent Early Shipments      4.7      3.5        5.6       5.6
Number of Overshipments           7       32         53       112
** Percent Overshipments        3.0      3.4        3.4       6.9

Total Dollars Purchased      72,452  480,302    732,242   722,272
Total Dollars at Std Cost    78,340  495,203    718,902   705,279
** Percent under Standard Cost  7.5      3.0       -1.8      -2.4
```

Figure 3.10
Buyer Performance Inquiry

```
Next Transaction: ___                                    Date: 10/11/91
This Transaction: PCP                                    Time: 10:13
                     Purchasing Control Parameter Inquiry

Part Number: EL29309            Buyer: 02

Description: 1/8 HP Motor       Standard Cost: $ 125.00

Inspection Required: Y          Sole Source: N
Applied/Unapplied Code: A       Type Unapplied Material: 01

Receiving Tolerances

                           Early Shipment Tolerance Parameter:  3 Days
                           Overshipment Tolerance Parameter:  0 Percent

Invoice Tolerances:

                           Invoice Tolerance Percent:  3.0
                           Invoice Tolerance Amount:  0.50
```

Figure 3.11
Purchasing Control Parameter Inquiry

Possible dispositions for overshipments are as follows:

- Accept the entire shipment.

- Return the excess quantity to the vendor at the vendor's expense.

Receiving exceptions are held in a temporary storage location pending disposition by the buyer. The buyer can view receiving exceptions on-line and enter authorization either to accept the shipment or to return part or all of the shipment to the vendor (Figure 3.12).

Inability to Schedule Just-in-Time Delivery of Material

Inability to Schedule Just-in-Time Delivery for Final Assembly

The inability to schedule just-in-time delivery of major subassemblies and expensive purchased components into final assembly can substantially increase inventory carrying costs. Some companies manufacture complex products that have long final assembly cycles. Many homegrown systems schedule all material required for final assembly to arrive at the beginning of the final assembly cycle, *even though some parts may not be needed until the end of the final assembly cycle.*

For example, a company may have a five-week final assembly cycle, but a $5000 transformer may not be needed until the last day of final assembly. Many homegrown systems would schedule delivery of the transformer five weeks prior to when it is actually needed!

```
Next Transaction: ___                                    Date: 11/11/91
This Transaction: REA                                    Time: 12:13
                      Receiving Exception Authorization

Buyer: 04

PO        It                      Receiving  Date              Days Quantity
Number    No Vendor   Part Number Control #  Received Category Early    Over

1C390490  01 23943    ADL309409   R304-301   11/10/91 Early      8
Disposition: Accept: Y Return:__  Partial Return:__  Quantity:__

1C394839  03 29302    MKL390209   R305-021   11/11/91 Over                20
Disposition: Accept: _ Return:__  Partial Return: X  Quantity:__ 20

1S920947  01 29304    MBL390189   R305-033   11/11/91 Early     25
Disposition: Accept: _ Return: X  Partial Return:__  Quantity:__

1C390203  02 39092    JSL309090   R305-040   11/11/91 Early/Over  9        23
Disposition: Accept: _ Return:__  Partial Return: X  Quantity:__ 23
```

Figure 3.12
Receiving Exception Authorization Screen

Solution

Provide the ability to stagger the delivery of parts throughout the final assembly cycle.

Most MRP II packages have a lead time offset feature in the Bill of Materials module. This feature helps to reduce inventory carrying costs by allowing parts to be scheduled for delivery a specified number of days *after* the assembly start date. The lead time offset feature is used most frequently to schedule high-value parts that are purchased or manufactured in discrete (one-for-one) quantities for use in final assembly. However, this feature can also be used to stagger the delivery of parts at any level of the bill of materials.

The number of offset days is specified by component on the product structure record. In Figure 3.13, part MBL100205 has a lead time offset of five days and part JSL380199 has a lead time offset of ten days. The MRP planning program adds five days to the assembly start date to determine the requirement need date for part MBL100205, and it adds ten days to the assembly start date to determine the requirement need date for part JSL380199. The requirement need date for all the other parts is the assembly start date.

Caveat

Most MRP II software packages do an excellent job of planning just-in-time deliveries but do a poor job of executing the plan. (In this case, the term **execution** refers to the ability to route just-in-time deliveries to final assembly.) A final assembly picklist will be produced by the system just prior to the beginning of final assembly. Parts having lead time offsets are not included on the final assembly picklist because they are not scheduled to arrive until after the order has been released to final assembly. Unfortunately, most MRP II packages have no facility for routing these parts directly to final assembly after they are received (and inspected, if necessary). The parts may be routed to the stockroom instead, resulting in a shortage in final assembly. A similar problem, that of routing receipts to fill material shortages, is discussed in Chapter 2.

One way to solve this problem is to add levels to the bill of materials instead of staggering delivery of parts within a single level of the bill of materials. This solution permits the normal manufacturing order/picklist routines to be used to route material to the shop floor. Figure 3.14 illustrates this approach.

In Figure 3.14, two new assemblies (FA100 and FA200) have been added to the bill of materials to accommodate the lead time offsets for parts MBL100205 and JSL380199. Manufacturing orders and

```
Next Transaction: ___                                    Date: 09/12/91
This Transaction: BMI                                    Time: 14:09
                  Single Level Bill of Materials Inquiry


Part Number: MAL230200        Effectivity Date Search:      Model Code: Eng
Description: Module           Make/Buy/Phantom Code: M   Used by MRP?: Y

                                          Make
Line  Oper   Component    Quantity        Buy    LT    Start      End
Nbr   No     Part Number  Per Assy   U/M  Phan   Off   Eff Date   Eff Date

0010         MBL100205    1.000      EA   M      5
0020         MAL487665    5.000      EA   B
0030         ADL230459    2.000      EA   B
0040         JSL380199    1.000      EA   B      10
0050         MBL239023    2.000      EA   M
0060         EL2303       1.000      EA   B
```

Figure 3.13
Single Level Bill of Materials Inquiry

picklists will be created for each of the new assemblies at the appropriate time.

This approach will work, but it adds unnecessary complexity and costs to the manufacturing process, and the bill of materials no longer reflects the way the product is really manufactured. This solution is also in conflict with the JIT management philosophy which employs "flatter" bills of materials (i.e., bills of materials with fewer levels) to help reduce cycle times and streamline the manufacturing process.

Another approach is to adapt the solution that is presented in Chapter 2 for routing receipts to fill material shortages. This can be accomplished by modifying the system to create shortage records for parts that have lead time offsets. The shortage records would be created at the time the final assembly picklist is produced. When material is received, the on-line receiving transaction can route the receipt to fill these pseudo-shortages using the method described in Chapter 2. (The term **pseudo-shortage** is appropriate because these

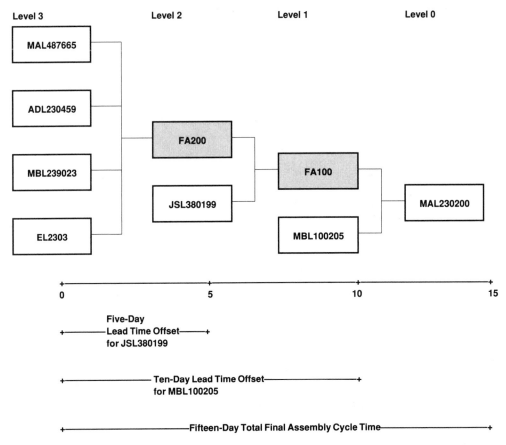

Figure 3.14
Multiple-Level Bill of Materials Diagram

parts are not scheduled to be available when the final assembly picklist is generated.) If this approach is used, a code should be added to the shortage record to differentiate between pseudo-shortages and real shortages. This code can then be used to exclude the pseudo-shortages from certain shortage reports. If the part has not been delivered to final assembly by its need date, the code should be automatically removed from the shortage record, and the part should be treated as a real shortage.

Inability to Schedule Multiple Deliveries against a Single Purchase Order Line Item

A common purchasing practice is to order parts in large quantities to take advantage of quantity discounts offered by vendors. By scheduling multiple deliveries, the buyer can minimize the impact on inventory carrying costs without losing the quantity discount, which is usually based on the total order quantity.

Some homegrown purchasing systems do not allow multiple deliveries to be scheduled against a single purchase order line item. If the buyer places a large order to obtain a quantity discount, a portion of the order will arrive before it is needed, resulting in higher carrying costs.

Solution

Provide the ability to schedule multiple deliveries against a single purchase order line item.

Some MRP II systems allow buyers to take advantage of quantity discounts without impacting inventory carrying costs. Figure 3.15 shows the difference between the database of a typical homegrown purchasing system and an MRP II system. Both systems store purchase order header information and purchase order line item information, but only the MRP II system has the ability to go to a lower level of detail to store multiple ship schedules.

Figures 3.16, 3.17, and 3.18 illustrate how an MRP II system enables a buyer to obtain the lowest price without impacting inventory carrying costs. The buyer creates the purchase order line item and enters the total item order quantity (Figure 3.16). The system automatically retrieves the correct item price from the price break information stored in the vendor-item-quote record (Figure 3.17).

In this example, the buyer has specified an order quantity of 500 pieces, and the system has selected a price of $8.95 each from the vendor-item-quote record. The buyer enters multiple ship schedules (Figure 3.18), and the system verifies that the sum of the quantities on the individual ship schedules is equal to the total item order quantity. The ship schedules are printed on the hard copy of the purchase order that goes to the vendor.

Typical Homegrown Purchasing System Database

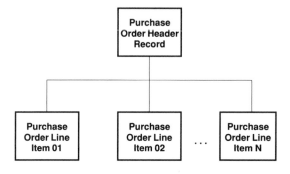

Typical MRP II Purchasing System Database

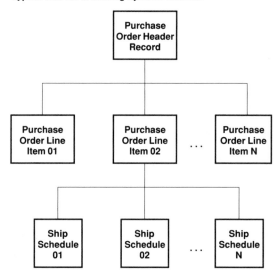

Figure 3.15
*Comparison between a Typical Homegrown and a
Typical MRP II Purchasing System Database*

Inability to Schedule Deliveries around
Nonworking Days

Some manufacturers schedule plant shutdowns once or twice a year for one or two weeks. Material should not be scheduled for delivery during these periods, because it will not be used until the plant resumes production.

Some homegrown systems do not take nonworking days into consideration when scheduling materials. This can have a significant

---

```
Next Transaction: ___                                    Date: 12/01/91
This Transaction: API                                    Time: 09:45
                        Add Purchase Order Line Item

PO Number: 1R400100 PO Line Number: 01 Buyer: 05

Vendor: 30030 Name: Electric Distributors

Part Number: TQL110025        Quantity:     500 Unit: EA  Price:    8.95 PER: E

Description: 25-Amp Circuit Breaker

Required Ship Date: __/__/__    Ship Promise Date: __/__/__

Lot Trace Receipts?      Inspection Required?      Vendor Require Print?

GL Account Number: 001-0293-10293 Ship to Code: DSD

Multiple Ship Schedules? Y Additional Text? N

Standard Message Codes: 01 04
```

Figure 3.16
Add Purchase Order Line Item Screen

impact on inventory carrying costs. Consider a $200 million business that purchases about $100 million worth of material per year and has an annual inventory carrying cost of 20 percent. Such a company receives about $2 million of material each week. If the company closes down for four weeks each year and is unable to stop deliveries during the shutdown weeks, the company may incur up to $30,000 in additional carrying costs each year, as follows:

4 weeks × $2 million/week × 0.20/52 weeks = $30,769

Solution   *Provide the ability to define and schedule around nonworking days.*

All MRP II systems schedule manufacturing operations from a plant calendar that is stored in the database. The user can define any nonworking days (scheduled shutdowns, holidays, and weekends) on the plant calendar by means of an on-line transaction (Figure

3.19). The system schedules all manufacturing-related activities, including the receipt of purchased material, around these nonworking days.

Caveat   The plant calendar assumes that all work centers will be operational on every workday. However, this may not be the case. For example, certain areas of the plant may have different work schedules than other areas. Unfortunately, most MRP II systems do not provide the ability to define individual calendars for each work center.

Large Economic Lot Sizes for Purchased Parts

Buyers sometimes have to order more inventory than is needed because minimum billing charges and/or high ordering costs inflate economic order quantities.

```
Next Transaction: ___                                  Date: 12/01/91
This Transaction: IQI                                  Time: 09:45
                           Vendor Quote Inquiry

Part Number: TQL110025  Quote Number: 49059      Quote Effective: 09/05/91
                                                 Quote Expires: 09/05/92
Description: 25-Amp Circuit Breaker

Vendor: 30030 Name: Electric Distributors
Vendor Part Number:               Vendor Unit of Purchase: EA

Price Per: Each        Base Price:        Setup Charge:
Minimum Order Quantity:

                        Price Break Information

Price                      Percent off
Break    Quantity    Price Base Price

  01           1    12.95
  02         100    10.95
  03         250     9.95
  04         500     8.95
  05        1000     7.95
```

Figure 3.17
Vendor Quote Inquiry

```
Next Transaction: ___                               Date: 12/01/91
This Transaction: MSS                               Time: 09:46
                   Add Multiple Ship Schedules

PO Number: 1R400100  PO Line Number:  01  Buyer: 05
Vendor: 30030  Name: Electric Distributors

Part Number: TQL110025  Quantity:  500  Unit: EA    Price:  8.95    Per: E


Ship                      Required        Ship
Schedule       Ship         Ship       Promise
Number       Quantity       Date         Date

  01            100       01/07/92
  02            100       01/14/92
  03            100       01/21/92
  04            100       02/05/92
  05            100       02/12/92
```

Figure 3.18
Add Multiple Ship Schedules Screen

Minimum Billing Charges

Some vendors have a minimum billing charge policy to compel customers to place orders large enough to cover their internal order processing costs. Minimum billing charges vary from vendor to vendor, but they typically range from $25 to $100 per purchase order. A purchase order may contain multiple line items, but the total value of the purchase order must meet a specified dollar amount to avoid the minimum billing penalty (which is the difference between the value of the purchase order and the minimum billing charge). Rather than pay a penalty, the buyer will increase the order quantity so that the extended purchase order dollar value just equals the minimum billing charge. The buyer avoids the penalty but creates an inventory problem in the process.

The easiest way to avoid minimum billing charges without incurring extra inventory carrying costs is to place multiple-item purchase orders that meet the minimum billing criteria. Some homegrown

```
Next Transaction: ___                                          Date: 11/01/91
This Transaction: PCM                                          Time: 12:12
                           Plant Calendar Maintenance

12/01/91   12/02/91   12/03/91   12/04/91   12/05/91   12/06/91   12/07/91
Off                                                                Off

12/08/91   12/09/91   12/10/91   12/11/91   12/12/91   12/13/91   12/14/91
Off                                                                Off

12/15/91   12/16/91   12/17/91   12/18/91   12/19/91   12/20/91   12/21/91
Off        Shutdown   Shutdown   Shutdown   Shutdown   Shutdown   Off

12/22/91   12/23/91   12/24/91   12/25/91   12/26/91   12/27/91   12/28/91
Off        Shutdown   Holiday    Holiday    Shutdown   Shutdown   Off

12/29/91   12/30/91   12/31/91   01/01/92   01/02/92   01/03/92   01/04/92
Off                              Holiday                           Off

01/05/92   01/06/92   01/07/92   01/08/92   01/09/92   01/10/92   01/11/92
Off                                                                Off
```

Figure 3.19
Plant Calendar Maintenance Screen

purchasing systems don't allow multiple-item purchase orders, and some systems have restrictions on how individual line items for the same vendor can be combined into multiple-item purchase orders.

For example, some purchasing systems cannot do inventory accounting at the line-item level. Such systems require that all items on a purchase order be charged to the same inventory account. The chargeable inventory account is specified in the purchase order header record or may be indicated by a significant digit in the purchase order number. The inability to combine items from different inventory accounts on the same purchase order may cause the buyer to place several small orders to a vendor instead of one large multiple-item order. If any of these orders fails to meet the minimum billing charge, the buyer will have to increase the order quantity to bring the order up to the minimum amount.

Solution   *Provide the ability to place multiple-item purchase orders, and provide inventory accounting at the line-item level.*

Most MRP II systems allow up to 999 items per purchase order and provide inventory accounting at the line-item level. An inventory account number can be specified for each item on the purchase order, eliminating the restrictions on combining across inventory accounts.

High Ordering Costs

Even if vendors don't impose minimum billing charges, buyers may have to order excess inventory to offset high purchase order processing costs. The administrative activities associated with the life cycle of a purchase order are listed below. Actual administrative costs vary from company to company, but they typically range from $50 to $100 per order. Scheduling multiple deliveries per line item does not really solve this problem because many of the administrative costs (expediting, receiving, inspection, material handling, and invoice processing) are proportional to the number of deliveries associated with a purchase order. The real solution lies in reducing the costs of the activities in the following list to make it economical for buyers to place frequent orders for small quantities.

1. Vendor selection

2. Purchase order generation

3. Purchase order distribution

4. Acknowledgment posting

5. Change order processing

6. Expediting

7. Receiving

8. Inspection

9. Material handling

10. Invoice data entry

11. Invoice matching

12. Invoice reconciliation (discrepant invoices)

13. Invoice payment

   Note: A similar problem, high set-up costs, exists in many factories. High set-up costs cause factories to manufacture more inventory than is needed. Set-up reductions are not achieved by implementing MRP II or any other software package. They are achieved by a combination of analyzing the setup, revising procedures and tooling, and implementing flexible manufacturing systems.

Solution   *Reduce economic lot sizes by providing the ability to automate or eliminate the administrative activities associated with the purchasing cycle.*

MRP II software systems have features that help automate most of the activities associated with the purchasing cycle. Table 3.4 provides a list of the features found in MRP II packages that help automate administrative purchasing activities. These features are discussed in more detail in Chapter 6, which addresses the productivity problem (except for on-line inspection, which is discussed in Chapter 4).

Improper Allocation of Finished Goods Inventory to Customer Orders

A few years ago, I was consulting for a manufacturer of power supplies who had a serious inventory problem. One day, the Manager of Customer Service proudly showed me his company's new on-line order entry system. The system had taken two years and over $1 million to develop. We watched as an order entry clerk took a phone order for 50 of a particular power supply and entered it into the system. The customer requested shipment on July 1, which was three months away. The order entry system confirmed that the

Table 3.4
*MRP II Features That Help Automate Administrative
Purchasing Activities*

Activity	Relevant MRP II Feature	MRP II Module
1. Vendor selection	Automatic purchase order processing	Purchasing
2. Purchase order generation	Automatic purchase order generation	Purchasing
3. Purchase order distribution	Electronic data interchange	EDI
4. Expediting	Vendor Action Report	Purchasing
5. Receiving	On-line receiving	Purchasing
6. Inspection	On-line inspection	Purchasing
7. Material handling	(Not addressed by MRP II packages)	N/A
8. Invoice data entry	On-line invoice data entry	Accounts Payable
9. Invoice matching	Automatic three-way matching	Accounts Payable
10. Invoice reconciliation	Electronic review and approval of discrepant invoices	Purchasing and Accounts Payable
11. Invoice payment	Automatic generation of payments	Accounts Payable

product was in stock and reserved 50 pieces of finished goods for shipment on July 1.

"Did you see how quickly we were able to process that order?" the Manager of Customer Service asked.

But I was too puzzled by what I had observed to respond to the question.

"Why did the system do that?" I asked.

"Do what?" the Manager of Customer Service replied.

"Why did the system reserve 50 pieces of finished goods inventory?"

"Why, to make sure that we meet the customer's requested ship date," he answered.

"But now you've committed to hold 50 units in inventory for three months. If another customer places an order and requests immediate shipment, you may not have enough inventory to satisfy the order. Meanwhile, the inventory you just reserved will be on the shelf gathering dust and carrying charges for three months."

"That may be true, but we can't give the second customer preference over the first customer," he said. "We have to satisfy the customers on a first come, first served basis. We can't call the first customer back and say, 'We're sorry, but we have a customer who can accept immediate shipment, and we want to turn our inventory.' We need to keep our promises to our customers."

"But it's not really a case of first come, first served or broken promises," I explained. "The order entry system only checked finished goods inventory—it never considered allocating inventory from scheduled production runs. Let's go take a look at the Master Production Schedule for this product."

We walked over to the master scheduler's office and checked the production schedule. A run of 300 units was scheduled for the week ending July 1.

"If the order entry system had access to this information, inventory could have been allocated from the production run. This would keep your finished-goods inventory available for immediate shipment," I explained. "You'll be able to turn your inventory faster while keeping your promises to both customers."

This company had too much finished-goods inventory because the order entry system was reserving available inventory for *any* customer order, regardless of the requested ship date. The order entry system allowed clerks to process orders quickly, but it was a major cause of the company's inventory problem.

Solution   *Provide Order Entry with visibility to the Master Production Schedule.*

The Order Entry module in an MRP II system is integrated with both the Inventory Control module and the Master Production Schedule module to provide order entry clerks with visibility to both finished-goods inventory and future production schedules. If a customer requires immediate shipment or shipment before the next scheduled production run, the Order Entry module allocates finished-goods inventory. Otherwise the Order Entry module attempts to allocate inventory from future production runs.

The Master Production Schedule module keeps track of the following information for each product by week (or day):

- The quantity scheduled

- The quantity promised to customer orders

- The quantity that is available-to-promise (ATP) to customer orders

This information is updated as customer orders are processed.

In Table 3.5, there are 64 units of product MAL100278 available for immediate shipment. For the week ending July 1, there are 300 units scheduled for production. Of these, 135 units have already been promised to customer orders, leaving 165 units available to promise.

Chapter 5, which addresses the customer service problem, contains a detailed discussion of how inventory is allocated to customer orders. It also includes a discussion of make-to-stock and assemble-to-order solutions.

Recursivity on Bills of Materials

I was sitting at my desk one day when someone from Production Control wheeled a wagon into my office. The wagon was filled with stacks of manufacturing orders.

"What in the world is that?" I asked.

"All these are orders for the same part," he replied. "If I release these orders to the shop, we'll produce about three years' worth of inventory. I don't know what caused all these orders, but it must be some kind of system problem."

I investigated the problem and found that the avalanche of orders had been caused by a recursivity (looping) problem on the bill of materials. The part was calling for *itself* as a component on the bill

Table 3.5
*Available-to-Promise Information from the Master
Production Schedule*

Part Number: MAL100278

Available Inventory: 64

Week Ending	Quantity Scheduled	Quantity Promised	Quantity Available to Promise
05/06/91	300	280	84
05/13/91	300	250	50
05/20/91	300	270	30
05/27/91	400	400	0
06/03/91	300	200	100
06/10/91	300	182	118
06/17/91	300	165	135
06/24/91	300	150	150
07/01/91	300	135	165
07/08/91	300	100	200
07/15/91	300	80	220
07/22/91	0	(Plant shutdown)	
07/29/91	0	(Plant shutdown)	
08/06/91	200	55	145
08/13/91	300	35	265
08/20/91	300	0	300

of materials, and the system was caught in an infinite loop trying to explode the bill of materials. We were able to correct the problem and cancel all the manufacturing orders, but not before $50,000 worth of lower-level purchased parts had been ordered and received.

Figure 3.20 illustrates the recursivity problem. Part *A* at Level 1 on the bill of materials is calling for part *A* at Level 5. Each time the bill of materials is exploded down to Level 5, the explosion process begins again. Clearly, the explosion process never ends.

Most systems limit the number of levels that are exploded in a single batch run. If the limit is 20 levels, the bill of materials in Figure 3.20 will be exploded four times each time the system is run. This process will go on forever, or until somebody notices and corrects the problem.

Solution   *Provide for automatic recursivity checking.*

All MRP II systems automatically check for recursivity whenever bills of materials are maintained. If the system detects a looping

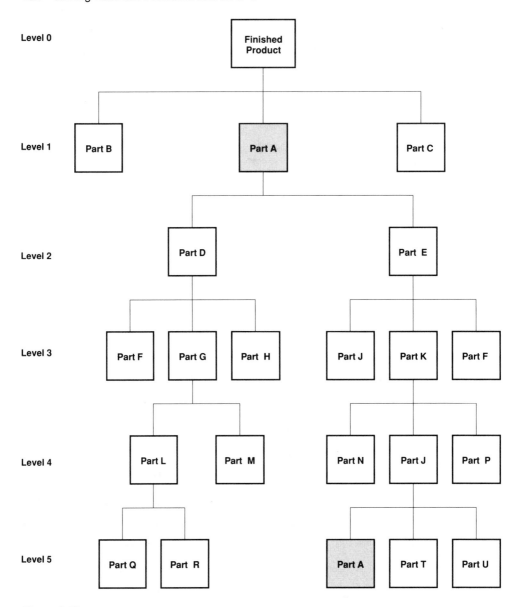

Figure 3.20
Recursivity on the Bill of Materials

condition, an error message is displayed (Figure 3.21). The user must correct the error before the transaction can be processed.

Lost Inventory

The following scenario is all too familiar at some companies:

Stockroom Manager: "We can't find the part."

Production Control Manager: "What do you mean you can't find the part? According to the stock locator report, the part is in location SJ2939."

Stockroom Manager: "That's just it! Location SJ2939 doesn't exist."

Production Control Manager (incredulously): "Of course it does! It's right here on the report!"

```
Next Transaction: ___                                      Date: 10/02/91
This Transaction: BMM                                      Time: 11:10
                          Bill of Materials Maintenance


Part Number:   REL200423          Model Code: ENG
Description:   Pump               Make/Buy/Phantom Code: M        Used by MRP?: Y


Line   Oper   Component     Quantity           LT    Start         End
Nbr    No     Part Number   Per Assy    U/M    Off   Eff Date      Eff Date

0010          MBL100849      1.000      EA
0020          JSL989405      5.000      EA
0030          ADL294569      2.000      EA
0040          BJL134532      1.000      EA
0050          REL200423      1.000      EA
```

MSG0120: Part REL200423   is calling for itself as a component.
Transaction cannot be processed until part is deleted or changed.

Figure 3.21
Bill of Materials Maintenance Screen

Stockroom Manager: "You don't understand. Our system doesn't validate data input. Occasionally the stockkeeper writes down an incorrect location or the keypunch clerk misinterprets the stockkeeper's writing. When that happens, invalid locations get into the system and appear on the stock locator report."

Production Control Manager: "So you don't know where you put the material."

Stockroom Manager: "That's right."

Production Control Manager: "That's great! What the heck am I supposed to do now?"

Stockroom Manager: "Well, we've been looking high and low and we know it's in the stockroom somewhere. But so far we've been unable to find the part. But don't worry, I asked Purchasing to place another order. We should get more inventory tomorrow."

Eventually the part is found, but not before the misplaced inventory has been replaced.

```
Next Transaction: ___                                    Date: 12/02/91
This Transaction: SMM                                    Time: 12:10
                      Storage Location Master Maintenance

Action      Storage     Location
Code        Master      Description

  A         HR100       High Rise Storage
  A         HR200       High Rise Storage
  A         RF100       Refrigerated Storage Room 1
  A         RF101       Refrigerated Storage Room 1
  A         EC323       Elec Components, Row 3, Bin 23
```

Figure 3.22
Storage Location Master Maintenance Screen

```
Next Transaction: ___                                    Date: 12/11/91
This Transaction: PMI                                    Time: 11:30
                        Put Material into Inventory

Part Number: JSL394042

                    Quantity:   50
                    Location: SV100
                    Status: AM
                    MRP Avail: Y
                    Reason Code:
                    Shelf Life Expiration Date:
                    Lot Trace?:
```

```
MSG6294: Location SV100                  is an invalid storage location.
Create storage location master record, or correct location and proceed.
```

Figure 3.23
Put Material into Inventory Screen

Solution   *Provide the ability to validate storage locations on inventory
                      transactions.*

                      As an option, some MRP II packages provide the ability to validate
                      storage locations on transactions that put material into inventory.
                      Valid storage locations can be predefined by using an on-line trans-
                      action to create storage location master records (Figure 3.22).
                        If the validation option is used, all inventory transactions validate
                      storage locations against storage master records. If the stockkeeper
                      specifies a location that does not exist (i.e., a location that has no
                      storage master record), the system will display an error message
                      (Figure 3.23). The stockkeeper must either create a new storage
                      master record before processing the transaction or correct the data
                      entry error and continue processing.

Inability to Verify the Accuracy of Inventory Records

The inability to verify inventory record accuracy can lead to material shortages or high inventory. If inventory balances are overstated, the material planner may not order enough material to satisfy future requirements. If inventory balances are understated, the planner may order material that isn't needed. Because material shortages impact quality, customer service, and productivity, planners tend to err on the safe side and order too much material when they suspect that inventory records are inaccurate. High inventory is a serious problem, but on a day-to-day basis, planners are criticized more for material shortages than for high inventory. Unless there is a way to confirm that inventory records are at least 98 percent accurate at all times, planners will opt to create an inventory problem rather than risk a material shortage problem.

Solution   *Provide the ability to verify inventory record accuracy through cycle counting.*

```
Next Transaction: ___                                    Date: 12/11/91
This Transaction: CCD                                    Time: 11:30
                         Part Cycle Count Data

Part Number:   BJL081023

                    Cycle Count Frequency:  20 Days

                    Cycle Count Tolerance Parameter:   5 Percent

                    Date of Last Count: 08/05/91

                    Next Scheduled Count Date: 08/20/91
```

Figure 3.24
Part Cycle Count Data Screen

The Inventory Control module of an MRP II software package provides a cycle counting capability to audit and maintain inventory record accuracy. The user specifies how often each part is to be counted by entering the cycle count frequency (the number of days between cycle counts) on the part master record.

Some packages provide the ability to assign cycle count frequencies automatically to part numbers based on the A-B-C inventory classification codes. High-value A parts are counted more frequently than low-value C parts.

During the initial load of the database, the user also specifies the last count date. Subsequently the system automatically updates the last count date each time the stockkeeper enters the results of a cycle count.

The system selects parts to be cycle-counted based on the last count date and the cycle count frequency. In Figure 3.24, part BJL081023 was last counted on 08/05/91 and has a cycle count frequency of 20 days. The next scheduled count date is 08/20/91.

Most MRP II packages also provide an on-line transaction to allow the material planner to request an unscheduled cycle count of any part. The planner may want to enter a cycle count request if a part has had an unusual amount of activity, or if there is any reason to suspect that the inventory records are not accurate.

Each day the system produces a cycle count report that lists all the parts to be cycle-counted, along with the inventory locations where the parts are stored (Figure 3.25). The stockkeeper counts the inventory in each location and enters the results into the system. Some MRP II systems display a warning message if the counted quantity differs from the system on-hand quantity by more than a specified percentage, known as the **part cycle count tolerance parameter** (Figure 3.26). The stockkeeper can either recount or ignore the message and proceed with the update. The system automatically updates the on-hand quantity, the last count date, and the next scheduled count date.

Some companies are becoming so successful at using cycle counting to monitor and improve inventory record accuracy that they no longer need to perform an annual "wall-to-wall" physical inventory. When this level of accuracy is demonstrated, planners gain enough confidence to order just-in-time quantities of material instead of just-in-case quantities.

• •

```
Date: 09/15/91                                        Page: 01
                            Cycle Count Report

              Inv     _____ Location Data_____
Part Number   U/M  Lot   Location   Status   Qty on Hand    Qty Counted


ADL102293     EA   001   SA200        AM          123            -

              002   SA201        AM          110            -

              003   SB202        AM           34            -


JSL203043     EA   001   SJ909        AM           23            -

              002   SJ390        AM           30            -


MBL390923     LB   001   SJ390        AM           39            -

              002   SB039        AM          230            -
```

• •

Figure 3.25
Cycle Count Report

Philosophies of Cycle Counting

In Figure 3.25, the quantity on hand is displayed next to the storage location for each part number. Some MRP II software vendors believe that showing the quantity on hand on the cycle count report encourages a thorough count. For example, if the stockkeeper initially sees 30 pieces in a location and the cycle count report indicates that there should be 40 pieces, the stockkeeper will search for, and often find, the additional 10 pieces before reporting the cycle count results.

On the other hand, some MRP II software vendors believe that showing the quantity on hand encourages stockkeepers to be lax in the performance of their cycle-counting duties. Indeed, if so inclined, a stockkeeper can "fool the system" by entering the quantity that is on the cycle count report.

Each theory has its supporters and detractors. I believe that it is impossible to force people to be conscientious, and that it is better to provide people with any information that will help them do a better job. However, if your philosophy differs from the philosophy of your MRP II software vendor, the quantity field is easy enough to add to or delete from the cycle count report.

Caveat   The cycle count feature in some MRP II packages is so poorly designed that it is useless for all practical purposes. Instead of comparing the cycle count quantity to the current on-hand quantity, some MRP II packages compare the cycle count results to a day-old "snapshot" of the on-hand quantity. If any inventory transactions take place after the snapshot is taken and before the location is cycle-counted, the cycle count results will not agree with the day-old snapshot. The inventory records will appear to be inaccurate when, in fact, they may be 100 percent accurate. (Don't look for any rationale as to why some MRP II packages use the snapshot approach—there isn't any!) MRP II vendors that use the snapshot

---

```
Next Transaction: ___                              Date: 09/15/91
This Transaction: CYC                              Time: 11:30
                        Post-Cycle Count Results

Part Number: ADL102293    Inventory Lot: 001

          Location: SA200
          On-Hand Quantity:     123
          Status: AM

          Counted Quantity:     132
```

```
MSG6294: Counted quantity exceeds cycle count tolerance parameter.
Recount or press enter to proceed with update.
```

Figure 3.26
Post-Cycle Count Results Screen

approach to cycle counting tell their customers to tag the locations that are being cycle-counted so that no inventory transactions are performed against a location until it has been counted. This approach is not feasible because it can easily result in material shortages.

Most MRP II packages fail to keep statistics on cycle count results. Because these statistics are not available, it is impossible to obtain reports that indicate trends in inventory-record accuracy. Without these reports, it is difficult to determine when the objective of 98 percent inventory-record accuracy has been achieved.

Excessive Safety Stock

Many companies carry large amounts of safety stock as a buffer against long lead times. This is particularly true of purchased parts, where long internal lead times can add several weeks to the replenishment cycle.

Solution   *Provide the ability to reduce internal lead times.*

MRP II systems provide features that compress the three major components of internal lead time:

1. The time required to forward a requisition to Purchasing

2. The time required to generate purchase orders

3. The time required to distribute orders to vendors

These features (the electronic link between the planner and buyer, automatic purchase order generation, and electronic data interchange) can compress internal lead times from three weeks to one day. These features are discussed in detail in Chapter 2.

Summary

Table 3.6 summarizes the causes of and solutions to the high inventory problem that were presented in this chapter.

Table 3.6
Summary of Causes of and Solutions to
High Inventory

Causes	Solutions
1. Material shortages	See Chapter 2.
2. Inability to determine when or how much material to order	The Planner Action Report helps the material planner determine when and how much to order and enables the planner to manage by exception.
3. Inability to deexpedite and cancel orders	The MRP module delays placing orders until the lead time has been reached. The Planner Action Report prints exception messages to alert the planner when orders need to be deexpedited or canceled.
4. Excessive obsolete inventory, caused by:	
- Inability to phase in global engineering changes	- Provide the ability to phase in changes using effectivity dates on bills of materials.
- Inability to prevent obsolete parts from being used on bills of materials	- Use the part status code to validate bill of materials maintenance. Only parts with a status code of A can be added to bills of materials.
- Excessive expired inventory	- Provide the ability to allocate material by shelf life expiration date.
- Inability to identify slow-moving inventory	- Use the Slow-Moving Parts Report.
5. Early shipments and over-shipments from vendors	The Purchasing module maintains statistics on early shipments and overshipments to help buyers select vendors that comply with company policies. Early shipments and overshipments are put on hold status in Receiving pending disposition by the buyer.
6. Inability to schedule just-in-time delivery of material	The lead time offset feature allows parts to be scheduled for delivery a specified number of days after the final assembly start date. The Purchasing module provides the ability to schedule multiple deliveries against a single purchase order line item.
7. Inability to schedule deliveries around nonworking days	The MRP II system uses a plant calendar to schedule around nonworking days.
8. Large economic lot sizes for purchased parts, caused by:	
- Minimum billing charges	- Provide the ability to place multiple-item purchase orders and combine items from different inventory accounts on the same purchase order.
- High ordering costs	- MRP II systems have features that automate or eliminate many of the administrative activities that cause high ordering costs. See Chapter 6 for details.

Table 3.6
Summary of Causes of and Solutions to
High Inventory (continued)

Causes	Solutions
9. Improper allocation of finished-goods inventory to customer orders	Integration of the Order Entry module with the Master Production Schedule module helps to increase inventory turns on goods.
10. Recursivity (looping) on bills of materials	The Bill of Materials module provides for automatic recursivity checking.
11. Lost inventory	The Inventory Control module validates storage locations on inventory transactions.
12. Inability to verify the accuracy of inventory records	The cycle count feature helps companies audit and maintain inventory record accuracy.
13. Excessive safety stock	MRP II systems help reduce internal lead times by providing: - Electronic link between the material planner and buyer - Automatic purchase order generation - Electronic data interchange of purchase order documents

The Quality Problem

*T*he Manager of Customer Service had been receiving an unusual number of complaints from customers about product quality. The number of failures within the warranty period had tripled within the last three months, and Quality Control's lack of success in solving the problem had the entire management team concerned. Already under siege from foreign competition, the company was now in danger of losing one of the few competitive edges it had: its reputation for quality. Unless the problem was solved quickly, the damage might be insurmountable.

The answer came from an unexpected source. One day, a buyer received a call from a supplier informing him that a lot of material that had been manufactured and shipped several months ago was discovered to be defective. Unfortunately, the defect did not become apparent until the product was in use for some time. The supplier, eager to help solve the problem he had caused, was able to tell the buyer that the defective material had been shipped on purchase order numbers 1S153200 and 1S200150. The buyer quickly relayed this information to Quality Control.

"That's great news!" said the Manager of Quality Control. "Now all we have to do is purge all the bad material out of the stockroom and the factory and replace all the bad components out in the field."

But the task did not prove to be as easy as it sounded. The company did not keep the kind of detailed records that would allow them to determine if any material from these two purchase orders was in the stockroom or in work-in-process inventory. Nor was the company able to determine which customers had received shipments that contained the defective components. Lacking this data, the company was forced to take a conservative approach to solving the problem. The company scrapped $10,000 worth of inventory to make absolutely certain that the bad lots had been purged from stock. All work-in-process was reworked to replace components that might be defective. The company's field service organization made service calls on all customers that might have received shipments *containing the defective component. Even with this conservative approach, the corrective actions were only about 80 percent effective, and the 80 percent solution had cost the company more than $100,000! A 100 percent solution could have been achieved at a much lower cost if the company had been able to trace how the material from the two purchase orders had been used.*

Introduction

In the 1950s and early 1960s, the word "Japan" was synonymous with poor quality, just as the word "America" was synonymous with high quality. In the space of only one generation, the perception of quality has been reversed. Today, American manufacturers that have made improvements in quality proudly (and ironically) compare themselves to their Japanese competitors to try to win back American consumers.

The costs of poor quality show up in rework, scrap, inspection costs, warranty costs, and lost orders. Poor quality has cost the American automobile industry 30 percent of its market share, and it has virtually eliminated the American consumer electronics industry.

Most people think of MRP II systems as scheduling and priority planning systems. An MRP II system is certainly no substitute for a quality management system, but MRP II software packages do have a number of features that can help companies solve their quality problems.

Some of the causes of poor quality are listed below. These causes, along with the solutions characteristic of MRP II systems, are discussed in the sections that follow.

1. Inability to assess the quality of purchased parts

2. Failure to route receipts to incoming inspection

3. Inaccurate incoming inspection instructions

4. Lack of an incoming inspection audit trail

5. Inability to identify expired material

6. Inability to create and maintain accurate manufacturing bills of materials

7. Inability to trace the origin and use of defective material

8. Material shortages

9. Invalid production schedules

Inability to Assess the Quality of Purchased Parts

Theoretically, buyers select vendors based on value, which is the lowest total cost in use. Value is a function of price, quality, and delivery. The low-price vendor may not be the low-cost vendor if late deliveries and poor quality cause increased production costs.

All manufacturing companies have an incoming inspection department to inspect the quality of purchased material. Unfortunately, few companies have systems that capture and analyze incoming inspection data to provide vendor quality performance ratings. This makes it difficult for buyers to factor quality into their purchasing decisions. Instead, buyers tend to focus heavily on price, which tends to have a negative impact on quality. Lack of quality data also makes it difficult for the Manager of Purchasing to measure how good a job a buyer is doing relative to finding high-quality suppliers.

Solution   *Provide the ability to calculate quality performance ratings.*

Quality Performance Ratings by Vendor

Most MRP II packages provide the ability to record the results of incoming inspection. This capability is usually incorporated into the Purchasing module, due to the need to track returns to vendors so that vendors are not paid for material that is rejected. Some MRP II systems use this data to calculate vendor quality performance ratings. The **vendor performance rating** is usually a simple calculation based either on the percentage of lots or on the percentage of pieces that pass inspection, as follows:

$$\text{Quality Rating} = \frac{\text{Number of Lots Passing Inspection}}{\text{Number of Lots Inspected}} \times 100$$

Or,

$$\text{Quality Rating} = \frac{\text{Number of Pieces Passing Inspection}}{\text{Number of Pieces Inspected}} \times 100$$

A perfect quality rating is 100. The quality rating is stored in the vendor master file and can be viewed on-line (Figure 4.1). Quality ratings are kept for several time periods to help buyers evaluate trends in vendor quality.

```
Next Transaction: ___                              Date: 08/21/91
This Transaction: VPI                              Time: 09:24
                      Vendor Performance Inquiry

Vendor Code: 35673        Group Code:        Name: Robertson Instruments

Street: 1020 Middle St.        City: Milford            State: CT
Zip: 06460-1453            Country: USA        Attn: Eddie Carpman

                            Current  Year to
                            Quarter   Date     1990     1989     1988

Number of Shipments Inspected    26      145      201      212      186
Number of Shipments Rejected      0        2        5        7       10
** Quality Performance Rating   100     98.6     97.5     96.7     94.6
Total Number of Shipments Received 35    153      245      234      212
Number of Early Shipments         1        3        7       12       12
** Percent Early Shipments       2.9      2.0      2.1      5.1      5.7
Number of Overshipments           2        5        7        8       10
** Percent Overshipments         5.8      3.3      2.9      3.4      4.7
Total Dollars Purchased       12,692   80,302  132,242  132,272  134,669
Total Dollars at Std Cost     13,340   85,203  128,902  123,289  143,203
** Percent under Standard Cost   4.9      5.8     -2.6     -7.3      5.6
```

Figure 4.1
Vendor Performance Inquiry Screen

Quality Performance Ratings by Vendor by Part

Most companies buy many different parts from the same vendor. While it is useful to know a vendor's overall quality rating, it is sometimes more important to know the vendor's quality rating for a *specific* part. A vendor may have an excellent overall quality rating but may have a very low rating on one or two parts. A system that keeps only overall quality ratings for each vendor may obscure quality problems on specific parts.

In Table 4.1, the vendor has an overall rating of 97.4 percent, but one part has a quality rating of only 50 percent. The buyer needs to be aware of this situation to take corrective action (e.g., find another source of supply for parts with low quality ratings).

To satisfy this need, some MRP II software packages also calculate quality ratings by vendor by part. Quality ratings by vendor by

Table 4.1
Vendor Quality Ratings by Part

Vendor: 20349
Barker Stamping Company

Part Number	Number of Shipments Received	Number of Shipments Passing Inspection	Quality Rating for Part (Percent)
ADL071951	200	198	99.0.
ADL071960	156	155	99.4
MBL070784	20	10	50.0
JSL022582	125	122	97.6
MAL101078	223	220	98.6
Overall Rating:	724	705	97.4

part are stored in the MRP II database in a record commonly known as the **vendor-part record**.

Table 4.2 differentiates between the vendor master record, the part master record, and the vendor-part record.

The **vendor master record** contains general information about a vendor that applies to all part numbers purchased from that vendor (e.g., the vendor name and address). The **part master record** contains general information about a part that applies to all vendors that supply the part (e.g., the buyer code and planner code). The **vendor-part record** contains information about a part that applies to a specific vendor (e.g., the minimum order quantity that must be purchased from that vendor).

Quality ratings by vendor by part make it possible for a buyer to view and compare quality performance ratings among vendors for a particular part (Figure 4.2). This helps the buyer factor quality into purchasing decisions.

The Management Reporting System can be used to produce a report of quality ratings for each part purchased from a vendor (Figure 4.3). This report can be used to determine which parts should be exempt from incoming inspection and which parts should be purchased from other, higher-quality sources.

Quality Performance Ratings by Part

Some MRP II packages also track quality performance ratings by part. Quality ratings by part are stored in the part master record. A low part quality rating may indicate that several vendors are having

Table 4.2
Differences between the Vendor Master Record, Part
Master Record, and Vendor-Part Record

Vendor Master Record Data	Part Master Record Data	Vendor-Part Record Data
Vendor number (key)	Part number (key)	Vendor number and part number (key)
Vendor name	Part description	Vendor's internal part number
Vendor address	Buyer code	Unit of purchase
Vendor phone number	Planner code	Minimum order quantity
Vendor contact	Make/buy code	Vendor-part inspection code
Vendor quality rating	Part status code	Vendor-part quality rating
	Inspection code	
	Part quality rating	

```
Next Transaction: ___                                    Date: 08/01/91
This Transaction: VCI                                    Time: 11:30
                    Vendor-Part Quality Comparison Inquiry

Part Number: ADL071976

                      Number of    Number of     Part Quality      Best/
                      Shipments    Shipments      —Rating—          Worst
                      Inspected    Rejected                Prior    Rating
Vendor Short Name        Ytd          Ytd        Ytd      Year       Ytd

38482  Mallory Mfg Co    150           2         98.7     98.5
28394  Stuart Fabrica     50           0        100.0     98.0       Best
83787  Trails Corp       120           8         93.3     93.3      Worst
```

Figure 4.2
Vendor-Part Quality Comparison Inquiry Screen

• •

```
Date: 08/01/91                                              Page: 01
                    Vendor Quality Ratings by Part Report
                         (Sorted by Part Number)

Vendor Number: 29384              Name: Plainville Bearing Co.

Asterisk (*) in Column 1 Indicates Ytd Quality Rating of Less Than 98.5%
```

Part Number	Number of Shipments Inspected Ytd	Number of Shipments Rejected Ytd	Ytd	Prior Year	Delta
* ADL071829	35	1	97.1	98.8	−1.7
ADL394058	120	1	99.2	100.0	−0.8
* ADL394090	85	8	91.8	95.8	−4.0
BJL049598	42	0	100.0	99.8	+0.2
* BJL405037	90	10	88.9		
JSL490859	105	0	100.0	100.0	0.0
MAL490595	92	1	98.9	100.0	−1.1
MBL394058	20	0	100.0		
REL394090	72	1	98.6	99.3	−0.7

Note: The "Part Quality —Rating—" spans the Ytd, Prior Year, and Delta columns.

• •

Figure 4.3
Vendor Quality Ratings by Part Report

difficulty meeting quality specifications. The Management Reporting System can be used to produce an exception report of parts that have low quality ratings (Figure 4.4). A quality review board consisting of Design Engineering, Engineering Standards, Quality Control, and Purchasing can use this report to identify parts that require some action to improve the part quality rating. Possible actions include:

- Redesigning the part
- Changing the quality specifications
- Finding an acceptable substitute that has a high part quality rating
- Finding a qualified source
- Working with the vendors to improve their process capabilities and process control

Quality Performance Ratings by Buyer

Some MRP II packages also calculate quality performance ratings by buyer. This is easy to do, because each part is associated with a specific buyer. This enables the Manager of Purchasing to evaluate exactly how well each buyer is doing relative to finding high-quality suppliers.

Quality performance ratings by buyer are stored in the buyer record in the MRP II database and can be viewed on-line (Figure 4.5). The performance ratings may be divided into time periods to help the Manager of Purchasing evaluate buyer performance for a specific performance evaluation period.

Caveat Some MRP II packages capture incoming inspection data but do not use the data to calculate vendor quality performance ratings. Some packages calculate overall vendor quality performance ratings but

```
Date: 08/01/91                                          Page: 01
              Part Low Quality Rating Exception Report
                     (Sorted by Part Number)
        Selection Criterion: Ytd Part Quality Rating Less Than 98.5%


              Number of   Number of   Overall      Ytd Quality
              Shipments   Shipments      Part       Ratings by
              Inspected    Rejected    Rating    Part by Vendor

Part Number      Ytd         Ytd         Ytd     Vendor   Rating

ADL054829        135           6        95.6      45069     97.5
                                                  38948     96.0
                                                  45904     95.4


ADL062839        200          10        95.0      49504     95.8
                                                  45940     93.8


BJL390490        150           8        94.7      39403     94.7


JSL394078        125           7        94.4      39405     95.7
                                                  28938     92.7


MAL39489          80           5        93.8      39504     96.7
                                                  45050     85.0
```

Figure 4.4
Part Low Quality Rating Exception

```
Next Transaction: ___                                    Date: 08/21/91
This Transaction: BPI                                    Time: 09:24
                        Buyer Performance Inquiry

Buyer Code: 03      Name: Jack Coulter         Phone: 703-384-2834

                                      Year
                            Current    to
                            Quarter   Date     1990     1989      1988

Number of Shipments Inspected   180    745     1201     1212
Number of Shipments Rejected      2      8       14       20
** Quality Performance Rating   98.9   99.1     98.8     98.3

Total Number of Shipments       235    953     1545     1634
Number of Early Shipments        11     33       87       92
** Percent Early Shipments      4.7    3.5      5.6      5.6
Number of Overshipments           7     32       53      112
** Percent Overshipments        3.0    3.4      3.4      6.9

Total Dollars Purchased      72,452 480,302  732,242  722,272
Total Dollars at Std Cost    78,340 495,203  718,902  705,279
** Percent under Standard Cost  7.5    3.0     -1.8     -2.4
```

Figure 4.5
Buyer Performance Inquiry Screen

do not calculate quality ratings by vendor by part, by part, or by buyer. However, if you select an MRP II package that has a vendor-part record and buyer record, it may be relatively easy to modify the package to provide these other quality ratings.

Failure to Route Receipts to Incoming Inspection

Shipments requiring incoming inspection need to be routed to the inspection area from the receiving dock. If the receiving clerk does not know which shipments require inspection, shipments that should be inspected may be sent directly to the stockroom. This can result in defective material being used in production.

Solution *Provide a method of automatically notifying the receiving clerk when a shipment requires inspection.*

Most MRP II systems provide an inspection code on the part master record. This is where the quality control engineer indicates whether a part requires incoming inspection. When material is received, the Purchasing module prints a receiving label on a printer located at the receiving dock. This label identifies the shipment and provides routing instructions. If the part requires inspection, the message "DELIVER TO INCOMING INSPECTION" is printed on the receiving label (Figure 4.6).

Some companies require more flexibility in determining whether or not a shipment requires incoming inspection. For example, if a part is purchased from two vendors, shipments from vendor *A* may be exempt from inspection if vendor *A* has a high quality rating for that part, whereas shipments from vendor *B* may require inspection. Some MRP II packages accommodate the need to have different inspection policies for different vendors by allowing inspection codes to be entered by vendor by part on the vendor-part record (refer to Table 4.2).

Some systems provide even more flexibility by allowing inspection codes to be entered on individual purchase orders. This feature is

• •

Receiving Identification Label

Receiving Report Number: R552-304

Part Number: ADL390349   Buyer: 01

Purchase Order: 1S394045   Item: 03

Vendor: 92783   Name: Osborne Metal Fab

Quantity Received: 23   U/M: PCS

Received by: P484   Date Received: 09/12/91

Notes: Deliver to Incoming Inspection

Incoming Inspection Results:

• •

Figure 4.6
Receiving Identification Label

especially useful when a buyer wants to qualify a new source for a part that does not normally require inspection. The buyer can place an order for sample parts and set the inspection code on the purchase order to require incoming inspection (Figure 4.7).

MRP II packages that allow inspection codes to be entered on the purchase order, part master record, or vendor-part record process receipts in the following manner. When a shipment is received, the system first checks the purchase order for an inspection code. If no inspection code is found on the purchase order, the system checks the vendor-part record. If no inspection code is found, the system checks the part master record for an inspection code.

Caveat   Some MRP II packages provide an inspection code only on the part master record. They do not provide the flexibility to define inspection policies by vendor by part, or to establish inspection codes on individual purchase orders.

```
Next Transaction: ___                                    Date: 10/11/91
This Transaction: API                                    Time: 08:45
                      Add Purchase Order Line Item

PO Number: 1S394048   PO Line Number:  01    Buyer: 05

Vendor: 34534    Name: General Instrument Corp.

Part Number: ADL39045    Quantity:    10  Unit: EA Price:    224.00 Per: E

Description: Power Supply

Required Ship Date: 11/15/91     Ship Promise Date:__/__/__

Lot Trace Receipts? Y   Inspection Required? Y   Vendor Require Print?

GL Account Number:              Ship to Code: DSD

Multiple Ship Schedules? N   Additional Text? N

Standard Message Codes: 01 04
```

Figure 4.7
Add Purchase Order Line Item Screen

One MRP II package provides the ability to define inspection codes by part, by vendor by part, or by purchase order. Unfortunately, this information is of little use because the Purchasing module does not print a receiving label! Providing the ability to input this information is of little benefit if it cannot be output in a useful format.

If you are evaluating MRP II systems, don't assume that the Purchasing module prints a receiving label. Before you select a package, verify that it is capable of producing the hardcopy documents required to support the system.

Inaccurate Incoming Inspection Instructions

While some parts require only a visual inspection for appearance or damage, many parts require several tests to verify their physical, mechanical, and/or electrical characteristics. The Incoming Inspection department needs to have up-to-date instructions (routings) on how a part is to be inspected. Many companies keep this information on hardcopy files in the inspection area. These instructions are not always kept up to date because of the manual effort required to maintain the files. If shipments are inspected using obsolete instructions, defective parts may pass inspection and be used in production.

Solution

Provide the ability to define, maintain, and view inspection routings on-line.

Some MRP II systems provide the ability to define routings for incoming inspection. These routings define the tests to be performed and the test equipment to be used. Quality Control engineers maintain this information on-line, and inspectors have access to up-to-date routings from terminals in the inspection area (Figure 4.8).

Lack of an Incoming Inspection Audit Trail

It would be ideal if defective purchased components were found during incoming inspection, but occasionally problems are not detected until production is in process or until final inspection is under way.

When a part is found to be defective during the production process, it is reasonable to ask the following questions:

```
Next Transaction: ___                                      Date: 10/02/91
This Transaction: IRI                                      Time: 13:23
                        Inspection Routing Inquiry

Part Number: ADL071976  Description: Circuit Breaker Trip Latch
Last Updated:  07/12/91  Inspection Sample Size: 5%

       Insp  Labor  Test
Seq    Dept  Class  Equipment    Test Instructions

010    I100  R05    OPT-100      Visual inspection for burrs.
020    I100  R05    OPT-100      Measure angle of trip surface. 10 degrees from
                                 vertical toward front of latch, plus or minus 2
                                 degrees.
030    I100  R05    OPT-100      Measure height of trip surface 0.125 in plus or
                                 minus 0.005 in.
040    I110  R10    CB-100       Measure trip characteristics. Insert in test
                                 breaker.
                    TQL110       Apply 10A of current. Breaker should trip
                                 between 80 seconds and 100 seconds.
```

Figure 4.8
Inspection Routing Inquiry Screen

- Was the lot inspected?
- Who inspected the lot?
- What test equipment was used?
- What were the results?
- Did Incoming Inspection perform all the required tests?

Reasonable as these questions are, some companies lack the documentation to answer them. This makes it difficult to take the appropriate corrective action.

The problem may have been caused by any number of reasons:

- The receiving clerk may have sent the lot directly to the stockroom instead of to Incoming Inspection.
- The inspector may have been unqualified to perform the required tests.
- The test equipment may have been defective.

- The lot may have been of marginal acceptable quality.
- The inspector may have omitted one of the required tests.
- The inspector may have been working from old, inaccurate instructions.
- The lot may have passed inspection. This would indicate that the inspection instructions need to be modified so that future lots do not pass incoming inspection, only to fail in production.
- The parts that failed may have been damaged after incoming inspection.

Solution

Provide a means of capturing the detailed information about incoming inspections.

Some MRP II packages allow inspection work orders to be created to track the results of the inspection process. The inspector can report the results of each test in the inspection routing against the inspection order, in much the same way that the factory reports progress against manufacturing orders. If a problem is found subsequent to incoming inspection, any questions about how the lot was inspected can be answered.

Caveat

Some MRP II packages allow inspection routings to be defined for informational purposes only. Inspection orders cannot be created and updated, so no audit trail is provided.

Inability to Identify Expired Material

Most companies have certain parts or materials that have a limited shelf life. For example, some chemicals may become unstable if they are not used by a specified date. Product quality can be seriously affected if expired material is used in production.

It is relatively easy to prevent material that is awaiting inspection or rejected material from being used in production, because such material is usually segregated from inventory that is available for manufacturing. However, it is not easy to prevent expired material from being used in production. **Expired material** is good material that became bad material overnight, when the expiration date was reached. Hence, expired material may still be stored with good material.

Solution   *Provide a method of ensuring that expired lots of material are not released to production.*

Some MRP II packages allow a shelf life expiration date to be associated with an inventory (Figure 4.9). When the expiration date is reached, the system automatically changes the inventory status code from AM (available for manufacturing) to EX (expired), the reason code to EXPIRE, and the MRP available code to N. This prevents the Inventory Control module from allocating expired material and causes the MRP Planning program to exclude expired inventory from netting calculations.

When the system generates a picklist, inventory is allocated only from lots that have an inventory status code of AM. In Figure 4.9, there are 140 pieces available to be allocated: 50 from lot 002, 30 from lot 003, and 60 from lot 004. Expired material will not be allocated for use in manufacturing.

```
Next Transaction: ___                                    Date: 08/01/91
This Transaction: IDI                                    Time: 11:30
                          Inventory Detail Inquiry

Part Number: GH022543    Qty Available to Be Allocated:      140
                         Qty Unavailable for Manufacturing:  280
                         Qty Available for MRP Planning:      310
                         Qty Unavailable for MRP Planning:    180
```

Lot Nbr	Location	Quantity on Hand	Quantity Alloc	MRP Avail?	Inv Stat	Reason Code	Date Received	Shelf Exp Date	Order Number	Lot Trc
001	SB137	100	0	N	EX	Expire	04/15/90	07/01/91	1S239328	
002	SB147	50	0	Y	AM		05/01/91	10/15/91	1S239348	
003	SB167	100	70	Y	AM		05/11/91	10/15/91	1C393842	
004	SB167	60	0	Y	AM		06/02/91	11/20/91	1C239493	
005	RM421	80	0	N	RJ	Reject	07/15/91	12/05/91	1R324993	
006	IN220	100	0	Y	II	Ininsp	08/01/91	01/05/92	1W230402	

Figure 4.9
Inventory Detail Inquiry Screen

```
Date: 08/01/91                                          Page: 01
                     Shelf Life Expiration Report
                  (Sorted by Shelf Life Expiration Date
              in Sequence from Latest to Oldest Expiration Date)

Asterisk (*) in Column 1 indicates expired lots appearing in
this report for the first time.

                 Inv                        Inventory
                 Lot                        Value at    Expiration
Part Number      Nbr   Location   Quantity  Std Cost    Date

*ADL029384       010   SR293           100  $1000.00    08/01/91
*MBL293854       010   SR324             5      5.25    07/28/91
 JSL289347       001   SR232           200   2050.00    07/01/91
 MAL029384       005   SR223            10    100.00    05/08/91
 REL212454       008   SR328           200   1730.00    04/15/91
 BJL285741       004   SR132          1000   8600.00    03/01/91


Total Value of Expired Inventory:     $ 13,485.25
```

Figure 4.10
Shelf Life Expiration Report

An MRP II system may also produce a Shelf Life Expiration Report that lists all lots of expired material (Figure 4.10). The Stockroom Manager can use this report to identify inventory lots that should either be scrapped or be segregated from good inventory.

Caveat

Some MRP II systems provide the ability to specify a shelf life expiration date but do not automatically change the inventory status code from AM to EX when the expiration date is reached. If the user forgets to change the inventory status code, expired material may be issued to production by mistake.

Inability to Create and Maintain Accurate Manufacturing Bills of Materials

Some companies have two types of bills of materials: engineering BOMs and manufacturing BOMs. The engineering bill of materials is the design engineer's view of the way a product is manufactured.

A manufacturing bill of materials may be required if the actual method of manufacture differs from the engineer's view.

Consider a repetitive (high-volume) manufacturing environment. The engineering bill of materials may contain several intermediate subassemblies. However, the product may be built on an assembly line without making and stocking the intermediate subassemblies specified on the engineering bill of materials. In fact, groups of parts *from different subassemblies on the engineering BOM* may be issued together to a work station on the assembly line.

The manufacturing bill of materials groups parts together into **phantom subassemblies**. As the name implies, a phantom subassembly is not a real subassembly but rather a collection of parts that are issued together to production. Each phantom subassembly on the manufacturing BOM represents a group of parts that are issued to a work station on the assembly line.

Figure 4.11 shows the engineering BOM and the manufacturing BOM for the same product. Note that engineering subassemblies B, C, D, E, and F do not exist on the manufacturing BOM. Note also that parts from different engineering subassemblies are released together on a manufacturing phantom subassembly.

It should be obvious that while the engineering and manufacturing BOMs may differ in the way parts are grouped together, they each must have the same component parts. That is, the manufacturing BOM must have the same parts in the same quantities that are specified on the engineering BOM. *If the two bills are not in agreement, the product built from the manufacturing BOM will have serious quality problems.*

It has been argued that the engineering and manufacturing organizations should work together to agree on one bill of materials that reflects the method of manufacture. Indeed, things *should* be done this way, but this may not be possible for several reasons:

- Engineering may take place in a location remote from manufacturing, making it difficult for the two organizations to work closely together. More and more, companies perform engineering functions domestically, and manufacturing is carried out in offshore facilities in places like Puerto Rico, Singapore, Malaysia, Taiwan, Hong Kong, and Korea.

- If the same product is manufactured in more than one location (or on more than one assembly line in the same plant), it might even be necessary to have more than one manufacturing bill of materials.

Engineering Bill of Materials for Product A

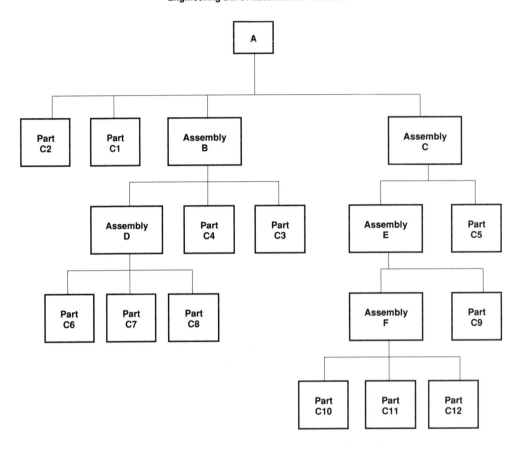

Manufacturing Bill of Materials for Product A

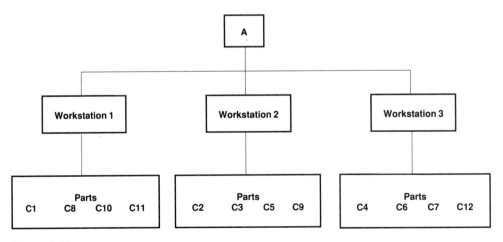

Figure 4.11
Comparison between Engineering and Manufacturing Bills of Materials

For example, I used to work in a plant that assembled television sets. The plant had eight assembly lines. The older assembly lines were less automated than the newer lines. Often, the same product was manufactured on old and new assembly lines. Two manufacturing bills of materials were required because parts were issued in different groups to the old and the new assembly lines.

- The intermediate assemblies on an engineering bill of materials may occasionally be manufactured as service parts. An engineering BOM allows manufacturing orders to be created for service parts.

- In high-volume manufacturing environments, there may be no way to avoid having two bills of materials. From a design point of view, Engineering needs to think in terms of intermediate assemblies even if manufacturing never builds and stocks these assemblies.

The inability to create and maintain accurate manufacturing bills of materials is a serious problem for many companies. Most homegrown systems do not allow engineering and manufacturing BOMs to coexist in the same database unless they are assigned different part numbers. The manufacturing bill of materials is maintained either in a separate system from the engineering BOM or in a manual file. This makes it extremely difficult to compare both BOMs to verify that they are in agreement. Even if the BOMs are stored in the same database under different part numbers, most companies do not have a method that compares the manufacturing BOM with the engineering BOM and reports any differences.

Solution   *Provide a way to create and maintain accurate manufacturing bills of materials.*

Most MRP II packages are designed to allow multiple versions of a bill of materials to coexist in the product structure file. A code known as a **version code** or **model code** is used to differentiate between different versions of a bill of materials (Figure 4.12). The **key** (information that uniquely identifies a record) to the product structure file is the combination of part number and model code. Thus, any number of different BOMs can be established for the same part, as long as each BOM has a different model code.

For example, the engineering BOM might have a model code of ENG, and the manufacturing BOM might have a model code of

```
Next Transaction: ___                                      Date: 08/01/91
This Transaction: BMI                                      Time: 11:30
                    Single Level Bill of Materials Inquiry


Part Number: ADL394893          Effectivity Date Search:       Model Code: ENG
Description: Volt Meter         Make/Buy/Phantom Code: M       Used by MRP?: Y


                                          Make
Line  Oper  Component   Quantity          Buy     LT   Start      End
Nbr   No    Part Number Per Assy   U/M    Phan    Off  Eff Date   Eff Date

0010        MBL293849   1.000      EA     M
0020        JSL349485   5.000      EA     B
0030        MAL393898   2.000      EA     B
0040        BJL239382   1.000      EA     M
```

Figure 4.12
Single Level Bill of Materials Inquiry Screen

MFG. One model is defined as the model that will be used by the MRP planning program.

Some MRP II packages provide a bill of materials comparison program in the Bill of Materials module. This program compares two bills of materials (specified by the user) and reports any differences between the two on a Bill of Materials Comparison Report (Figure 4.13). (The program may be written to exclude subassemblies optionally from the comparison process. This option is especially useful in comparing an engineering BOM with a manufacturing BOM.) The person responsible for maintaining the manufacturing BOM (usually a process planner) can review the report and make any necessary changes to the manufacturing BOM. Engineering and manufacturing bills of materials should be compared frequently to ensure that the latest, approved engineering changes are incorporated into the manufacturing BOM. Most companies compare engineering and manufacturing BOMs on a weekly basis to ensure that the manufacturing BOMs are 100 percent accurate.

．．

```
Date: 08/01/91                              Page: 01
              Bill of Materials Comparison Report

Part Number: ADL071957      Model: ENG
Compared with:
Part Number: ADL071957      Model: MFG


Assemblies Excluded from Comparison

Differences in components and/or quantities are as follows:



                   Bill:  ADL071957  Bill:  ADL071957
                   Model: ENG        Model: MFG

 Part Number      Quantity          Quantity          Difference
 MBL293848           5                 0                   5
 JSL923823           4                 3                   1
 BJL293898           1                 0                   1
 REL293784           3                 0                   3


All Other Components Match
```

．．

Figure 4.13
Bill of Materials Comparison Report

Caveat

Some MRP II software packages take a different design approach to supporting engineering and manufacturing bills of materials. Instead of using a model code on the product structure header record to distinguish between versions of a bill of materials, they provide a **view code** at the component level of the product structure record (Figure 4.14). The view code can be set to M, E, or B to indicate that a component is associated with the manufacturing BOM, engineering BOM, or both, respectively.

This design does not work well because it does not allow Manufacturing and Engineering to group parts together in different assemblies, and it only allows two views of a bill of materials.

Some bill of materials comparison programs are capable of performing only a single-level comparison. This is useless in comparing engineering and manufacturing bills of materials. To be effective, the comparison program must "explode" through all levels of the bill of materials, summarize the quantity required for each component, and compare the summarized bills of materials. These steps are illustrated in Figure 4.15.

If you are evaluating MRP II software packages, and if you have engineering and manufacturing bills of materials, be careful to select a package that has a multilevel bill of materials comparison program. A multilevel comparison program is difficult to write, and you would probably not want to select a package that does not have this feature.

Inability to Trace the Origin and Use of Defective Material

Quality problems are sometimes detected by the customer. If a problem is caused by defective material, it is important to be able to trace the origin of such material and to determine where else the defective material was used. The company can then take the necessary corrective actions to purge the bad material from inventory and

```
Next Transaction: ___                              Date: 08/01/91
This Transaction: BMI                              Time: 11:30
                  Single Level Bill of Materials Inquiry


Part Number: ADL394893          Effectivity Date Search:
Description: Volt Meter         Make/Buy/Phantom Code: M


                                        Make
Line   Oper   Component   Quantity      Buy    LT    Start      End        View
Nbr    No     Part Number Per Assy  U/M  Phan  Off   Eff Date   Eff Date   Code

0010          MBL293849   1.000   EA   M                                   E
0020          JSL349485   5.000   EA   B                                   B
0030          MAL393898   2.000   EA   B                                   B
0040          BJL239382   1.000   EA   M                                   E
```

Figure 4.14
Single Level Bill of Materials Inquiry Screen

Step 1: **Explode the bill of materials.**

Engineering Bill of Materials for Product X

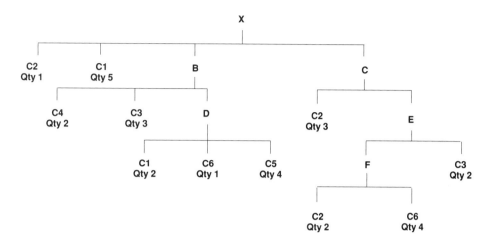

Manufacturing Bill of Materials for Product X

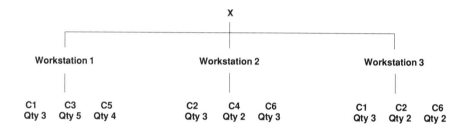

Step 2: **Summarize the quantity required for each component.**

Component	Quantity on the Engineering BOM	Quantity on the Manufacturing BOM
C1	7	6
C2	6	5
C3	5	5
C4	2	2
C5	4	4
C6	5	5

Step 3: **Report the differences on the Bill of Materials Comparison Report.**

Component	Quantity on the Engineering BOM	Quantity on the Manufacturing BOM	Difference
C1	7	6	1
C2	6	5	1

Figure 4.15
Steps Required to Produce Bill of Materials Comparison Report

work-in-process and to fix or recall defective products that have been shipped to other customers.

Solution

Provide the ability to trace the origin and use of a material lot.

Many MRP II packages have a **lot tracing feature** that can trace the origin and use of material. This feature is sometimes incorporated into the Inventory Control module, although some MRP II software vendors sell Lot Tracing as a separate module.

Lot tracing is analogous to two features found in the Bill of Materials module: the indented bill of materials and the where-used bill of materials. An Indented Bill of Materials Inquiry or Report is used to trace an assembly *downward* to all lower-level parts that comprise the assembly. A Where-Used Bill of Materials Inquiry or Report is used to trace a part *upward* to all higher-level assemblies that use the part. The product structure records are used to trace upward and downward through the bill of materials.

Lot tracing operates in a similar fashion. An Indented Lot Tracing Report is used to trace a specific customer order or manufacturing order downward to lower-level orders and inventory lots that comprise it. A Where-Used Lot Tracing Report is used to trace a specific inventory lot to all manufacturing orders and customer orders that use it. For example, using the Where-Used Lot Tracing Report, a company can determine that a part *A* lot procured on purchase order 1S389748 was used on customer orders CO189283, CO283674, and CO383474.

Lot tracing records are used to trace upward and downward through orders. Lot tracing records are similar to product structure records except for the following:

- Product structure records define relationships between components and assemblies. Lot tracing records define relationships between inventory lots and orders.

- Product structure records are created manually by the design engineer. Lot tracing records are created *automatically* by the system whenever material is received into inventory or is issued to a manufacturing order or customer order. In fact, the effort required to perform lot tracing would be prohibitive if lot tracing records had to be created manually for every receipt and issue.

Lot Tracing: An Illustration

To illustrate how the lot tracing feature works, consider the following example.

A customer calls to report that a switch (part number ADL2030) on a control panel is defective. The control panel was shipped on customer order CO374923. The following steps need to be taken to solve the quality problem:

1. Identify the origin (purchase order number) of the lot of switches that was used on customer order CO374923.

```
••••••••••••••••••••••••••••••••••••••••••••••••••••••••••••

Date: 08/01/91                                       Page: 01
                    Indented Lot Tracing Report


   Order to Be Traced:  CO374923     Part Number: ADL100200
                                     Desc: Control Panel
```

Level	——— Built from ——— Part Number	Order Number	Pulled from Location	Quantity Used	Date Pulled
1	MBL2039	M0102939	SA2118	1	05/15/91
.2	BJL2738	1C928392	SB2239	1	05/08/91
.2	MBL9283	M0288167	SA1233	1	05/08/91
..3	JSL3940	1C239092	SD1193	2	05/01/91
..3	REL2450	1S239092	SD1953	3	05/01/91
..3	ADL2093	M0203903	SA2239	1	05/01/91
...4	MBL1234	1W304092	SA3949	1	04/18/91
...4	JSL3940	1C239092	SD2223	1	04/18/91
...4	ADL2030	1S200300	SD2903	1	04/18/91
1	ADL2339	M0384956	SC3421	1	05/15/91
.2	REL2748	1S925672	SA0439	1	05/03/91
.2	JSL1243	M0234345	SB2950	2	05/03/91
..3	MBL3244	M0234672	SE1294	2	04/14/91
...4	REL1139	1W304769	SX9242	2	04/07/91
...4	JPM3246	1C234578	SR3934	4	04/07/91
...4	JWL2336	1C457660	SA1234	4	04/07/91
..3	ADL3096	M0203673	SB3202	4	04/14/91
...4	EIL1356	1S454491	SE3429	4	04/05/91
...4	BJL3345	1R786892	SD2232	8	04/05/91
...4	REL2870	1S357680	SD2267	4	04/05/91

```
••••••••••••••••••••••••••••••••••••••••••••••••••••••••••••
```

Figure 4.16
Indented Lot Tracing Report

```
Next Transaction: ___                                Date: 08/01/91
This Transaction: IDI                                Time: 13:43
                        Inventory Detail Inquiry

Part Number: ADL2030      Qty Available to Be Allocated:         180
                          Qty Unavailable for Manufacturing:       0
                          Qty Available for MRP Planning:        180
                          Qty Unavailable for MRP Planning:        0

Lot           Quantity  Quantity  MRP   Inv Reason  Date     Shelf    Order    Lot
Nbr Location  on Hand   Allocated Avail? Stat Code  Received Exp Date Number   Trc

001 SD2903      30          0      Y     AM  04/15/90                 1S200300 Y
002 SB147       50          0      Y     AM  05/01/91                 1S239348 Y
003 SB167      100          0      Y     AM  05/11/91                 1C393842 Y
```

Figure 4.17
Inventory Detail Inquiry Screen

2. Determine if any more defective switches remain in inventory.

3. If any defective switches are still in inventory, change the inventory status code to prevent any more of the switches from being issued to production.

4. Identify all other manufacturing orders and customer orders that used the defective lot of switches.

5. Rework the work-in-process to replace the defective switches.

6. Make a service call to other customers who received products containing the defective switches.

The first four steps are described in more detail below.

Identify the origin of the lot of defective switches. The customer has reported that part number ADL2030 was defective on customer order CO374923. The Indented Lot Tracing Report (Figure 4.16) explodes customer order CO374923 to produce a listing of all parts that were lot-traced to that order. This report shows that part number ADL2030 was obtained on purchase order 1S200300 and was pulled from inventory location SD2903 on 04/18/91.

Determine if any defective switches remain in inventory. An inventory detail inquiry shows that there are still 30 pieces of part ADL2030 in inventory from purchase order 1S200300, and that the inventory status code is AM (available for manufacturing) (Figure 4.17).

Change the inventory status code. Use the Inventory Status Change screen (Figure 4.18) to change the status code from AM (available for manufacturing) to RC (rejected by customer). This will prevent the remaining inventory from being allocated for production. Change the MRP Avail? field from Y to N so that the defective inventory is excluded from netting calculations.

```
Next Transaction: ___                                    Date: 08/01/91
This Transaction: ISC                                    Time: 13:44
                         Inventory Status Change


Part Number: ADL2030          Inventory Record Number: 001


Inventory Status: RC    Reason: REJCUS        MRP Avail?: N


Shelf Exp Date: __/__/__                     Lot Trace?: Y
```

Figure 4.18
Inventory Status Change Screen

```
Date: 08/02/91                                    Page: 01
                    Where-Used Lot Tracing Report


Part Number and Order Number to Be Traced Upward:

Part Number      Order Number        Description

ADL2030              1S200300            Switch


              — Used on —           Pulled from Quantity      Date
Level    Part Number  Order Number  Location     Used      Pulled

.3       ADL2093      M0203903      SA2239         1       05/01/91
..2      MBL9283      M0288167      SA1233         1       05/08/91
...1     MBL2039      M0102939      SA2118         1       05/15/91
....0    ADL100200    C0374923      FG1000         1       05/23/91

4        JSL2350      M0354562      SD2463         1       05/01/91
.3       REL2353      M0203452      SB2349         1       05/04/91
..2      MBL1245      M0256457      SR4653         1       05/12/91
...1     MBL2039      M0134766      SZ2789         1       05/18/91
....0    ADL300100    C0288093      FG2000         1       05/30/91

.3       ADL2093      M0256983      SA2239         1       05/03/91
..2      MBL9283      M0258869      SA1233         1       05/10/91
...1     MBL2039      M0142736      SA2118         1       05/17/91
....0    ADL100200    C0294723      FG1000         1       05/25/91

.3       MAL2343      M0202323      SD6879         1       05/08/91
..2      JSL3533      M0282347      SF1973         1       05/15/91
...1     ADL2345      M0202439      SA3457         1       05/22/91
....0    ADL200450    C0963927      FG3000         1       05/29/91
```

Figure 4.19
Where-Used Lot Tracing Report

Identify all other manufacturing orders and customer orders that used the defective lot of switches. The Where-Used Lot Tracing Report (Figure 4.19) is used to trace the defective lot of inventory upward through all manufacturing orders to the customer order level to determine where the defective material was used. This report indicates that the defective lot of part ADL2030 was also used on customer orders CO288093, CO294723, and CO963927.

The Real Cost of Lot Tracing

An MRP II system can perform lot tracing easily and inexpensively, because all the necessary lot tracing records are automatically created by the system whenever material is received into inventory or issued to an order. The real cost of lot tracing is in the indirect labor associated with identifying, segregating, and picking specific lots of inventory. If a part does not need to be lot-traced, receipts can be mixed together in a single inventory location (unless each lot has a shelf life expiration date). No care or effort is required to issue material from a specific lot to a specific manufacturing order. Clearly, a great deal of effort is required to store and issue lot-traced inventory. Because of the indirect labor costs associated with lot tracing, some companies may only want to lot-trace certain parts. Some industries (e.g., the pharmaceutical industry) are required by law to lot-trace all inventory.

Activating the Lot Tracing Feature

The lot tracing feature in most MRP II software packages can be activated optionally by part. The feature is activated by setting the lot trace indicator on the part master record to Y. This allows companies to trace only those parts where product liability and/or reliability is critical.

Some MRP II packages provide the option to lot trace only specific orders for a part. The lot trace indicator on the part master record is left blank, indicating that the part is not normally lot-traced. However, a lot trace indicator on a purchase order (or manufacturing order) can be set to Y. When the order is received, the receipt will be lot traced automatically. This option is useful when a company is trying out a new source for a purchased part or a new process for a manufactured part. Problems can be traced to the new source or new process without incurring the costs of lot-tracing all inventory lots.

Caveat

Lot tracing is a feature that even some software vendors have difficulty understanding. One MRP II software vendor purports to have lot tracing, but in reality, the package only provides a lot number field on the inventory detail record. The system does not build the lot tracing records necessary to trace downward or upward to determine where a lot originated or how it was used.

Another MRP II software package does have lot tracing, but the inventory system does not recognize when the lot tracing feature is deactivated. The inventory system creates a new inventory record in the database for every receipt *even when the lot tracing feature is not activated*. Thus, if five lots of a part are received and mixed together in the same inventory location, the system still treats each receipt as if it were being segregated, and creates five inventory detail records in the database. The system traces the inventory logically even though no attempt is made to trace the inventory physically. When material is issued, lot tracing records are not created, but the stockkeeper may have to perform several transactions to update multiple inventory detail records even though the material was issued from one physical lot.

Material Shortages

Material shortages can have a significant impact on product quality. Pressures to meet production schedules in the face of material shortages can force companies to substitute components, which can result in quality problems. Shortages can also affect quality by causing companies to use reworked material or other marginal material. Solutions to the material shortages problem are presented in Chapter 2.

Invalid Production Schedules

Invalid production schedules can cause increased pressure to ship product that may meet only minimum quality standards. Invalid schedules also can cause companies to require increased overtime, and product quality may suffer when employees work longer than usual hours. Solutions to invalid production schedules are presented in Chapter 5.

Quality Management: Limitations of MRP II Systems

Many of the features presented in this chapter are concerned with detecting quality problems after they occur. This is because most MRP II packages were developed during the 1970s and early 1980s. At that time, the predominant American quality management philosophy was to *inspect* quality into the product. Little attention was given to the manufacturing process. Instead, the emphasis was on using statistical quality control techniques to detect quality problems *after* they occurred. Consequently, MRP II Shop Floor Control modules were designed to help control priorities, but they do little to help control quality on the shop floor.

Today, there is far more emphasis on controlling the manufacturing process to *build* quality into the product. The quality management philosophy has shifted from one of problem detection to problem prevention. A number of software companies now provide shop floor management systems and quality management systems to help manufacturers "do it right the first time."

Shop Floor Management Systems

Shop floor management systems help prevent quality problems by:

- Providing operators with detailed, up-to-date process instructions
- Preventing unqualified operators from performing operations
- Preventing operations from being performed out of sequence
- Guiding operators through complex procedures
- Providing quality management systems with the data needed for statistical process control and data analysis

Each of these aspects is discussed in more detail below

Providing operators with detailed, up-to-date process instructions. MRP II systems provide operators with only basic, textual instructions. However, more detail is often needed to ensure that quality is built into the product. Shop floor management systems provide electronic instructions that can include text files, graphics files, process specifications, and interactive video instructions. Because all this information is stored electronically, the latest approved changes to the process instructions are immediately available to the operator. This eliminates quality problems that can occur when operators don't have access to the latest process instructions.

Preventing unqualified operators from performing operations. Most MRP II systems are not integrated with the human resource database, which contains information about operator skill levels. These MRP II systems are therefore unable to determine if an operator is certified to perform an operation.

Some shop floor management systems have an employee master file that receives daily updates from the human resource system. When an operation is begun, the shop floor management system can verify that the operator is certified at the skill level required to perform the operation. If the operator is not certified, the shop floor management system will not provide the operator with the process instructions needed to perform the operation.

Preventing operations from being performed out of sequence. Most MRP II systems cannot prevent an operation from being performed out of sequence, even though this may cause serious quality problems.

Shop floor management systems help prevent quality problems by ensuring that operations are performed in the specified sequence. When an operation is begun, the shop floor management system can verify that all previous operations have been completed. It provides the operator with a warning message if the operation is being performed out of sequence. If the operator ignores the warning, the system can automatically notify the appropriate personnel by means of electronic mail that the operation is being done out of sequence.

Guiding operators through complex procedures. On-line activity in an MRP II Shop Floor Control module is limited to work-in-process status reporting. Operators cannot interact with the MRP II database to receive detailed, step-by-step instructions for performing complex manufacturing operations.

Shop floor management systems provide more interactive capabilities than Shop Floor Control modules. Shop floor management systems can guide operators step-by-step through complex operations and can require input from the operator to verify that each step is performed in sequence.

Providing quality management systems with the data needed for statistical process control and data analysis. MRP II software packages do not capture information about the manufacturing process. Shop floor management systems can collect process control data and report it to the quality management system for statistical process control and data analysis.

Quality Management Systems

A number of small software companies specialize in providing quality management systems. Quality management systems use data provided by the shop floor management system to maintain control of the manufacturing process. The Statistical Process Control (SPC) module detects unfavorable trends in the manufacturing process in time for the appropriate personnel to take action to prevent quality problems. Some SPC modules are expert systems that can analyze process data and recommend corrective actions.

Quality management systems may also include a Data Analysis module that provides statistical analysis of process data to help engineers continuously improve the manufacturing process.

Other modules of a quality management system overlap MRP II systems in the areas of vendor ratings, incoming inspection, and lot tracing.

Impact of JIT on the Use of MRP II Quality-Related Features

Four of the features presented in this chapter are related to the incoming inspection function. These features are as follows:

1. The ability to assess the quality of purchased parts from incoming inspection data

2. The ability to route receipts to Incoming Inspection

3. The ability to provide Incoming Inspection with up-to-date inspection instructions

4. The ability to provide an incoming inspection audit trail

From a JIT perspective, the incoming inspection function adds no value to the product and should therefore be eliminated. JIT purchasing programs focus on developing long-term, single-source relationships with quality suppliers to eliminate the need for incoming inspection. (This in turn eliminates the need to perform quality ratings based on incoming inspection results.) This is accomplished by implementing a supplier part certification program. **Supplier part certification** is "a process of granting ship-to-stock or ship-to-line privileges to a supplier who successfully demonstrates the ability to develop, operate, and control the production process."[1] It is a qualification process that is applied to each part (suppliers are not accorded blanket certification privileges). Certified suppliers are subject to periodic audits to retain their part certification privileges.

The part certification process begins by finding vendors who are considered likely candidates for certification. These are usually vendors who are considered to be quality suppliers by current criteria (i.e., incoming inspection results). MRP II packages help to identify candidates for part certification by providing performance ratings

---

1. Richard T. Lubben, *Just-In-Time Manufacturing.* New York, NY: McGraw-Hill Book Company, 1988, p. 221.

by vendor by part. Once a part is certified, periodic quality audits are performed at the supplier's plant in lieu of incoming inspection.

Few companies, if any, have developed certified suppliers for every part, so the incoming inspection and quality rating features found in MRP II packages will continue to be of benefit to most companies in the future.

Summary

MRP II systems are much more than scheduling and priority planning systems. They contain a number of quality-related features. Table 4.3 explains how these features can be applied to solve quality problems.

Table 4.3
Summary of Causes of and Solutions to Poor Quality

Cause	Solution
1. Inability to assess the quality of purchased parts	The Purchasing module calculates vendor quality ratings from incoming inspection data.
2. Failure to route receipts to Incoming Inspection	The inspection code indicates whether an item requires incoming inspection. If the item requires inspection, the Purchasing module prints the message "Deliver to Incoming Inspection" on the receiving identification label.
3. Inaccurate incoming inspection instructions	MRP II systems provide the ability to define and maintain inspection routings on-line. Inspectors can view up-to-date routings from computer terminals in the inspection area.
4. Lack of an incoming inspection audit trail	MRP II systems provide the ability to create inspection orders and track the results of the inspection process.
5. Inability to identify expired material	The shelf life expiration date of a part can be entered on the inventory detail record. When the shelf life expires, the inventory status is changed to prevent expired material from being released to production.
6. Inability to create and maintain accurate manufacturing bills of materials	The Bill of Materials module allows manufacturing bills of materials to be created. The bill of materials comparison program identifies discrepancies between the engineering and manufacturing BOMs.
7. Inability to trace the origin and use of defective material	The lot-tracing feature provides the ability to trace the origin and use of inventory lots.
8. Material shortages	See Chapter 2.
9. Invalid production schedules	See Chapter 5.

Some of the quality-related features in an MRP II system focus on problem detection, because this was the predominant quality management philosophy at the time MRP II software packages were developed. Deficiencies that MRP II packages have in the area of problem prevention are being addressed by other applications, such as shop floor management systems and quality management systems.

The Customer Service Problem

Orders at Gresh Technologies were down for the fourth consecutive month. At first, top management had attributed the downturn to a combination of seasonal and random fluctuations in customer ordering patterns. By the end of the fourth month, however, management had begun to suspect that some external force was responsible for the undesired trend.

The Manager of Customer Service began to study ordering patterns during the last four months. At first, the Manager of Customer Service was puzzled—orders from some customers were actually up 5 percent over the corresponding quarter the previous year. A more thorough investigation traced the overall decline to eight major customers. Curiously, all eight customers were from Gresh Technologies' original equipment manufacturer (OEM) customer segment. In fact, orders from these OEMs had been declining for more than four months, but increases in other market segments had obscured the problem for some time. In total, orders from these eight customers were down over $250,000 during the last six months, as compared to the corresponding six-month period the previous year.

The Manager of Customer Service called Bob Bryson, the buyer at one of the eight companies.

"Bob, this is Jane Carlson, Manager of Customer Service at Gresh Technologies. How are you today?"

"Just fine, thanks. To what do I owe the pleasure?"

"Well, Bob, I've been reviewing our records, and I see that you've been doing less than the usual volume of business with us over the last six months. Naturally, whenever we notice such a trend, we try to determine whether a customer service problem exists. Can you help me understand why orders from your company are down?"

"Well, Jane, like many manufacturers, our company is implementing a just-in-time program. To successfully implement JIT, we need our suppliers to provide us with accurate delivery dates."

"Haven't we always kept our promises?" replied Jane, puzzled.

"Well, yes and no," Bob answered.

"I'm not following you. What does 'yes and no' mean?"

"You often meet or beat your standard lead times on shipments," explained Bob. *"So in that sense, you keep your promises. But your promises are too vague, and vague promises are easy to keep. Quoting standard lead times isn't satisfactory anymore. When we place an order, we need to know exactly when you will be able to ship, and we need your promise to be accurate at least 95 percent of the time."*

"Well, who in the world can do that?" asked Jane.

"Your biggest competitor, that's who! Eight months ago they installed a new order entry system that is linked to their manufacturing planning and control system. When we place an order, they give us a firm delivery date over the phone, and they consistently meet that date."

"Why weren't we aware of the new requirements associated with your just-in-time program?"

"We had a meeting at our plant last year to kick off the JIT program. We invited the chief executives of all our major suppliers—including your company—to attend the meeting and participate in the program. For some reason your company failed to respond. Frankly, we had so many suppliers eager to become JIT partners, we didn't always have time to follow up with customers who didn't jump on the bandwagon right away."

There was nothing more the Manager of Customer Service could say. She thanked the buyer for the information and promised to investigate the matter further.

The Manager of Customer Service polled the other seven companies and heard similar responses. In every case, Gresh Technologies was losing business because a major competitor was providing customers with more accurate, timely information about shipments.

The situation was a hot topic at the CEO's next staff meeting.

"I'm glad you identified the cause of the problem so quickly, Jane," said the CEO. *"Frankly, I don't recall receiving an invitation to participate in any JIT programs. But that's water under the bridge. I want to understand the fundamental change that has occurred in the way our customers are doing business. For years we have been quoting standard lead times, and that has been good enough for our customers. Now some of our customers are telling us we need to do better. Can't we provide our customers with more accurate delivery dates when they place orders?"*

"Not without a lot of manual effort," the Manager of Customer Service replied. *"We've made various attempts to do that over the years. Every attempt has met with failure."*

"Why is that?" the CEO asked.

"To provide customers with accurate delivery dates, our order entry clerks would have to research every order manually to determine the status of finished-goods inventory. If an item is not in stock, the order entry clerk would then have to contact the master scheduler to determine when the next production run is scheduled.

"The results of such research would be highly suspect, because we keep no cumulative records of how much inventory and production is already committed to customer orders. This means that two order entry clerks conceivably could commit the same inventory to two different customers! Even if we researched every customer order, we would be making an educated guess at best as to when we could ship. And to top it off, to provide customers with estimated delivery dates, we would have to put the order on hold and call the customer back hours or days later. Why should our customers wait hours or days for an educated guess when they can get valid delivery dates from our competitor when they place the order?"

"Why indeed!" the CEO nodded agreement. *"How come our competitor is able to provide accurate delivery dates at the time of order entry?"*

"Well, according to my information, our competitor has recently implemented an MRP II system, which integrates the order entry function with manufacturing."

"MRP II," the CEO reflected. *"Mike, isn't that the project you've been trying to sell me on for the past two years?"* he asked the Manager of Manufacturing.

"That's right, Carl. We've been wanting to implement MRP II to help solve our material shortage and inventory problems, but an MRP II system would also provide the capabilities that Jane is talking about."

"Well, maybe it's high time I got behind you on this. Tell me more about these MRP II software packages you've been evaluating. . . ."

Introduction

Importance of Customer Service

There are two popular views on the importance of customer service:

1. *Customer service is a competitive weapon that can be used to achieve product differentiation.* This view assumes that customers recognize and value a high level of customer service.

2. *Customer service is a negative differentiator.* This view assumes that customers use poor customer service to classify a product or company as an unacceptable alternative but do not differentiate between two companies that provide acceptable service levels.

It is not really important which view you subscribe to, because both opinions point to the same inescapable conclusion: Poor customer service results in lost business either by preventing a company from winning new customers or by causing a company to lose existing customers.

Costs of Poor Customer Service

In the opening scenario to this chapter, the costs of poor customer service were easy to quantify—a competitor introduced a new customer service feature which cost the company $250,000 in lost sales over a six-month period. Rarely are the costs of poor customer service this easy to quantify. Popular rules of thumb dictate that it costs five times as much to gain a new customer as it does to keep one, and that it takes a dozen positive experiences to compensate for one negative experience. These rules seem logical, but it is difficult to use them to compute the *costs* of poor customer service. However, the fact that the costs of poor customer service are often difficult to quantify does not diminish the importance of this strategic competitive weapon.

Elements of Customer Service

Traditionally, the term "customer service" in a manufacturing environment is used to describe the availability of items when the customer needs them. This chapter takes a broader view of customer service, embracing the definition that "customer service consists of those activities that enhance or facilitate the sale and use of one's products and services."[1]

Using this definition of customer service, companies can develop a specific set of activities or elements that comprise a corporate customer service policy and establish a relative importance for each element. Some of the more common customer service elements, broken down into three categories, are as follows.

---

1. "A Sales Tool for All Seasons," *Sales Management,* Vol. 114, February 17, 1975, p.1.

Category 1 elements are those that can be implemented as a matter of policy. Some examples of Category 1 elements are as follows:

- Provide prepaid shipments.
- Provide daily shipments.
- Provide special packaging.
- Absorb the cost of freight on all returned items.
- Allow customers to return expired inventory at no charge.
- Stock inventory for preferred customers.
- Provide a technical staff to respond to customer questions.

Category 2 elements are those that require special-purpose systems to implement. For example, a customer complaint handling system may be needed to provide 24-hour resolution to customer complaints. Such a system would route all incoming phone calls to customer service representatives and track the status of each open complaint. The system might also keep historical data on complaints and produce reports that help the company take action to prevent, instead of respond to, complaints. Other examples of Category 2 elements are as follows:

- Provide toll-free telephone service.
- Provide information about product changes.
- Provide information about impending service failures.

Category 3 elements are those that can be either partially or fully addressed by an MRP II system. Some examples of Category 3 elements are as follows:

- Provide timely, accurate information about delivery dates.
- Provide the ability to process phone orders quickly.
- Provide the ability to receive orders electronically from those customers that are able to transmit orders in standard electronic formats.
- Provide reasonable minimum order amounts. (This can be implemented as a matter of policy, but an MRP II system can make the policy economically feasible.)
- Provide prompt responses to customer inquiries about the status of open orders.
- Provide 95 percent on-time shipments.
- Provide 99 percent accurate shipments.

The Category 3 elements are the focus of this chapter.

Causes of Poor Customer Service

Some of the causes of poor customer service are listed below. These causes, along with the solutions offered in MRP II systems, are discussed in the sections that follow.

1. Missed shipments, caused by:
   - Invalid production schedules
   - Inability to plan shipping activity
2. Inability to help customers configure orders to meet their business requirements
3. Inability to provide customers with timely, accurate delivery information
4. Inability to process customer orders quickly and accurately
5. Stockouts of service parts, caused by an inability to distinguish between service parts inventory and manufacturing inventory
6. High minimum order amounts
7. Inability to respond to customer inquiries about the status of open orders
8. Undershipments and overshipments, caused by counting errors

Missed Shipments

Customer service measurements are most commonly based on the timeliness of customer shipments. Typical measurements are

- Percentage of orders shipped on schedule
- Percentage of line items shipped on schedule

Because these measurements frequently are used externally to promote a company's emphasis on customer service, and because missed shipments can cost the company repeat business, missed shipments are of great concern to the CEO, Manager of Manufacturing, Manager of Marketing, and Manager of Customer Service.

Missed shipments can be caused by some of the business problems discussed in earlier chapters, such as material shortages (Chapter 2) and poor quality (Chapter 4). This section focuses on two other causes of missed shipments:

1. Invalid production schedules
2. Inability to plan shipping activity

Invalid Production Schedules

For many companies, the single largest cause of missed shipments is invalid production schedules. Customer promises based on invalid production schedules are destined to be broken as soon as they are made. Invalid production schedules occur when the Master Production Schedule represents a wish list of what a company would like to produce rather than a statement of what the company is capable of producing. Many companies lack the tools necessary to evolve from the wish list to a valid Master Production Schedule. Promises are made with the best of intentions, but orders are rarely shipped on schedule.

Some companies make a game out of customer service, measuring themselves against their latest promise. It's easy to obtain a 95 percent or better customer service rating playing such games, but customers aren't fooled, and not facing facts about performance is certainly no solution to the problem.

Solution   *Provide rough cut capacity planning.*

To help ensure valid production schedules, MRP II software packages have a rough cut capacity planning (RCCP) feature within the Master Production Schedule (MPS) module. (In some packages, RCCP is a separate module.) This capability allows a manufacturer to evaluate a proposed Master Production Schedule to determine whether there is enough capacity (labor and equipment) to meet the schedule.

As the name implies, rough cut capacity planning is a rough estimating tool used at the beginning of the planning process. It is intended to identify potential capacity problems at critical work centers (i.e., work centers that are known production bottlenecks).

Preparing to run RCCP   Prior to executing RCCP, the master scheduler must identify the critical work centers. For each work center, the master scheduler specifies the equipment and labor capacity (Figure 5.1).

Some MRP II packages also allow the master scheduler to specify the following information for each critical work center:

- Load tolerance parameters
- Changes to normal capacity

Load tolerance parameters are used to determine when a work center is underloaded or overloaded. For example, if the underload

```
Next Transaction: ___                              Date: 08/06/91
This Transaction: CWC                              Time: 10:44
                      Add Critical Work Center

Critical Work Center ID: FA200    Description: Final Assembly

Normal Machine Capacity:    0    Normal Labor Capacity: 400
Underload Parameter:  65%        Overload Parameter: 90%

Changes to Normal Capacity

 Effectivity Dates              Machine      Labor
Start         Stop             Capacity    Capacity
11/04/91      01/03/92                0         600
```

Figure 5.1
Add Critical Work Center Screen

parameter is 65 percent, the work center is considered to be underloaded when it is loaded to less than 65 percent of capacity. If the overload parameter is 85 percent, the work center is considered to be overloaded when it is loaded to more than 85 percent of capacity.

Changes to normal capacity are specified by entering the start and end effectivity dates for the work center capacity. Changes to normal capacity might be caused by scheduled maintenance or plans to run an extra shift for a period of time. The system automatically incorporates the capacity changes into all rough cut capacity planning performed between these dates.

After the critical work centers have been defined, the master scheduler (or an industrial engineer) defines rough cut routings for each product (Figure 5.2). A rough cut routing defines the following information for all operations performed at critical work centers:

- The work center where the operations are performed

- The number of equipment and/or labor hours required to perform each operation

Some MRP II packages allow generic rough cut routings to be defined. For example, if 25 products follow the same production process, one generic routing can be shared by all 25 products. This eliminates the need to create a rough cut routing for each product.

Running RCCP Once the critical work centers and rough cut routings have been defined, RCCP can "explode" the Master Production Schedule (i.e., backschedule the MPS, using the rough cut routings, to develop a week-by-week load profile at the critical work centers). This process produces three reports that help the master scheduler evaluate the feasibility of the Master Production Schedule:

- Critical Work Center Load Profile Report

- Critical Work Center Load Detail Report

- Critical Work Center Underload/Overload Exception Report

```
Next Transaction: ___                            Date: 08/06/91
This Transaction: RCR                            Time: 10:44
                        Add Rough Cut Routing

Part Number: MBL209309

                Critical        — Standard Hours —
Operation     Work Center      Machine      Labor

   0010          MS100          0.1500      0.1500
   0020          WS100          0.2000      0.3500
   0030          FB100          0.1000      0.1500
   0040          PT100                      0.4000
   0050          FA100                      1.5000
```

Figure 5.2
Add Rough Cut Routing Screen

Critical Work Center Load Profile Report
(Sorted by Work Center / Week)
Page Break on: Work Center

Work Center: MS200   Description: Turret Lathes   Underload Tol Parameter: 65%   Overload Tol Parameter: 85%

Machine Capacity Utilization

Week Starting	Capacity	Load	Percent Load	Under/Over	0........5.........0.........0
11/04/91	120.0	115.0	95.8	Over	*******************
11/11/91	160.0	120.0	75.0		****************
11/18/91	160.0	130.0	81.3		*****************
11/25/91	72.0	65.0	90.3	Over	******************
12/02/91	120.0	115.0	95.8	Over	*******************
12/09/91	120.0	110.0	91.7	Over	*******************
12/16/91	120.0	100.0	83.3		*****************
12/23/91	120.0	70.0	58.3	Under	**************

Labor Capacity Utilization

Week Starting	Capacity	Load	Percent Load	Under/Over	0........5.........0.........0
11/04/91	160.0	110.0	68.8		****************
11/11/91	200.0	165.0	82.5		*******************
11/18/91	200.0	153.0	76.5		*****************
11/25/91	120.0	85.0	70.9		****************
12/02/91	160.0	120.0	75.0		*****************
12/09/91	160.0	145.0	90.7	Over	**********************
12/16/91	160.0	135.0	84.4		********************
12/23/91	160.0	100.0	62.5	Under	*************

Figure 5.3
Critical Work Center Load Profile Report

The Critical Work Center Load Profile Report (Figure 5.3) shows the weekly equipment and labor load for each critical work center. The load is displayed graphically to help the master scheduler identify underloaded and overloaded work centers.

The Critical Work Center Load Detail Report (Figure 5.4) provides a detailed report of the orders that comprise the weekly load at each work center. This report helps the master scheduler determine what adjustments to make in the Master Production Schedule to solve capacity problems in overloaded work centers.

The Critical Work Center Underload/Overload Exception Report has the same format as the Load Profile Report, except that it lists only those weeks in which a work center is underloaded or overloaded.

RCCP decouples the Master Production Schedule from the Material Requirements Planning module. This decoupling process is illustrated in Figure 5.5. The feasibility of the master schedule can be tested by running rough cut capacity planning prior to running MRP. If the plan is not feasible, the master schedule can be changed and RCCP can be performed again to test the feasibility of the revised plan. The master schedule is not passed to the Material Requirements Planning module for detailed planning and execution until a feasible plan has been demonstrated.

Limitations of Rough Cut Capacity Planning

Although RCCP is a useful tool, it has several inherent limitations, as follows.

RCCP takes too fine a cut too early in the planning process. In spite of its name, RCCP is a rather detailed scheduling and capacity planning tool. With RCCP, for example, it would be possible to determine that work center *A* was loaded to 130 percent of capacity during the week of March 23. This is useful information, but RCCP doesn't answer the most basic of all questions:

"Is there enough capacity, on average, to meet this year's production plans?"

In effect, RCCP takes too fine a cut too early in the planning process. Before you look for capacity problems in a specific work center in a specific week, you should look at average conditions over an extended period of time to determine the feasibility of the production plan.

RCCP does not allow the quick evaluation of many alternatives. RCCP takes several hours to run because of the volume of data and

Date: 11/04/91   Page: 01
                       Critical Work Center Load Detail Report
                  (Sorted by Work Center / Week / Scheduled Start Date)
                             Page Break on: Work Center

Work Center Number: MS200   Description: Turret Lathes

Week Starting: 11/04/91

Order Number	Part Number	Scheduled Start Date	Scheduled Comp Date	Oper No	Machine Hours	Labor Hours
32349	ADL674935	11/02/91	11/04/91	0010	14.0	14.0
12333	MBL33145	11/02/91	11/04/91	0020	12.0	10.0
34321	REL045023	11/04/91	11/04/91	0010	5.5	5.0
91231	ADL43547	11/04/91	11/05/91	0035	10.5	12.5
12343	EL290934	11/05/91	11/06/91	0010	12.0	13.0
12342	ADL201452	11/06/91	11/08/91	0030	14.0	12.0
22762	ADL353434	11/06/91	11/08/91	0010	15.5	13.0
15453	MAL34576	11/07/91	11/07/91	0020	8.0	7.0
25453	JSL434523	11/07/91	11/08/91	0010	9.5	9.5
25862	BJL33455	11/08/91	11/11/91	0035	8.5	8.5
13455	EL576676	11/08/91	11/12/91	0010	5.5	5.5
	**** Capacity Utilization Totals:				115.0	110.0

Week Starting: 11/11/91

Order Number	Part Number	Scheduled Start Date	Scheduled Comp Date	Oper No	Machine Hours	Labor Hours
25862	BJL33455	11/08/91	11/11/91	0015	5.5	5.5
13455	EL576676	11/08/91	11/12/91	0020	10.0	10.5
34549	ADL346335	11/11/91	11/12/91	0010	12.0	20.0
12345	MBL33464	11/11/91	11/12/91	0010	10.0	15.0
33451	SFL654523	11/12/91	11/12/91	0030	7.5	12.0
92451	BJL25465	11/12/91	11/13/91	0025	10.5	11.0
46545	MBL43434	11/13/91	11/14/91	0015	7.0	13.0
24643	ADL203232	11/13/91	11/15/91	0020	9.0	12.0
45345	BLD94034	11/13/91	11/15/91	0010	11.5	21.5
56422	ABL235434	11/14/91	11/15/91	0020	12.5	13.0
35343	MAL23544	11/14/91	11/18/91	0010	10.0	12.0
43453	JSL45444	11/14/91	11/19/91	0040	8.0	13.0
34654	JSL423423	11/15/91	11/19/91	0020	6.5	6.5
	**** Capacity Utilization Totals:				120.0	165.0

Figure 5.4
Critical Work Center Load Detail Report

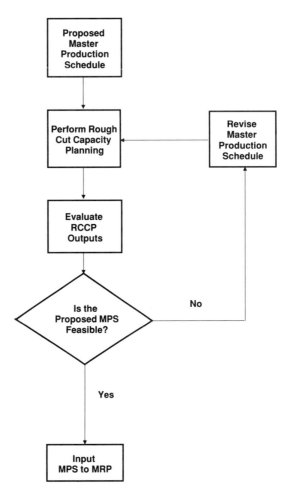

Figure 5.5
Rough Cut Capacity Planning Flowchart

the number of calculations involved in exploding the Master Production Schedule through rough cut routings. This does not allow sufficient time to perform a "what if" analysis of many alternatives. MRP II vendors' claims to the contrary, RCCP is *not* a viable "what if" analysis tool.

RCCP is a static analysis tool. Another limitation of RCCP is that it is a static analysis tool; that is, it requires fixed manufacturing lead times. In reality, lead times will vary because queue times will vary. Queue times are a function of resource availability, product mix, lot sizes, factory load, machine reliability, and the variability of job arrivals at a work center.

For example, consider the effect of machine reliability on queue times. If a machine breaks down ten times a day but can be fixed each time in six minutes, the impact on queue times is less than if the machine breaks down once a day and requires an hour to fix. Therefore, the mean-time-to-failure and mean-time-to-repair reliability estimates for a machine should be considered in a rough cut analysis.

Because RCCP requires fixed lead times, it is not possible to vary other parameters such as process yields, machine reliability, or lot sizes to observe the impact on lead times and capacity utilization.

What is needed, then, is a high-level planning tool to compensate for the limitations of RCCP. This supplementary tool should have the following characteristics:

- The ability to determine if there is enough capacity, on average, over an extended period of time to meet production plans
- The ability to allow the quick evaluation of many alternatives
- The ability to calculate and use actual lead times rather than require lead times to be arbitrarily fixed during the rough cut planning process

The solution to this problem has emerged in the form of **rapid modeling systems**. Rapid modeling software packages use **queuing network theory** and **reliability theory** to capture mathematically the queue-time dynamics of a manufacturing environment. Rapid modeling sits above RCCP in the hierarchy of capacity planning tools to provide quick insight into the feasibility of a production plan (Figure 5.6).

Data inputs to a rapid modeling system are as follows:

- Equipment types
- Equipment capacities
- Equipment reliabilities (mean-time-to-failure and mean-time-to-repair figures for each type of equipment)
- Product demands for the period being evaluated
- Process routings
- Lot sizes
- Process yields

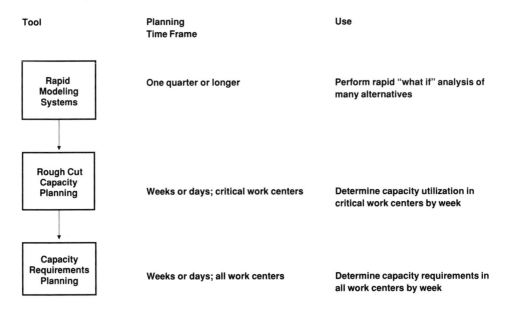

Tool	Planning Time Frame	Use
Rapid Modeling Systems	One quarter or longer	Perform rapid "what if" analysis of many alternatives
Rough Cut Capacity Planning	Weeks or days; critical work centers	Determine capacity utilization in critical work centers by week
Capacity Requirements Planning	Weeks or days; all work centers	Determine capacity requirements in all work centers by week

Figure 5.6
Hierarchy of Capacity Planning Tools

The equipment types, equipment capacities, process routings, and process yield information can be loaded into the model directly from the MRP II database.

The rapid modeling software package analyzes this data, applying queuing and reliability theory, to provide the following outputs:

- Estimated production rates

- Product lead times

- Work-in-process inventories

- Capacity utilization and downtimes

- Queues at each work center

Because this analysis is performed for one period of time (usually a quarter or longer), the rapid modeling analysis usually takes less than a minute to complete. If the desired results are not obtained, the input parameters can be changed and a number of "what if" scenarios can be evaluated in a minimum amount of time.

Some rapid modeling packages provide the ability to specify "what if" speed-up factors to further facilitate the rapid analysis of many alternatives. These factors allow the user to evaluate the impact of percentage changes in setup time, run time, and capacity for a particular work center.

Once a feasible plan has been generated, RCCP can be run to identify capacity problems on a week-by-week basis.

Rapid modeling systems do not provide 100 percent accurate answers, but a well-designed package provides answers that are 80 to 85 percent accurate within a minute. This is usually much more valuable than performing several weeks of analysis to obtain a 100 percent accurate answer.

Inability to Plan Shipping Activity

The inability to plan for the amount of time required to pick, pack, and ship a customer order is another cause of missed shipments. Depending on the products and the number of items in a customer order, the time required to pick, pack, and ship an order may be anywhere from a few hours to a week. If the picking and shipping documents are not produced in advance of the actual required ship date, the shipment may be delayed several days.

Solution   *Provide the ability to plan when picking and shipping documents are generated.*

Some MRP II Order Entry modules provide the ability to specify the lead time required to pick, pack, and ship a customer order. In Figure 5.7, the order entry clerk has specified that it will take two days to pick the order, two days to pack the order, and one day to ship the order. The system automatically generates a picklist for the customer order five days prior to the required ship date to allow sufficient time to pick, pack, and ship the order. Shipping documents are generated automatically one day prior to the ship date to prompt the shipping clerk to ship the order.

Inability to Configure Special Customer Orders Properly

Some companies manufacture complex products that include a wide variety of options that the customer can order. For example, a manufacturer of personal computers can build dozens of different configurations depending on the customer's processing, storage, memory, printer interface, and graphics requirements. Even with the small number of choices available in Figure 5.8, the customer can order any of a total of 72 unique product configurations.

```
Next Transaction: ___                              Date: 10/29/91
This Transaction: OHE                              Time: 10:38
                    Order Entry: Header Information

Customer Number: 29039     Customer Name: Jacobson Valve Company
                                          1035 Summer Oaks Boulevard
                                          Roswell, GA 30076

Order Number: C029023     Order Type: Regular     Entered by: KWL
PO Number:    P030922

Picking   Lead Time:  2 days
Packing   Lead Time:  2 days
Shipping  Lead Time:  1 day

Freight Terms: Prepaid     Price at time of order or shipment? S

Customer Group Price Code:
```

Figure 5.7
Order Entry: Header Information Screen

Many manufacturers try to simplify the ordering process by manufacturing a number of standard configurations, but a large percentage of orders may still be for custom configurations.

When a customer places an order, the order entry clerk must select from among many product options to configure a product that meets the customer's business needs. The selection process can be extremely complex, because the selection of one option may dictate and/or preclude the selection of other options. For example, if a customer orders a personal computer with a color monitor, this dictates the selection of a color video adapter card and precludes the selection of a monochrome video adapter card.

Sometimes the clerk must select one and *only* one option from a group of options. For example, when a customer orders a personal computer with a color monitor, the clerk must select either an EGA or a VGA color video adapter card, but not both.

Sometimes the clerk must select at least one option from a group of options. For example, a customer must order at least one disk

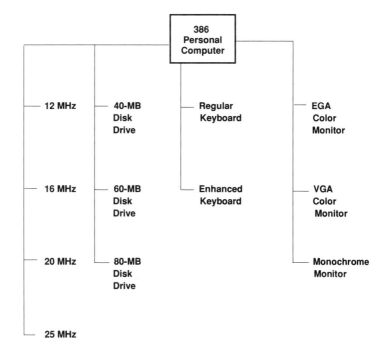

4 Choices × **3 Choices** × **2 Choices** × **3 Choices = 72 Choices**

There is a mathematical relationship between the number of product options and the number of unique product configurations.

Figure 5.8
Diagram of Product Options and Product Configurations

drive with a personal computer. However, the customer can order up to three disk drives for each computer.

Customer service problems result when an order entry clerk selects the wrong product options. This can result in the wrong product being shipped to the customer. When I ordered the computer that I used to write this book, the manufacturer shipped a monochrome monitor instead of a color monitor, even though the system had the correct color video adapter card. I had to return the monochrome monitor and wait two weeks for the color monitor to arrive.

Sometimes the incorrect selection of options can result in a product configuration that cannot be manufactured. If the order entry clerk configures a personal computer without any kind of disk drive, a working system cannot be assembled and shipped.

Many companies rely entirely on the skill and experience of their order entry clerks to properly configure customer orders. Whether or not the customer receives the right product depends entirely on the clerk's knowledge of the available options and the relationships between the options. Orders processed by inexperienced clerks can be a major source of customer service problems. Even experienced clerks can have difficulty configuring orders when there are hundreds of options from which to choose and dozens of relationships to remember. Systems that require order entry clerks to be perfect "if/then" processors ("if the customer picks option *A*, then he must also select either option *B*, *C*, or *D*") don't work very well in practice.

Solution

Provide the ability to specify configuration bills of materials.

Some MRP II systems provide the ability to specify configuration bills of materials (also called **planning bills of materials** or **family bills of materials**). These are bills of materials (BOMs) that define the rules on how product options can be grouped together to create specific product configurations within a product family.

Creating Configuration Bills of Materials

Configuration BOMs are typically multilevel bills of materials comprised of

1. A product family at the top level

2. Option group-level parts at the intermediate levels

3. Master Production Schedule (MPS) parts at the bottom level

Configuration codes are used to identify each part on a configuration BOM as a product family, option group-level part, or MPS part.

Product family The product family is located at the top of the configuration bill of materials. It represents a group of similar products, such as a particular model of a computer or automobile. Product family part numbers are identified by a configuration code of FAM.

Option group-level parts These are parts that represent groups of product options. A well-designed MRP II package should allow four different types of option group-level parts. Each type has a different configuration code that defines how the options within the group can be selected. The four types are described below:

1. A configuration code of ALL means that all options under the group are automatically selected when the group is selected. For example, an automobile manufacturer may offer special option packages (i.e., groups of options that can be ordered as one part number at a special price). When the option group-level part is selected, all the individual options under the group are automatically selected.

2. A configuration code of ANY means that any number of options in the group *can* be selected. These are usually add-on options that can be ordered in any combination. Examples of add-on options in an automobile product family are power locks, power windows, and power seat controls.

3. A configuration code of ALO means that At Least One of the options in the group *must* be selected. However, any number of options in the group *can* be selected. For example, a customer must order at least one disk drive with a personal computer. The customer can also order more than one disk drive.

4. A configuration code of ONE means that one and *only* one option in the group *must* be selected. For example, a particular model of automobile is available with either a four-cylinder or a six-cylinder engine. The customer must select one and only one engine when ordering a car.

Master Production Schedule parts   These parts are at the bottom of the configuration BOM. They represent specific stocked parts or kits of parts that appear on the Master Production Schedule. MPS parts are identified by a configuration code of either STK or KIT to differentiate between stocked MPS parts and nonstocked kits of parts. An example of a nonstocked kit is a group of parts that are common to all configurations within a product family.

Figure 5.9 shows a sample configuration bill of materials for a product family of 386 personal computers.[2] The following observations can be made from the way the configuration bill of materials is structured:

- All models in the family share a group of common parts.

- The customer must select either a 16-MHz, 20-MHz, or 25-MHz processor speed.

2. The configuration BOM presented in Figure 5.9 is not intended to be complete. An actual configuration BOM for a 386 personal computer would be more complex. For example, a manufacturer might offer several more types of monitors, graphics cards, printer interfaces, disk drives, etc.

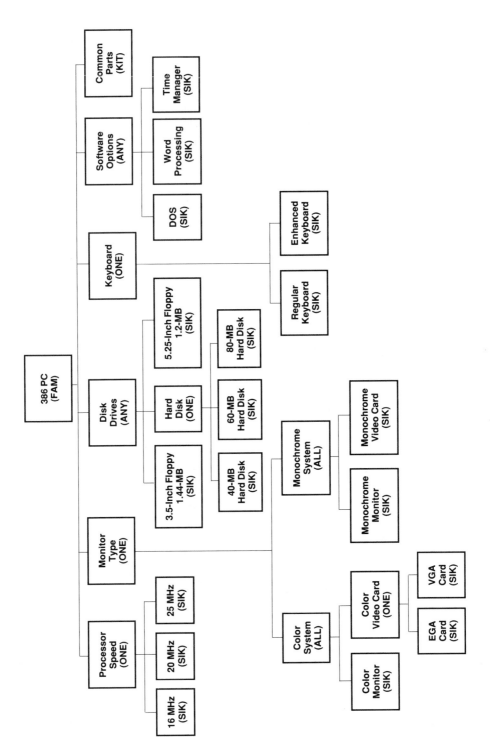

Figure 5.9
Sample Configuration Bill of Materials

- The customer must select either a color or a monochrome system. If the color system is selected, the customer must also select either an EGA or a VGA color graphics card.

- The customer can select up to three different disk drives, including a 3.5-inch floppy drive, a 5.25-inch floppy drive, and a hard drive. If a hard disk drive is selected, the customer must specify either a 40-MB, 60-MB, or 80-MB capacity drive.

- The customer must select either the regular or the enhanced keyboard.

- The customer can select any or all of three add-on software options.

Table 5.1 summarizes the configuration codes used in configuration bills of materials.

Integrating Configuration Bills of Materials into the Order Entry Module

When the configuration BOMs are integrated with the Order Entry module, the system becomes an if/then processor, prompting the order entry clerk to choose options in accordance with the configuration codes on the configuration bill of materials. For example, if the order entry clerk enters an order for a 386

Table 5.1
Configuration Codes Used in Configuration Bills of Materials

Configuration Code	Description
FAM	Identifies a product family. Located at the top of the configuration bill of materials.
Option Group Level Parts	
ALL	All options under the group are automatically selected when the group is selected.
ANY	Any number of options in the group can be selected.
ALO	At Least One of the options in the group *must* be selected.
ONE	One and *only* one option in the group *must* be selected.
MPS Parts	
STK	Stocked MPS option.
KIT	Nonstocked MPS option (such as a kit of common parts).

```
Next Transaction: ___                              Date: 08/06/91
This Transaction: CBM                              Time: 10:38
            Configuration Bill Order Entry: Option Selection

Order Number: CO390904   Item: 0001   Order Type: Assemble-to-Order
Customer Name: Business Computing   Customer Number: 39041
Product Family: 386    Family Name: 386 PC   Order Quantity:      10

Sel Part Number          Cfg Code  Description             Unit Qty
    Processor            ONE
    8038616              STK       16-MHz Processor            1
 x  8038620              STK       20-MHz Processor            1
    8038625              STK       25-MHz Processor            1
    Monitor              ONE
 x  Color System         ALL
 x  CM1280               STK       Color Monitor               1
    Video Card           ONE
    CAEGA100             STK       EGA Card                    1
 x  CAVGA100             STK       VGA Card                    1
    Mono System          ALL
    MM1920               STK       Monochrome Monitor          1
    MA290                STK       Monochrome Card             1

Page 1 of 3   Press enter to select more options
```

Figure 5.10
Configuration Bill Order Entry: Option Selection Screen

personal computer, the system prompts the clerk to select either a 16-MHz, 20-MHz, or 25-MHz processor. Even inexperienced order entry clerks can configure orders perfectly, because the system does not allow the clerk to mismatch options or configure an order that cannot be manufactured.

Figure 5.10 illustrates how a multilevel configuration bill of materials is displayed on an order entry screen. The configuration BOM is displayed as an indented bill of materials to help the order entry clerk visualize which options belong under an option group-level part number. The configuration codes guide the clerk in selecting options. The system displays the appropriate error message if the clerk violates the configuration code rules.

Caveats   Some MRP II software packages allow only single level configuration bills of materials to be created. With single level configuration BOMs, it is impossible to group options together under option group-level part numbers. Therefore, it is impossible to define the rules on how product options can be selected from a group of related options. Single level configuration BOMs are of some help because they at least provide the order entry clerk with a complete list of options. However, the clerk must still remember the relationships between product options. In contrast, multilevel configuration BOMs provide a complete, foolproof solution to the problem of configuring customer orders.

Some MRP II packages provide the ability to define multilevel configuration BOMs *but do not integrate the configuration BOMs with the Order Entry module.* The configuration BOMs are used for information purposes only.

Some MRP II packages use numeric configuration codes instead of alphabetic configuration codes like ONE, ANY, and ALL. Numeric configuration codes are not as easy for the order entry clerk to interpret.

Order Configuration: Limitations of MRP II Systems

MRP II systems are not expert systems that can help an order entry clerk configure a customer order based on a description of functional requirements. An MRP II Order Entry module cannot engage in an interactive session with an order entry clerk, in which the system prompts the clerk to input functional requirements and automatically develops the proper product configuration.

Expert product configuration systems do exist, but they are homegrown systems because they are unique to the product being manufactured. These systems can act as a front-end processor to an MRP II Order Entry module.

Inability to Provide Customers with Timely, Accurate Delivery Information

Next to missed shipments, the inability to provide customers with accurate delivery dates[3] at the time of order entry is the most common cause of poor customer service. Quoting standard lead times is unsatisfactory if a competitor can tell the customer precisely when the order can be shipped. Asking a customer to wait several

---

3. The terms "delivery date" and "ship date" are often used interchangeably, although the two dates are actually quite different. The delivery date should refer to the date the customer *receives* the shipment. In this section, the term delivery date refers to the ship date.

days for a delivery date isn't acceptable if a competitor can provide delivery dates while the customer is still on the phone.

Many companies are unable to provide customers with timely, accurate delivery dates for one of two reasons:

1. They are unable to calculate how much inventory is available-to-promise (ATP) to customers in a given week.

2. They do not have realtime access to ATP information at the time of order entry.

Solutions

Provide the ability to calculate available-to-promise inventory.

MRP II systems use information about booked orders, on-hand inventory, and scheduled production to calculate how much inventory is available-to-promise (ATP) in a given week. The ATP quantity is calculated as follows:

For the current week:

ATP
= On-Hand Balance + MPS Quantity – Booked Customer Orders

For any future week *n*:

$$\text{ATP}_{\text{Week } n}$$
= MPS Quantity$_{\text{Week } n}$ – Booked Customer Orders$_{\text{Week } n}$

The information required to calculate the ATP quantity comes from the following MRP II modules:

Information	*Source*
On-hand balance	Inventory Control module
MPS quantity	Master Production Schedule module
Booked customer orders	Master Production Schedule module (updated by the Order Entry module)

The ATP quantity is calculated only for periods that have scheduled production, because if a customer's requested ship date falls between two production runs, the order must be promised from one of the two runs (Figure 5.11).[4] This decision is made at the time of order entry. If the customer will accept an earlier ship date, the order entry clerk will promise the order from the earlier production run. If the customer will not accept an earlier ship date, the order entry clerk will attempt to negotiate a later ship date so that the order can

4. The ATP quantity is calculated for the current period even if there is no scheduled production, provided that there is a balance in on-hand inventory.

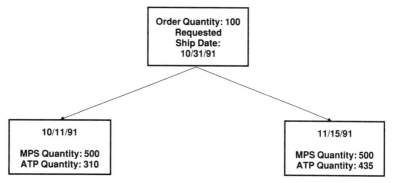

The customer order must be promised from either the 10/11/91 MPS lot or the 11/15/91 MPS lot, because there is no production scheduled for 10/31/91.

Figure 5.11
Order Promising from MPS Lots

be promised from the later production run. If the customer will not accept either an earlier or a later ship date, the order must be promised from the earlier production run and product must be held in finished-goods inventory until the customer will accept shipment.

In most MRP II packages, the ATP quantity is stored in the Master Production Schedule record in the MRP II database. This is a logical place to store the ATP quantity, because the MPS module is designed to store information in a matrix fashion. Table 5.2 shows how the MPS quantity, booked customer order quantity, and ATP quantity are stored in the Master Production Schedule matrix.

Provide realtime access to ATP information at order entry.

Calculating the ATP quantity is of little value if the Order Entry module does not have realtime access to this information. Realtime access is needed:

- To allocate (commit) ATP inventory to customer orders.
- To perform realtime updating of ATP quantities as inventory is committed.
- To provide customers with firm delivery dates.

If the system is unable to commit ATP inventory and provide customers with firm delivery dates, the order entry clerk's only recourse is to quote standard lead times. As stated earlier, this is a practice that is no longer acceptable in today's just-in-time competitive environment.

MRP II Order Entry modules provide realtime access to ATP information so that order entry clerks can perform the order promising function. Order promising solutions are commonly available in MRP II packages for two types of manufacturing environments:

1. Make-to-stock environments

2. Assemble-to-order environments

Order Promising in Make-to-Stock Environments

In a make-to-stock environment, ATP inventory is allocated to customer orders in the following manner.

The order entry clerk enters a requested ship date for each item on the customer order. If the customer requests immediate shipment, the system will attempt to satisfy the order by allocating finished-goods inventory. If the customer requests shipment on a future date, the system will attempt to allocate inventory from a future production run. If there is sufficient ATP inventory to meet the customer's requested ship date, the system automatically will commit the inventory and update the ATP quantity. If there is insufficient ATP inventory or if the customer's requested ship date falls between two scheduled production runs, the system will display the ATP Inventory screen (Figure 5.12). From this the order entry clerk can immediately determine a ship date.

In Figure 5.12, the customer has requested a ship date of 10/10/91. The system has displayed the ATP Inventory screen because there is no production scheduled during that week. The order entry clerk may commit ATP inventory from the 09/06/91 production run or may try to negotiate a ship date of 10/25/91. The order entry clerk

Table 5.2
MPS Record Showing ATP Quantities

Part Number: DAD102938
On-Hand Inventory: 100

	MPS Period							
	05/06	*05/13*	*05/20*	*05/27*	*06/03*	*06/10*	*06/17*	*06/24*
Booked Orders	180	—	—	85	—	70	—	35
MPS Quantity	100	0	0	200	0	200	0	100
ATP Quantity	20	—	—	115	—	130	—	65

```
Next Transaction: ___                              Date: 08/06/91
This Transaction: ATP                              Time: 10:44
                    Available-to-Promise Inventory

Order Number: C0390478   Line Item: 0001   Order Type: Regular
Part Number: MBL309094   Order Quantity: 35   Requested Ship Date: 10/10/91

Select   ATP         ATP        MPS      Select    ATP      ATP        MPS
Period   Date     Quantity   Quantity    Period    Date   Quantity   Quantity

         Current     150        175        -     10/18/91     -          0
         08/16/91     -           0        x     10/25/91    180        200
         08/23/91     -           0        -     11/01/91     -          0
         08/30/91     -           0        -     11/08/91     -          0
         09/06/91    120         200       -     11/15/91     -          0
         09/13/91     -           0        -     11/22/91     -          0
         09/20/91     -           0        -     11/29/91     -          0
         09/27/91     -           0        -     12/06/91    100        100
         10/04/91     -           0        -     12/13/91     -          0
         10/11/91     -           0        -     12/30/91     -          0
```

Figure 5.12
Available-to-Promise Inventory Screen

commits ATP inventory by entering an "x" in the SELECT PERIOD column.

Order Promising in Assemble-to-Order Environments

Manufacturers of complex products that include a wide variety of options don't maintain a large inventory of finished goods. Instead, these companies make and stock standard product options. These options can be assembled to produce a configuration that has been ordered by the customer. An earlier section of this chapter discussed how configuration bills of materials are used to help order entry clerks properly configure customer orders in assemble-to-order environments.

The order promising solution is more complex for assemble-to-order environments than for make-to-stock companies. To provide customers with accurate delivery dates, the order entry system must consider the availability of each option required for final assembly of the customer order. In addition, the order entry system must consider the final assembly lead time when calculating ship dates.

Some MRP II systems provide order promising solutions for assemble-to-order environments. The order entry clerk configures an order from the configuration bill of materials and enters the customer's requested ship date. The system responds by calculating a ship date for the end item based on the ATP date of each of the selected options and the final assembly lead time. (There is no standard approach for calculating ship dates in assemble-to-order environments; each MRP II package uses its own algorithm for determining ATP dates.)

In Figure 5.13, the customer has ordered ten of a particular configuration of 386 model personal computer. The customer has requested shipment on 10/15/91. The system has determined an ATP date for each option based on the customer's requested ship date. In addition, the system has calculated the ATP date for the end item by

```
Next Transaction: ___                               Date: 08/06/91
This Transaction: ATO                               Time: 10:44
                  Assemble-to-Order Order Promising

Order Number: C0390904   Item: 0001   Order Type: Assemble-to-Order
Customer Name: Business Computing   Customer Number: 39041

Product Family: 386          Family Name: 386 PC
Order Quantity:       10      Unit Price:    2,389.00  Ext Price:    23,890.00
Requested Ship Date: 10/15/91 Final Assembly Lead Time:   5
ATP Date: 11/08/91            Scheduled Ship Date:

                               Extended              View ATP
Part Number   Description      Quantity   ATP Date   Inv Screen?

8038620       20-MHz Processor    10      10/04/91      -
CM1280        Color Monitor       10      10/04/91      -
CAVGA100      VGA Card            10      11/01/91      x
HD251-1       40-MB Hard Disk     10      10/04/91      -
FDHD350       1.44-MB 3 1/2 Floppy 10     09/27/91      -
KB101         Enhanced Keyboard   10      10/04/91      -
CPU001        CPU Unit (Common Part) 10   09/20/91      -
```

Figure 5.13
Assemble-to-Order Order Promising Screen

adding the final assembly lead time (five days) to the latest ATP date of the selected options. In this case, the calculated ATP date is three weeks later than the customer's requested ship date. If this is not acceptable to the customer, the order entry clerk can review the ATP Inventory screen for the limiting item (part CAVGA100 in Figure 5.13) to see if this item can be promised from an earlier MPS period. In this case, part CAVGA100 can be promised from the 08/16/91 MPS period (Figure 5.14). In this way, the customer's requested ship date can be met.

Note that the order promising algorithm did not commit inventory of option CAVGA100 from the 08/16/91 MPS period automatically because this requires part CAVGA100 to be held in inventory for eight weeks. However, the order entry clerk can commit inventory from an earlier period to meet the customer's requested ship date.

Caveats   Some MRP II systems only provide order promising solutions for make-to-stock environments. If you are evaluating MRP II packages,

---

```
Next Transaction: ___                                    Date: 08/06/91
This Transaction: ATP                                    Time: 10:44
                        Available-to-Promise Inventory

Order Number: C0390904   Item: 0001   Order Type: Assemble-to-Order
Customer Name: Business Computing   Customer Number: 39041
Product Family: 386              Family Name: 386 PC
Option Part: CAVGA100        Order Quantity: 10
Option Need Date: 10/08/91
```

Select Period	ATP Date	ATP Quantity	MPS Quantity	Select Period	ATP Date	ATP Quantity	MPS Quantity
-	Current	20	0	-	10/18/91	-	0
x	08/16/91	213	500	-	10/25/91	-	0
-	08/23/91	-	0	-	11/01/91	385	500
-	08/30/91	-	0	-	11/08/91	-	0
-	09/06/91	-	0	-	11/15/91	-	0
-	09/13/91	-	0	-	11/22/91	-	0
-	09/20/91	-	0	-	11/29/91	-	0
-	09/27/91	-	0	-	12/06/91	500	500
-	10/04/91	-	0	-	12/13/91	-	0
-	10/11/91	-	0	-	12/30/91	-	0

Figure 5.14
Available-to-Promise Inventory Screen

make certain that you select a package that provides a solution for your manufacturing environment.

Some MRP II systems separate the order promising function from the order entry function. The customer order must be completely processed before a promise date can be determined. This is not a valid approach, because the customer will usually decide whether or not to place the order based on the quoted delivery date. If the order has to be processed before a delivery date can be determined, the order may have to be canceled immediately if the delivery date is unacceptable to the customer.

Some MRP II packages do not dynamically recalculate ATP quantities. There are a number of transactions that should cause the ATP inventory quantity to be recalculated. These transactions are listed below.

Order Entry Transactions

- New customer order
- Cancellation of a customer order
- Change in order quantity
- Change in the delivery date

Inventory Transactions

- Cycle count adjustments
- Receipts into finished-goods inventory
- Issues from finished-goods inventory
- Any other transaction that adjusts the on-hand inventory balance

MPS Transactions

- Changes to MPS quantities

Whenever one of these transactions is performed, the ATP quantity should be updated immediately. Realtime updating is essential to providing customers with accurate delivery dates.

Some MRP II packages perform realtime updating of ATP quantities only when ATP inventory is committed to new customer orders. A 100 percent accurate ATP quantity is calculated only once a day when a nightly batch program is executed. This undermines the primary objective, which is to provide customers with *accurate* delivery dates. Make certain that you select an MRP II system that dynamically keeps the ATP quantity up to date.

*Order Promising: Limitations of MRP II
Systems*

Most MRP II systems do not provide closed-loop order promising solutions. A closed-loop solution provides feedback to the order entry clerk when changes occur after a customer order has been entered into the system, as illustrated in the following two examples.

On July 1, customer *A* places an order for 10 units of product *X* and requests shipment on August 10. The earliest ATP date is September 10. The customer agrees to the later date. The next day, customer *B* cancels an order for 15 units of product *X* that was to have been shipped on August 10. The cancellation makes inventory available to meet customer *A*'s requested ship date. A closed-loop order promising solution would notify the order entry clerk that customer *A*'s requested ship date of August 10 can now be met. Without a closed-loop solution, the inventory of product *X* may sit on the shelf for a month while it is needed by customer *A*. But that's not the worst of it. Customer *A* may call back a few days later to cancel the order if he can find another company that can meet the required ship date.

In the second example, the master scheduler changes the MPS quantity for the week of 10/18/91 from 200 to 100 to make capacity available for another product line. A closed-loop order promising solution would provide the order entry clerk with a list of all customer orders affected by the change.

Inability to Process Customer Orders Quickly and Accurately

The inability to process customer orders quickly and accurately can be a major source of customer dissatisfaction and a direct cause of lost orders. Any of the following time elements in the order entry process can impact the order entry clerk's ability to provide fast, accurate service:

- The time required to identify the customer number
- The time required to enter the line items that comprise the customer order
- The time required to price the order
- The time required to check inventory availability and provide the customer with ship promise dates
- The time required to check customer credit

Assuming an average of 2.5 items per customer order, the above elements can add more than 30 minutes to the order entry process. Each of these elements is discussed in more detail below.

Identifying the customer number. The clerk begins the order entry process by identifying the customer number. At most companies, this entails looking up the customer name on an alphabetized customer list to cross-reference the customer name to a customer number—a process that usually takes about a minute.

Entering line item information. This includes entering the part number, quantity, and required ship date for each item. Depending on the nature of the product, the order entry clerk may also have to enter descriptive information or special notes. The time required to enter a line item varies from company to company, but a reasonable average is two minutes per item (five minutes per customer order). It is here that many errors are introduced into the order entry process, by entering either the incorrect part number or the incorrect order quantity.

Order pricing. Order pricing is still done manually at many companies. The time required to price an item varies from company to company, but a reasonable average is one minute per item (2.5 minutes per customer order). Manual pricing also tends to introduce errors into the order entry process. At one company I worked with, the price lists and policies were so confusing that five order entry clerks calculated a different price for the same item!

Order promising. At many companies, the order entry clerk has to contact other people in the organization (e.g., the stockkeeper or the master scheduler) to check inventory availability and determine a ship promise date for the customer. A very conservative estimate of the time required to determine a ship promise date is five minutes per item (12.5 minutes per customer order).

Credit checking. At most companies, the order entry clerk is required to check the customer's credit status before accepting the order. First, this entails checking the customer's accounts receivable balance, unbilled orders amount, and the amount of the new order. Then the clerk must ensure that the sum of these three amounts does not exceed the customer's established credit limit. Locating and adding these numbers easily can take five minutes per item (12.5 minutes per customer order).

The following list (based on an average of 2.5 items per customer order) summarizes the impact that these tasks have on the time required to enter customer orders:

Task	Time Estimate (Minutes)
Customer number identification	1.0
Line item entry	5.0
Order pricing	2.5
Order promising	12.5
Credit checking	<u>12.5</u>
Total Time	33.5

Naturally, few customers are going to remain on the phone for 30 minutes or more while the order entry clerk performs all these steps. Typically, inventory availability checking and credit checking are done "off-line," necessitating a return call to the customer to provide either delivery information or the bad news that the customer has exceeded his credit limit.

Solution

Provide features that streamline the order-entry process.

MRP II Order Entry modules contain several features that can compress the order entry function into a few minutes, and in many cases a few seconds! These features are described below.

Automatic Customer Identification Feature

Most MRP II Order Entry modules provide an automatic customer identification feature that eliminates the need for the order entry clerk to look up a customer number. The order entry clerk simply enters the customer name (or the first few characters of the name) on the order entry screen. If a unique match is found in the customer file, the customer information (full name, address, customer number, etc.) is automatically displayed on the order entry screen. If more than one match is found, the system automatically displays a Customer Name Search screen (Figure 5.15) to help the order entry clerk locate the correct customer.

In Figure 5.15, the clerk has entered COR on the order entry screen and the system has found and displayed all vendors whose name begins with COR. Using an "x" the clerk "tags" the correct customer and the system automatically returns to the order entry screen with the correct customer information.

```
Next Transaction: ___                                    Date: 08/06/91
This Transaction: CNS                                    Time: 10:44
                        Customer Name Search

Search String: COR
                                        Customer
Select    Customer Name                 Number
          Corben Equipment              34223
   X      Corbin Industries             44552
          Corner Electric               23567
          Corsini Power                 42300
          Cort Equipment Rental         20343
```

Figure 5.15
Customer Name Search Screen

Customer Profile Feature

Some MRP II Order Entry modules provide the ability to store customer profile information in the database. This feature allows the order entry clerk to store information about products and quantities normally ordered by the customer. Therefore this information does not have to be keyed in every time the customer places an order.

The order entry clerk uses historical data about customer ordering patterns to create the **customer profile record**. The customer profile typically includes a list of the items and quantities that the customer usually orders. However, if there is too much variation in either the products or quantities that a customer orders, the profile may contain only partial information. (For example, the customer profile may contain a list of products without order quantities.)

When the customer places an order, the order entry clerk enters the customer name or number, and the customer profile is automatically displayed on the Customer Order Line Item Entry screen

(Figure 5.16). If no changes are required, the order entry clerk simply presses the Enter key to process the order. If the customer decides not to order a particular item, the order entry clerk can change the quantity to zero. If the customer decides to order more or less than the usual quantity, the order entry clerk can also make this adjustment on the screen. If the customer wants to order items that are not currently on the customer profile, the order entry clerk can enter additional items on the order entry screen to tailor a custom order from the standard profile. In Figure 5.16, the customer has decided not to order one of the items on the customer profile (part KNC039404, brass door knocker), and the order entry clerk has changed the order quantity to zero.

The customer profile feature is a significant customer service differentiator. When customers place multiple-item orders, this feature can greatly reduce the time required to enter line item information. An added benefit is improved accuracy. Because the items and

---

```
Next Transaction: ___                              Date: 09/05/91
This Transaction: LIE                              Time: 09:14
                       Customer Order Line Item Entry

Order Number     Customer Name          Customer Number   Order Type
CO100390         Miller Merchandising    39023            Regular

Line   Quantity/  Part Number/  Requested    Scheduled      ATP      Unit     Ext
Item     U/M      Description   Ship Date    Ship Date      Date     Price    Price

0001      100     HNG390289      10/16/91     10/16/91    09/20/91   2.50    250.00
          EA      Decorative Brass Hinge Style #290

            0     KNC039404
          EA      Brass Door Knocker Style #124

0002      200     HND037548      10/16/91     10/16/91    10/11/91   4.00    800.00
          EA      Brass Handle Style #029

0003       10     SWP310238      10/16/91     11/08/91    11/08/91   5.00     50.00
          EA      Brass Switch Plate
```

Figure 5.16
Customer Order Line Item Entry Screen

quantities are already stored in the customer profile record, the order entry clerk is less likely to make an error in processing the order.

Automatic Order Pricing

All MRP II Order Entry modules provide the option to automatically price customer orders. Prices can be established for each product, and most MRP II systems allow prices to be established by customer by product. In this way, each customer can receive unique pricing.

When the order entry clerk enters a line item, the system automatically calculates the correct unit price and extended price, eliminating the time and errors associated with manual pricing. (The order entry clerk can still override the system price with a manual price, if necessary. Such manual intervention is rarely required if prices have been established correctly in the database.)

Most MRP II systems contain a number of other pricing-related features that help ensure customer satisfaction through accurate, low pricing. These features are discussed below.

Base pricing. Most MRP II software packages provide the ability to establish base prices and derive actual selling prices from the base price. This helps to ensure accurate pricing because only one price, the base price, needs to be updated when a price change occurs. All prices derived from the base price are automatically calculated correctly.

Pricing by effectivity date. This feature ensures that price changes (increases or decreases) are automatically and consistently implemented on the proper date. Figure 5.17 illustrates how prices are entered with start and end effectivity dates.

Pricing by order date or ship date. This option tells the system to price a line item based on the price that is in effect on either the order date or the ship date.

Automatic repricing. If a customer increases an order quantity, the customer may be eligible for a quantity discount. Most MRP II systems automatically reprice an order when any of the following conditions occur:

- Change in order quantity
- Change in required ship date
- Change in the pricing database

The system verifies the price during the billing cycle to ensure that the latest changes have been reflected in the price. *Orders that were priced manually are not automatically repriced.*

```
Next Transaction: ___                                    Date: 11/12/91
This Transaction: UPP                                    Time: 03:45
                              Update Product Pricing

Part Number: JSL304909   Description: Power Supply
Pricing U/M: EA

Start       End         Quantity    Price
01/01/91    12/31/91           1    250.00
                              10    225.00
                              25    200.00
                              50    175.00
                             100    150.00
01/01/92    12/31/92           1    260.00
                              10    235.00
                              25    210.00
                              50    185.00
                             100    160.00
```

Figure 5.17
Update Product Pricing Screen

Customer group pricing. Some MRP II systems allow different price lists to be established for different groups of customers. This helps to ensure accurate and consistent pricing by eliminating the need to enter unique prices for each customer.

Price tolerance parameters. Some MRP II systems provide price tolerance parameters to help reduce errors when the order entry clerk overrides the system-calculated price with a manual price. These parameters help to reduce errors by accepting a manual price only when it is within a specified percentage range of the system price. For example, a price increase parameter of 10 percent would allow the order entry clerk to increase the system price a maximum of 10 percent. Similarly, a price decrease parameter of 10 percent would allow the order entry clerk to reduce the system price a maximum of 10 percent.

Realtime Order Promising Capability

Order promising solutions for make-to-stock and assemble-to-order manufacturing environments are discussed earlier in this chapter. It is worth noting that these order promising solutions significantly reduce the time required to process customer orders.

Automatic Credit Checking

In most MRP II systems, the Order Entry module is integrated with the Accounts Receivable module to perform automatic credit checking. When the order entry clerk enters a customer order, the system automatically calculates the total value of the customer order and adds it to the unbilled totals amount and the accounts receivable amount to calculate the total credit exposure. This total is then compared to the credit limit that has been established for the customer. If the total exceeds the limit, the order is automatically placed on credit hold. Otherwise the order is automatically approved and processed.

Some MRP II systems provide the flexibility to do two types of credit checks. **Order limits** establish the maximum amount for an individual order, and **credit limits** establish the maximum amount of credit that can be extended to a customer.

Electronic Data Interchange

Many MRP II packages provide the ability to receive customer orders electronically, thereby eliminating the manual order entry process. The Electronic Data Interchange (EDI) module receives customer orders that are transmitted in industry-standard electronic formats and converts them into the format required by the MRP II Order Entry module. The converted orders are then loaded (by means of a batch program) into the Order Entry module.

Because EDI bypasses the interactive order promising capabilities described earlier in this chapter, EDI works best where realtime order promising is not an important requirement.

Stockouts of Service Parts

Manufacturers of repairable products often have a large and highly profitable service parts business. This is especially true of manufacturers of custom-engineered products, because customers have no alternative but to purchase service parts from the original equipment manufacturer (OEM).

Stockouts of service parts are a serious customer service problem because they can result in costly field failures.

Stockouts of service parts can result from the inability of most homegrown systems to distinguish between service parts inventory (also called **distribution inventory**) and manufacturing inventory. If the planning system is unable to make this distinction, the system will consider all inventory to be available for manufacturing. Thus, even if 100 pieces of a part are stored in service parts inventory, the planning system will consider the 100 pieces as manufacturing inventory. An inflated inventory balance will appear on the Part Activity Report (see Chapter 2), and the material planner will not order enough material to cover the material requirements for manufacturing. When the manufacturing inventory is consumed, Manufacturing will attempt to pick and release the service parts inventory, even if it is physically segregated from the manufacturing inventory. At this point, the inevitable conflict between the Manufacturing and Service Parts organizations arises: Should a $50 part that is in short supply be used to complete a factory order worth $300,000, or should it be used to ship a service parts order worth $300? Even if the profit margin on the service parts order is ten times that of the factory order, a $300,000 shipment will take priority over a $300 shipment every time. Unfortunately, the decision to ship the factory order may cause the service parts customer to incur a costly field failure.

Solution

Provide the ability to distinguish between service parts (distribution) inventory and manufacturing inventory.

Most MRP II systems provide the ability to identify inventory as either distribution or manufacturing inventory. Inventory that is available for manufacturing is assigned an inventory status code of AM. Service parts inventory is assigned an inventory status code of SP. Service parts inventory is treated as nonnettable inventory (see Chapter 2), so that the MRP module will not consider service parts inventory in the planning process.

When a picklist for a manufacturing order is generated, the system allocates only manufacturing inventory, that is, inventory with a status code of AM. When a picklist for a service parts customer order is generated, the system allocates only service parts inventory, that is, inventory with a status code of SP.

This solution eliminates service parts stockouts caused by an inability to distinguish between manufacturing inventory and service parts inventory. It also eliminates conflicts between the Manufacturing and Customer Service organizations because (1) MRP plans enough replenishment orders to meet manufacturing requirements, and (2) service parts inventory is never allocated on manufacturing picklists.

High Minimum Order Amounts

Some manufacturers establish high minimum order amounts to offset the administrative costs of processing customer orders. Administrative order-processing costs vary from company to company but typically range from $50 to $100 per customer order. Most of the administrative costs are related to the time required to perform the following order-entry tasks:

- Customer number identification

- Line item entry

- Order configuration (in assemble-to-order environments)

- Order pricing

- Order promising

- Credit checking

The features that help to automate these tasks are discussed earlier in this chapter. These features can reduce administrative costs to the point where minimum order amounts of $10 or less are still economically feasible.

Inability to Respond to Customer Inquiries About the Status of Open Orders

The ability to provide customers with up-to-date status information about open orders is essential to good customer service. In some companies, customer orders fall into a "black hole" from the time of order entry to the time of shipment, because Manufacturing has no means of communicating status information to Order Entry. When a customer inquires about the status of an order, order entry clerks are unable to confirm that the order will be shipped on schedule.

```
Next Transaction: ___                                    Date: 10/08/91
This Transaction: OSI                                    Time: 03:23
                          Order Status Notes Inquiry

Order Number: C0390904   Item: 0001   Order Type: Assemble-to-Order
Customer Name: Business Computing   Customer Number: 39041

Product Family: 386              Family Name: 386 PC
Order Quantity:        10        Unit Price:   2,389.00  Ext Price:   23,890.00
Requested Ship Date: 10/15/91    Scheduled Ship Date: 10/15/91


Status Notes:  Order delayed due to shortage of 40-MB hard disks.  Order will be
shipped on 10/22/91.  Contact Joe Franklin X2934 for latest status.
```

Figure 5.18
Order Status Notes Inquiry Screen

Solution

Provide Manufacturing with the ability to communicate order status information to Order Entry.

Some MRP II systems provide the ability to allow Manufacturing to enter status information about customer orders. This feature is especially useful in assemble-to-order and make-to-order environments, where it is not expected that the order can be shipped immediately from stock. The production control specialist or final assembly foreman enters status information on the Order Status Notes Inquiry screen (Figure 5.18), and this information immediately becomes available to the order entry clerk. When a customer inquires about the latest status, the order entry clerk can display the Order Status Notes Inquiry screen and provide the customer with a quick, accurate response.

Undershipments and Overshipments

Undershipments and overshipments are often caused by counting errors made when the customer order is picked and assembled for shipment. Such errors often go undetected because most companies cannot afford the time and expense to manually recount every order prior to shipment.

Solution

Provide the ability to automatically detect shipment variances.

In some MRP II systems, the Order Entry module provides the ability to automatically detect weight variances when an order is weighed prior to shipment. Weight variances indicate an undershipment (actual weight less than the calculated weight) or an overshipment (actual weight greater than the calculated weight).

The unit shipping weight is defined for each product on the part master record. When the system prints shipping documents, the total weight of the shipment is calculated and stored in the database. In Table 5.3, the total calculated weight for the example shipping unit is 16.1 lb.

When the order is ready to ship, the shipping clerk weighs the shipment and enters the value on the Shipment Activity Reporting screen (Figure 5.19). The system compares the actual weight to the calculated weight. If the variance exceeds the acceptable limit, the system displays an error message.

In Figure 5.19, the system has detected an overshipment condition. The cause of the error must be determined and corrected before the transaction can be completed.

Some MRP II systems allow the shipping clerk to override the error message if the variance falls within certain limits. Accepted variances are reported on a Shipment Variance Report (Figure 5.20). The Manager of Customer Service can use this report to monitor shipment accuracy levels.

Table 5.3
How Shipment Weights Are Calculated

Part Number	Shipment Quantity	Unit Weight (lb)	Total Weight (lb)
ADL329034	10	1.20	12.0
MBL300343	5	0.42	2.1
REL930394	20	0.20	4.0
Total Calculated Weight:			16.1

```
Next Transaction: ___                              Date: 11/01/91
This Transaction: SAR                              Time: 01:45
                     Shipment Activity Reporting

Order Number    Customer Name          Customer Number  Order Type
C0391016        Miller Merchandising   39023            Regular

Shipment Date: 11/01/91    Shipped by: SLD    Number of Units:  1

Carrier:  UPS

Freight:  Prepaid

Calculated Weight:  420.1 lb    Actual Weight: 433.3 lb

Accept Variance?  Y




MSG7880:  Overshipment Warning
```

Figure 5.19
Shipment Activity Reporting Screen

. . . .

```
Date: 11/04/91                                              Page: 01
                        Shipment Variance Report
                        (Sorted by Order Number)
                        Week Ending: 11/01/91

Total Number of Shipments: 250
Total Number of Variances: 16
Percentage Accurate Shipments: 93.6%

Order       Date        Calculated      Actual      Percent     Under/
Number      Shipped       Weight        Weight      Variance    Over

C0390233    10/28/91      200.4          210.3          5.1      Over
C0390239    10/28/91      290.2          280.2         -3.4      Under
C0390243    10/30/91      190.2          201.0          5.7      Over
C0391002    10/29/91       89.1           94.2          5.8      Over
C0391012    10/31/91      321.2          333.4          3.8      Over
C0391016    11/01/91      420.1          433.3          3.1      Over
C0392010    11/01/91       34.0           32.0         -5.9      Under
C0392012    10/28/91      120.2          112.3         -6.6      Under
C0392014    10/31/91      123.2          112.1         -9.0      Under
C0392123    11/01/91      402.2          423.2          5.2      Over
C0392212    10/31/91      121.2          105.4        -13.0      Under
C0393026    11/01/91      410.0          415.2          1.3      Over
C0393040    10/28/91       84.0           92.0          9.5      Over
C0394132    10/28/91      210.2          202.3         -3.8      Under
C0395314    10/31/91      112.2          118.1          5.3      Over
C0395623    11/01/91      412.0          423.2          2.7      Over
```

. . . .

Figure 5.20
Shipment Variance Report

Summary

Table 5.4 summarizes the causes of poor customer service that were discussed in this chapter, along with the solutions offered by MRP II systems.

Table 5.4
Summary of Causes of and Solutions to Poor Customer Service

Cause	Solution
1. Missed shipments, caused by	
- Invalid production schedules	Rough cut capacity planning (RCCP) helps the master scheduler develop valid production schedules.
- Inability to plan shipping activity	The Order Entry module produces picking and shipping documents in advance of the required ship date.
2. Inability to help customers configure orders to meet their business requirements	Configuration bills of materials use "if/then" logic to define how product options can be selected to configure customer orders.
3. Inability to provide customers with timely, accurate delivery information	MRP II systems provide order promising solutions for make-to-stock and assemble-to-order environments. The system calculates available-to-promise (ATP) inventory. The Order Entry module allocates ATP inventory to customer orders and provides customers with firm delivery dates.
4. Inability to process customer orders quickly and accurately	MRP II systems provide several features that reduce the time required to process customer orders and eliminate common order entry errors:
	- Automatic customer number identification
	- Customer profile feature
	- Automatic order pricing
	- Realtime order promising
	- Automatic credit checking
	The Electronic Data Interchange module provides the ability to receive orders electronically from those customers that are able to transmit orders in industry-standard electronic formats.
5. Stockouts of service parts, caused by an inability to distinguish between service parts inventory and manufacturing inventory	The Inventory Control module distinguishes between service parts inventory and manufacturing inventory. Service parts inventory is treated as nonnettable inventory and is not allocated to manufacturing orders.
6. High minimum order quantities	MRP II systems reduce administrative order processing costs, making low minimum dollar amounts economically feasible.
7. Inability to respond to customer inquiries about the status of open orders	MRP II systems allow Manufacturing to enter status information about customer orders. The order entry clerk can view up-to-date status information on the Order Status Notes Inquiry screen.
8. Undershipments and overshipments caused by counting errors	Some MRP II systems can automatically detect shipment weight variances and hold up shipments until the cause of the variance is determined and corrected.

The Productivity Problem

*T*he Manager of Manufacturing scrutinized the appropriation request that the Manager of Materials had presented for approval. The request was for a $2 million computer system. The cost justification section of the proposal described in glowing terms how the new system would help the company achieve a 20 percent reduction in inventory.

"I'm sick and tired of reviewing appropriation requests that use inventory reductions to justify costs," the Manager of Manufacturing complained to the Manager of Materials. "In the past three years, I've approved four major appropriation requests that were cost-justified by inventory reductions. Heck, we should be down to zero inventory by now!

"Well, I'm not going to approve any more requests of this nature. In the first place, I don't believe them. In the second place, I want to see some appropriation requests that are justified by a salaried headcount reduction. Three years ago, we had 75 salaried employees whose primary job was expediting. Today we have over 100 professional expediters on the payroll. They may have different job titles— we call some material planners, some production control specialists, and others customer service specialists—but they all spend most of their time expediting. Each of these people costs the company about $50,000 a year in salary and benefits. That's $5 million a year we spend on employees that add cost, not value, to the product.

"Don't get me wrong. The way we currently operate, we couldn't survive without these people. But we won't survive much longer if we continue to operate this way. If you want my signature on any appropriation requests in the future, you're going to have to show me how we can use technology to reduce our salaried headcount."

Introduction

In the 1970s, renowned MRP consultant Oliver Wight held the view that MRP systems were people systems made possible by computers. He stated that "the best computer systems are those that are designed to enhance—not to supplant—the capabilities of human beings."[1]

I have often wondered why Oliver Wight took this view. For decades, technology has been used to reduce direct labor costs. It seems natural to me that we should also apply technology to reduce salaried and indirect labor costs.

Mr. Wight was right in one respect: MRP II systems don't operate by themselves; they are tools designed to be used by trained, intelligent people. But MRP II systems should make the people who use them become more productive. Very simply, this means that the same number of people should be able to produce more, or that fewer people should be able to produce the same amount of work. Business conditions determine whether technology such as MRP II is used as a cost-reduction or a cost-avoidance tool. If demand for a company's products is increasing, MRP II systems can enable the company to produce more using the same number of people. If demand is constant or decreasing, MRP II systems can help the company eliminate jobs that it can no longer support.

Until recently, the productivity objective was often played down in MRP II implementations for fear that user support would crumble. Today, instead of making productivity improvements a hidden objective, many companies are using either cost avoidances or head-count reductions in Purchasing, Accounts Payable, Order Entry, Production Control, Receiving, and/or the stockroom to cost-justify appropriation requests for MRP II systems.

Sometimes, productivity improvements come from very unusual places. Few companies would think of using MRP II to reduce the headcount in reproduction services, but one company did just that. The Bill of Materials module provided users with on-line access to bills of materials. This eliminated the need to make and distribute updated hard copies of bills of materials whenever an engineering change became effective. Over 500,000 copies per year were saved—enough to eliminate a copy machine operator and save $15,000 per year in copy paper.

1. Wight, Oliver W. *Production and Inventory Management in the Computer Age.* Boston, MA: CBI Publishing Co., 1974, p. 206.

Another company eliminated several keypunch clerks in Data Processing when users began to enter data at terminals instead of filling out keypunch forms.

Naturally, cost avoidances are preferable to cost reductions. Optimally, a company grows fast enough so that technology doesn't eliminate jobs, but that doesn't diminish the need to reduce salaried and indirect labor costs to levels that the company can support.

Table 6.1 lists some of the major causes of poor salaried and indirect labor productivity that are addressed by MRP II systems. These causes, along with the solutions offered by MRP II systems, are discussed in the sections that follow.

Poor Productivity in Accounts Payable

Excessive Manual Effort Required to Perform Invoice Matching

For many companies, invoice matching is a manual task that keeps a dozen or more invoice clerks on the payroll. These clerks spend much of their time filing copies of purchase orders and packing slips in the Accounts Payable office. When an invoice is received, an invoice clerk pulls the corresponding purchase order and packing slip from the file. The clerk matches the three documents to make certain that the invoice is valid and accurate. For an invoice to be valid, the purchase order and packing slip must exist. For an invoice to be accurate, the invoice price must agree with the purchase order price, and the invoice quantity must agree with the packing slip quantity. Valid, accurate invoices are then processed for payment. Exceptions are sent to the buyer for resolution.

Solution *Provide electronic three-way matching of invoices, purchase orders, and packing slips.*

The Accounts Payable and Purchasing modules of MRP II systems are integrated to provide electronic three-way matching of invoices, purchase orders, and packing slips. Electronic invoice matching eliminates the need for invoice clerks:

1. To file and pull hard copies of purchase orders and packing slips

Table 6.1
Major Causes of Poor Productivity

Organization	Causes
Accounts Payable	Excessive manual effort required: - To perform invoice matching - To obtain invoice signature approvals - To approve large payments - To reconcile payments - To respond to vendor inquiries
Purchasing	1. Excessive manual effort required: - To place purchase orders - To perform file maintenance - To expedite purchase orders - To solicit bids from vendors 2. Excessive time spent responding to inquiries from material planners and production control personnel
Receiving	Excessive manual effort required to identify shipments
Stockroom	1. Excessive material handling caused by staging of partially picked orders 2. Excessive manual effort required: - To locate materials - To report picking activity - To receive materials into stores
Design Engineering	Excessive manual effort required to add and maintain bills of materials
Manufacturing Engineering	Excessive manual effort required to add and maintain shop routings
Material Control	1. Inability to manage by exception 2. Excessive manual effort required to track material in incoming inspection
Production Control	1. High level of expediting 2. Excessive manual effort required to employ alternate routings
Master Scheduling	Excessive manual effort required: - To develop a feasible production plan - To maintain the master schedule
Information Systems	Excessive effort required: - To maintain old systems - To process end-user requests for reports
Order Entry	Excessive manual effort required to enter customer orders

2. To verify that invoices are valid (physical document matching)

3. To verify that invoices are accurate (price and quantity matching)

The ability of the Accounts Payable module to access purchase order and receiving information from the Purchasing module is key to electronic invoice matching. The invoice clerk initiates electronic matching from the Invoice Data Entry screen (Figure 6.1). The clerk enters the purchase order number from the hard copy of the invoice. The purchase order line item information is then automatically retrieved and displayed on the screen.

Some MRP II packages do not display closed line items (i.e., line items that have already been received and invoiced). This improves productivity because the clerk does not need to page through closed items on multiple-item purchase orders to finally reach the open

```
Next Transaction: ___                                      Date: 08/06/91
This Transaction: IDE                                      Time:  10:15
                              Invoice Data Entry

Purchase Order Number: 1C903904

Vendor Number: 39092           Vendor Name: Alpha Electronics

Invoice Number: AE29039    Invoice Date: 08/02/91    Invoice Amount:    90.00
Sales Tax:          Freight:          Additional Charges:

PO                                          Invoice    Invoice
Line    Part Number   Vendor's Item Number  Quantity   Amount

002     ADL390233     AE200-230             25         75.00
004     MBL490934     AE320-203             10         15.00
005     JSL390293     AE034-284
006     ADL490309     AE349-278




Additional Items? N (Y = Yes, N = No)
```

Figure 6.1
Invoice Data Entry Screen

items. In Figure 6.1, line items 001 and 003 are not displayed because they are closed to invoicing.

To process the invoice, the invoice clerk needs to enter only the invoice quantity and invoice amount for each line item.

Many MRP II systems are designed to prevent data entry errors by requiring the invoice clerk to enter the total invoice amount on the Invoice Data Entry screen. If the sum of the line item amounts does not equal the total invoice amount, the system displays an error message. The invoice clerk can then correct the data entry error and proceed.

For each line item on the invoice, the Accounts Payable module automatically compares the invoice quantity to the quantity that is available for payment. The quantity that is available for payment is calculated as follows:

Quantity Available for Payment =
Quantity Received to Date − Quantity Invoiced to Date

Thus, if 50 pieces have been received to date but only 20 pieces have been invoiced, the system will accept an invoice for up to 30 pieces.

For each line item on the invoice, the Accounts Payable module also automatically compares the invoice amount to the amount that is available for payment. The amount that is available for payment is calculated as follows:

Amount Available for Payment =
Quantity Available for Payment × Unit Price

Invoice line items that meet the matching criteria are automatically approved for payment. Exceptions are put on hold until they are resolved by the buyer. Some Accounts Payable modules route exceptions electronically to the buyer for resolution.

Some MRP II Accounts Payable modules allow an **invoice tolerance amount** and an **invoice tolerance percent** to be defined. Invoice tolerance parameters improve productivity by reducing the number of exceptions that require manual intervention. The tolerances are applied to each line item on the invoice. Discrepancies that fall within the established amount and percent tolerances are automatically approved for payment. Discrepancies that exceed either the amount or percent tolerances are put on hold.

The following three examples illustrate how invoice tolerance parameters function.

Example 1

Invoice Tolerance Amount:	$10.00
Invoice Tolerance Percent:	5
Amount Available for Payment:	$50.00
Invoice Amount:	$58.00

The invoice amount falls within the tolerance amount of $10.00 but exceeds the tolerance percent of 5 ($2.50). Therefore, the invoice is handled as an exception.

Example 2

Invoice Tolerance Amount:	$10.00
Invoice Tolerance Percent:	5
Amount Available for Payment:	$400.00
Invoice Amount:	$415.00

The invoice amount falls within the tolerance percent of 5 ($20.00) but exceeds the tolerance amount of $10.00. Therefore, the invoice is handled as an exception.

Example 3

Invoice Tolerance Amount:	$10.00
Invoice Tolerance Percent:	5
Amount Available for Payment:	$200.00
Invoice Amount:	$210.00

The invoice amount falls within the tolerance percent *and* the tolerance amount. Therefore, the invoice is automatically approved for payment.

Excessive Manual Effort Required to Obtain Invoice Approval Signatures

Invoices for services cannot be matched against receipts, because services are not "received" the way material is received. Typically, invoices for services require the approval signatures of one or more people before payment can be made. In most homegrown accounts payable systems, approval signatures must be obtained before the invoice can be entered into the system. The invoice clerk must pull the hard copy of the purchase order to determine whose signature(s) is (are) required to authorize payment. The clerk sends the invoice to the appropriate individual(s) for approval. When the invoice is returned with the required signature(s), the invoice clerk must handle the invoice a second time. If the invoice is not returned promptly, the vendor may send a second invoice. The confusion created by duplicate invoices adds to the manual effort required to process invoices for services.

Solution   *Provide the ability to perform electronic signature approval.*

Some MRP II Accounts Payable modules provide the ability to perform electronic signature approval. When a purchase order for services is created, the buyer specifies one or more approvers (Figure 6.2). When an invoice is entered, the Accounts Payable module automatically routes the invoice for electronic signature approval.

```
Next Transaction: ___                              Date: 12/01/91
This Transaction: APH                              Time: 12:45
                         Add Purchase Order Header

PO Number: 1R390100    PO Type: Service    Buyer: 001

Vendor Number: 30030    Vendor Name: Electric Distributors

Ship-to Code: DSD    Ship-via Code: UPS

Standard Message Codes:___  ___  ___  ___  ___

Electronic Signature Approval? Y

Approval Codes:   LSK    DLF    DKE    DFL
```

Figure 6.2
Add Purchase Order Header Screen

```
Next Transaction: ___                                    Date: 12/18/91
This Transaction: ESA                                    Time: 12:20
                      Electronic Signature Approval Queue

Approver: LSK


Invoice   Invoice     PO                              Invoice    Approve for
Number    Date        Number    Vendor               Amount     Payment?

OL29093   12/02/91    1S390490  Osborne Landscaping   2230.00        Y
MJ39023   12/02/91    1S233234  Martin Janitorial Service 392.33     Y
GG39023   12/03/91    1S390239  Good Guys Pest Control  200.00       Y
```

Figure 6.3
Electronic Signature Approval Queue Screen

Figure 6.3 shows the Electronic Signature Approval Queue for approver LSK. System security prevents an unauthorized individual from approving an invoice that has been routed to LSK for approval. The approver enters a code (i.e., an electronic signature) to authorize payment. When all electronic signatures have been received, the invoice is automatically prepared for payment. No further manual effort by the invoice clerk is required.

Excessive Manual Effort Required to Approve Large Payments

In most companies, checks that exceed a certain dollar amount must be signed by an officer of the company. Some homegrown systems require that a clerk look through all the checks that were printed to find those requiring an authorized signature.

Solution   *Provide the ability to print checks in sequence by dollar amount.*

Some MRP II systems provide the option of printing checks in ascending or descending order by dollar amount. All checks requiring an authorized signature are printed together, eliminating the effort required to sort through them manually.

Excessive Manual Effort Required to Reconcile Payments

Most people go through the monthly chore of balancing their personal checking accounts. Even though most people issue fewer than 100 checks per month, it may take an hour or more to balance the checkbook. Viewed from this perspective, it is easy to understand how much manual effort is required to reconcile payments in companies that issue thousands of checks each month from several different accounts.

Solution   *Provide the ability to do automatic payment reconciliation.*

Some MRP II Accounts Payable modules are set up to receive a magnetic tape of cleared payments from the bank. The tape is applied against a file of open payments to automate the reconciliation process.

Caveat   The features of the Accounts Payable module vary greatly among MRP II software packages. Some Accounts Payable modules have limited on-line functionality and are not well integrated with the Purchasing module. Some Accounts Payable modules provide little more than the ability to write checks. In general, the better Accounts Payable modules are offered by software vendors that started out as financial software vendors.

Excessive Manual Effort Required to Respond to Vendor Inquiries

Accounts payable clerks may respond to hundreds of inquiries each month from vendors wanting to know the status of unpaid invoices. In companies that do not have on-line accounts payable systems, these clerks spend many hours locating hardcopy documents to obtain payment status information.

Solution   *Provide on-line access to invoice status information.*

MRP II Accounts Payable modules provide users with on-line access to accurate invoice status information. When a vendor requests payment status information for a specific invoice, the accounts payable clerk enters the invoice number on the Invoice Status Inquiry screen (Figure 6.4). This screen displays detailed payment status information, including:

- Invoice status

- Scheduled payment date (if the invoice has not been paid)

- Actual payment date (if the invoice has been paid)

```
Next Transaction: ___                                    Date: 12/03/91
This Transaction: ISI                                    Time: 12:20
                          Invoice Status Inquiry

Vendor Number: 39029    Vendor Name: Patane Manufacturing
Invoice Number: 490394

Invoice Amount: $423.20    Invoice Date: 11/06/91

Date Entered into System: 11/22/91
Payment Status: Approved for Payment
Scheduled Payment Date: 12/24/91

Actual Payment Date:        Amount Paid:        Discount Taken:
Payment Reference Number:

Payment Terms: 2/15   Net Thirty
```

Figure 6.4
Invoice Status Inquiry Screen

Poor Productivity in Purchasing

Excessive Manual Effort Required to Place Purchase Orders

In many purchasing organizations, buyers and purchasing clerks spend more than half of their time placing purchase orders. To convert a requisition into a purchase order, the buyer must select a vendor, determine the price, and complete a purchase order request form. The buyer submits the request form to a clerk (if purchase orders are typed manually) or to Data Processing (if purchase orders are printed by a batch processing computer system). After the purchase order is generated, a clerk compares the purchase order to the purchase order request form to make sure that no typing or keypunching errors were made. Finally, the clerk inserts the purchase order in an envelope and mails it to the vendor.

Solution   *Provide for automatic generation of purchase orders.*

Most MRP II software packages provide the ability to generate purchase orders without manual buyer intervention. To activate the automatic purchase order feature for a specific purchased part, the buyer must perform the following tasks:

1. Enter a valid quote from a vendor to the purchasing database.

2. Identify the vendor as the preferred vendor on the part master record.

3. Set the automatic purchase order code on the part master record to Y (yes).

When a requisition is approved by the material planner, the Purchasing module automatically creates a purchase order for the preferred vendor. The system automatically prices the order by matching the order quantity to the appropriate price break quantity on the vendor quote.

It is worth noting that the automatic purchase order feature in most MRP II systems has three major limitations:

1. The system does not automatically select the vendor that has the highest vendor performance rating; the buyer must specify the preferred vendor in advance. If a part can be purchased from more than one vendor, the buyer must review vendor performance ratings often to ensure that the preferred vendor is the vendor with the highest performance rating.

2. The system does not perform a quantity discount analysis and automatically adjust the order quantity to the next lot size when a net savings can be obtained. For example, consider an item that has the following price breaks:

Order Quantity	Unit Price
1	$10.00
25	8.00
50	7.00
75	6.00

If the buyer places an order for 70 pieces, the extended purchase order price will be:

$$70 \times \$7.00 = \$490.00$$

However, if the buyer increases the order quantity to 75, the extended purchase order price will be:

$$75 \times \$6.00 = \$450.00$$

Thus, 75 pieces can actually be purchased for less money than 70 pieces. This pricing anomaly occurs when the order quantity approaches the next higher price break quantity. However, the automatic purchase order feature still generates the purchase order for 70 pieces because it cannot perform a quantity discount analysis to determine if 75 pieces can be purchased for less than 70 pieces.

3. The system cannot automatically split an order among two or more vendors in accordance with predefined percentages. For example, a buyer may want to allocate 80 percent of an order to a primary source and 20 percent to a secondary source. However, most MRP II systems do not provide an automatic order-splitting feature.

Because of the limitations of the automatic purchase order feature, the buyer may decide to create purchase orders from requisitions manually using on-line screens provided for that purpose. MRP II systems provide a number of features that reduce the effort required to generate purchase orders from requisitions. These features include the ability to define:

- Purchasing defaults
- Standard purchase order messages
- Unit of measure conversion factors

Ability to define purchasing defaults   MRP II systems provide the ability to specify purchasing defaults (i.e., default values for shipping instructions, payment terms, invoice tolerance parameters, and receiving tolerance parameters). Purchasing defaults improve productivity because the buyer does not need to enter this information manually for each purchase order line item.

Some MRP II systems allow purchasing defaults to be specified on the vendor master file and the part master file. Defaults at the part master level override defaults at the vendor level. This allows general defaults to be established by vendor and exceptions to the general defaults to be established by part number. For example, the invoice tolerance percent for a vendor may be 5. However, for an expensive part, the invoice tolerance percent may be 0.

When a purchase order line item is created, the system first checks the part master file for purchasing defaults. If a default is not found, the system checks the vendor master file. The defaults are automatically entered on the purchase order line item. The buyer has the option of overriding the default values for a specific purchase order line item.

Table 6.2 illustrates the purchasing default selection process.

Table 6.2

How the MRP II System Assigns Default Values to a Purchase Order Line Item

	Vendor Master Purchasing Defaults	Part Master Purchasing Defaults	Default Values Assigned to the PO Line Item
Shipping Instructions			
Ship-via Code	UPS		UPS
Ship-to Code	MAC		MAC
FOB Code	ORG		ORG
Payment Terms			
Net	30		30
Discount Percent	1		1
Discount Days	15		15
Invoice Controls			
Invoice Tolerance Percent	5	0	0
Invoice Tolerance Amount ($)	10	0	0
Receiving Controls			
Early Shipment Tolerance Days	10	5	5
Overshipment Tolerance Percent	10	0	0

Some MRP II packages also allow purchasing defaults to be defined at the system level. System-level defaults are also called **global defaults**. If a default is not found at the vendor level, the global default is used.

One currently available MRP II system allows purchasing defaults to be established at six different levels within the database. However, this much flexibility can be confusing. The buyer may have to look at six different screens to determine how a particular default value was assigned to a purchase order line item. Three default levels—system, vendor, and part—should provide more than enough flexibility for any purchasing organization.

Ability to define standard messages   Some MRP II systems provide the ability to define standard messages. Standard messages save time because the buyer no longer needs to enter long messages on purchase orders.

The buyer adds a standard message to the database by entering a message code and the detailed message text on the Add Standard Messages screen (Figure 6.5). For a standard message to be printed on a purchase order, the buyer enters the appropriate message code on the Add Purchase Order Header screen (Figure 6.2) or the Add Purchase Order Line Item screen (Figure 4.7). If the buyer enters a standard message code on the Add Purchase Order Header screen, the message will appear at the top of the purchase order. If the buyer enters a standard message code on the Add Purchase Order Line Item screen, the message will appear on the appropriate line item.

Ability to define unit of measure conversion factors   The purchasing unit of measure for an item often may be different than the manufacturing unit of measure. For example, the manufacturing unit of measure may be feet but the item may be purchased by the pound. If one foot weighs 0.60 lb, a requisition for 300 feet must be converted into a purchase order for 180 lb.

MRP II systems allow the buyer to specify a purchasing unit of measure and a unit of measure conversion factor. This information is stored on the Vendor Part Record (instead of the Part Master Record) because, if a part is purchased from more than one vendor, each vendor may use a different unit of measure or conversion factor.

For example, consider an item that has a manufacturing unit of measure of EACH and a purchasing unit of measure of BOX. One vendor may have a standard box of 10 pieces and another vendor

```
Next Transaction: __                                    Date: 12/03/91
This Transaction: ASM                                   Time: 08:20
                        Add Standard Messages

Message Code: CON

Detailed Message: This is a confirming purchase order document.
Do not duplicate this purchase order.
```

Figure 6.5
Add Standard Messages Screen

may have a standard box of 12 pieces, necessitating different conversion factors for each vendor.

The Purchasing module uses the unit of measure conversion factor
to convert the requisition quantity to the purchase order quantity
automatically. This eliminates the effort required to perform the unit
of measure conversion manually.

Provide for electronic exchange of purchase orders with vendors.

MRP II packages can eliminate the clerical costs associated with
mailing purchase orders by electronically transmitting purchase
orders in standard electronic data interchange formats. On the
receiving end, the vendor must be able to convert the standard
electronic format into that required by the vendor's order entry
system.

Excessive Manual Effort Required to Perform File Maintenance

In most companies, the Purchasing organization performs more computer file maintenance than any other organization. This is because buyers and purchasing clerks have to maintain at least four important, dynamic master files:

1. Part Master File
2. Vendor Master File
3. Vendor Quote Master File
4. Purchase Order Master File

A tremendous amount of manual effort is required to perform file maintenance in many homegrown purchasing systems. This is evidenced by large professional and clerical staffs in many purchasing organizations. Some common causes of poor productivity in this area are as follows:

- The inability to detect and prevent errors at the point of data entry
- The lack of file maintenance productivity tools
- The inability to prevent the mathematical and/or logical relationships among data fields from being corrupted by improper file maintenance
- The lack of file maintenance audit trails

Inability to detect and prevent errors at the point of data entry Many homegrown purchasing systems only provide the ability to perform batch updates to the purchasing database. To perform file maintenance, the buyer or purchasing clerk must complete a data entry form and submit it to Data Processing for keypunching and batch processing. Any errors made in completing and/or keypunching the data entry form are not discovered until after batch processing. The only way for the user to be sure that the database was updated successfully (and correctly) is to compare a copy of the data entry form to batch reports that are produced by the system. Some companies employ a full-time clerk to verify all file maintenance in this manner.

Lack of file maintenance productivity tools Homegrown purchasing systems often lack file maintenance productivity tools. For example, the Manager of Purchasing may decide to reassign a commodity from Buyer 001 to Buyer 003. If there are 200 purchased parts within the commodity, a purchasing clerk may have to complete 200 data entry forms to change the buyer code associated with each part.

Inability to prevent the mathematical and/or logical relationships among data fields from being corrupted Some homegrown purchasing systems lack the logic that automatically maintains the integrity of the purchasing database. For example, consider the following four data fields associated with a purchase order line item:

1. Item status code

2. Order quantity

3. Quantity received

4. Balance due quantity

The balance due quantity can and should be derived from the order quantity, quantity received, and item status code using the following logic:

If the item has been canceled (item status code is CA), then:

Balance Due = 0

Otherwise:

Balance Due = Order Quantity – Quantity Received

Clearly, it is not necessary to store the balance due quantity in the database, since it can be derived for reporting purposes.

Unfortunately, some homegrown systems not only store all three quantity fields (order quantity, quantity received, and balance due quantity), but *they require the user to maintain each field independently*. This puts the onus on the user to preserve the mathematical and logical relationships between the item status code, order quantity, quantity received, and balance due.

Thus, if a buyer performs a maintenance transaction to increase the order quantity by ten, the buyer must remember to perform another transaction to increase the balance due by ten. If the buyer cancels an item, the buyer must also remember to change the balance due to zero. If the buyer forgets to perform either transaction or makes an error in calculating the balance due, the purchase order file will become corrupted with bad data. When this happens, a line item may look something like this:

Order Quantity: 100

Quantity Received: 50

Balance Due: 70

Once the mathematical and logical relationships among data fields have become corrupted, a great deal of manual effort may be required to set things right. In the above example, the buyer can correct the problem either by increasing the order quantity to 120 or by decreasing the balance due to 50. But the *correct* solution is not obvious. To determine the correct solution, the buyer may have to examine hard copies of change orders and other documents to determine if the original intent was to increase the order quantity from 100 to 120 or decrease the order quantity from 120 to 100.

Lack of file maintenance audit trails Of the four master files mentioned earlier, the purchase order master file is by far the most dynamic. During the life cycle of a purchase order, dozens of maintenance transactions may be performed. A record of all maintenance transactions is required for two reasons:

1. A purchase order represents a legal contract between two companies for products or services. During its life, this contract may be amended many times. Detailed records of all changes must be kept, in the same manner that amendments to any contract must be documented.

2. If the buyer suspects that an error has been made in maintaining the purchase order, it may be necessary to review all maintenance that has been performed on the purchase order. This will help the buyer discover the nature of the error, who made the error, and when the error occurred.

Unfortunately, most homegrown systems do not provide audit trails of purchase order maintenance activity. The buyer must create an audit trail either by keeping a manual log of all purchase order maintenance or by keeping a file (for each purchase order) of all data entry forms that were submitted for maintenance. A significant amount of manual effort is required for either approach.

Solutions   *Provide the ability to perform on-line, realtime file maintenance.*

MRP II Purchasing modules provide the ability to perform on-line, realtime updates to the purchasing database. Errors are detected at the time of data entry, and meaningful error messages are displayed to help the user correct errors and complete the transaction. On-line, realtime maintenance eliminates the time required to verify that batch updates have occurred.

Provide file maintenance productivity tools.

Some MRP II Purchasing modules contain productivity tools (features) that reduce the effort required to perform file maintenance manually. These features include the ability:

- To perform mass maintenance
- To automatically close purchase orders that are received short
- To define default values for data fields
- To automatically calculate actual prices from discounts off a base price

Ability to perform mass maintenance   Mass maintenance is the ability to perform mass updates to the database by keying off a field that relates items having common characteristics. This capability eliminates the need to perform thousands of individual maintenance transactions.

Some MRP II Purchasing modules allow mass maintenance to be performed on certain data fields by keying off the commodity code field. The user performs a single transaction, and all part numbers within the specified commodity code are automatically updated.

In Figure 6.6, mass maintenance is being performed on the procurement lead time for commodity code 10020050. The system has displayed a message indicating that 242 part master records will be updated if the user proceeds with the transaction.

Clearly, the mass maintenance feature cannot be used if commodity codes are defined too broadly. If lead times vary greatly within a commodity code, mass maintenance cannot be used to update the procurement lead time. Because mass maintenance is such a powerful productivity tool, commodity codes should be defined with this feature in mind.

For example, it may be necessary to define several commodity codes to identify different types of resistors or capacitors. Of course, no commodity coding system is perfect. For example, if there are 1000 items in a commodity, 990 items may have a lead time of 20 days and 10 items may have a lead time of 40 days. Provided the number of exceptions is small, exceptions can be updated individually after the mass maintenance transaction has been performed.

```
Next Transaction: __                                          Date: 12/17/91
This Transaction: MMC                                         Time: 09:32
                       Mass Maintenance by Commodity Code

Commodity Code:  10020050         Description: Fasteners

Lead Time:  40 Days
Buyer Code:
Planner Code:
Inspection Code:
Order Policy Code:
Cycle Count Frequency:
Cycle Count Tolerance Parameter:
Early Shipment Tolerance Parameter:
Overshipment Tolerance Parameter:
Invoice Price Tolerance Percent:
Invoice Price Tolerance Amount:




MSG0390:     242 Part Master Records will be updated.  Continue? Y (Y or N)
```

Figure 6.6
Mass Maintenance by Commodity Code Screen

A mass maintenance exception code on the Part Master Record would be useful. This code could be used to exempt a part from any mass maintenance. However, I am not aware of any MRP II package that provides such a code.

The ability to perform mass maintenance to pricing by vendor by commodity code would also be useful. Thus, if a vendor raises prices 5 percent on a commodity, the vendor quote master file could be updated by a single mass maintenance transaction that multiplies all item pricing for that vendor and commodity by 1.05. However, no MRP II software vendor currently provides this capability.

Ability to automatically close purchase orders that are received short Occasionally vendors ship less than the purchase order quantity and consider the order to be complete. For example, if an order is placed for 100 pieces and the vendor has only 98 pieces in stock, the vendor may ship the 98 pieces and close out the purchase order.

Some MRP II systems provide the option of automatically closing orders when the cumulative receipts are within a specified percentage of the order quantity. This eliminates the need for the buyer to review daily receipts and manually close purchase orders that vendors consider to be complete.

Ability to define default values for data fields   Some MRP II packages reduce the effort required to create new Part Master Records manually by providing the ability to specify default values (by commodity code) for certain data fields. The user also has the option to override the default values on an item-by-item basis.

In Figure 6.7, default values for commodity code 10020050 have been specified for the buyer code, material planner code, preferred vendor code, inspection code, purchasing unit of measure, and procurement lead time. These values will be automatically assigned when a new part is added to the database for commodity code 10020050.

```
Next Transaction: ___                           Date: 12/15/91
This Transaction: PMD                           Time: 12:23
                         Part Master Defaults

Commodity Code: 10020050      Description: Fasteners

Buyer Code: 001
Planner Code: 001
Preferred Vendor: 29093
Inspection Code: 2
Purchase Unit of Measure: EA
Lead Time: 40 Days
```

Figure 6.7
Part Master Defaults Screen

Ability to automatically calculate actual prices from discounts off a base price   In some industries, vendors provide quotes by specifying percentage discounts off a base price at different order quantities. Some MRP II Purchasing modules are designed to accommodate this common industry practice easily. Instead of requiring the buyer to calculate and enter an actual price, some MRP II systems allow the buyer to enter the base price and the percentage discount quoted by the vendor. The system automatically calculates and displays the actual price, and the buyer can see both the percentage discount and the actual price on the Vendor Quote Inquiry screen (Figure 6.8).

Provide the required system logic to ensure data integrity

MRP II Purchasing modules do not allow the user to corrupt the mathematical and logical relationships among data fields. The Purchasing module automatically calculates the value of derived data fields and does not allow the derived fields to be maintained directly by the user. This eliminates the manual effort required to maintain

---

```
Next Transaction: __                                    Date: 11/12/91
This Transaction: VQI                                   Time: 10:13
                          Vendor Quote Inquiry

Part Number: REL230025    Quote Number: 49234    Quote Effective: 12/01/91
                                                 Quote Expires:   12/01/92
Description: Relay

Vendor: 30030   Name: Electric Distributors
Vendor Part Number:                          Vendor Unit of Purchase: EA

Price Per: EACH   Base Price: $50.00    Setup Charge:
Minimum Order Quantity:
                              Price Break Information

Price                          Percent
Break    Quantity    Price     Discount

01              1    50.00         0
02            100    45.00        10
03            250    42.50        15
04            500    40.00        20
05           1000    37.50        25
```

Figure 6.8
Vendor Quote Inquiry Screen

derived fields and to resolve data integrity problems caused by improper file maintenance.

Note that most MRP II systems do not store derived fields in the database. Instead, derived fields are calculated "on the fly" for display on screens and batch reports.

Provide on-line file maintenance audit trails.

Some MRP II systems provide an audit trail of all purchase order file maintenance activities. This eliminates the need to maintain audit trails manually.

The Purchase Order History Inquiry screen (Figure 6.9) provides on-line access to the audit trail. This screen displays all changes to purchase order header information or all changes to a specific purchase order line item. The following information is displayed for each change:

- Date the change was made

```
Next Transaction:__                                    Date: 11/13/91
This Transaction: POH                                  Time: 12:12
                       Purchase Order History Inquiry

Purchase Order Number: 1S290390   Line Item: 001
Vendor: Gresh Containers          Part Number: EL90239

Select by: (Leave blank to select and display all records)

Date: __/__/__      Field Name:_____      Operator Initials:__

           Ship
Date       Sched   Field Changed      ——Old Value——   ——New Value——   Init

10/16/91    01     Order Quantity              75               100    LSK
10/17/91           Price                     7.50              7.00    LSK
10/17/91    01     Ship-Promise-Date                        12/11/91   BED
10/21/91    01     Required-Ship-Date     12/04/91          01/09/92   LSK
10/21/91    01     Ship-Promise-Date      12/11/91          01/09/92   BED
10/22/91    02     Order Quantity              50               100    BED
```

Figure 6.9
Purchase Order History Inquiry Screen

- Name of the field that was changed
- Value of the field prior to the change
- Value of the field after the change
- Initials of the person who made the change (automatically obtained by the system from the user's password)

To reduce the effort required to review the audit trail, some MRP II packages allow users to specify selection criteria to limit what is displayed on the Purchase Order History Inquiry screen. For example, the buyer may only be interested in viewing all changes to the order quantity field or all changes performed by a particular user.

The user enters the selection criteria in fields at the top of the Purchase Order History Inquiry screen. If these fields are left blank, all history records are displayed.

Excessive Manual Effort Required to Expedite Purchase Orders

In most companies, buyers and purchasing clerks spend a significant amount of time expediting purchase orders. The inability to expedite by exception is a major cause of high expediting costs. This causes many companies to expedite reactively instead of proactively.

Reactive expediting requires a significant amount of effort because an immediate solution is required to a material shortage problem. Proactive expediting (i.e., expediting to prevent a material shortage) requires far less effort. By way of analogy, it is always more expensive to put out a fire than it is to prevent the fire.

Solution   *Provide expediting exception reports.*

The Vendor Action Report, which is described in Chapter 2 as one way to help solve the material shortages problem, is a proactive expediting tool that enables the buyer to expedite by exception. The Vendor Action Report is a combination of four separate subreports, three of which focus on proactive expediting:

Report	Type of Expediting
Late Acknowledgment Report	Proactive
Potential Late Shipments Report	Proactive
Pending Shipments Report	Proactive
Overdue Shipments Report	Reactive

By working the proactive sections of the Vendor Action Report, the buyer can reduce the number of overdue shipments that require reactive expediting.

Excessive Manual Effort Required to Solicit Bids from Vendors

When companies decide to automate the purchasing function, they invariably begin by automating purchase order processing. However, many companies never progress beyond this stage. Other aspects of the buyer's job, such as the task of soliciting bids from vendors, continue to be performed manually at great expense. At these companies, the purchasing clerk must type a separate request for quote (RFQ) form for each vendor that is asked to submit a quote for an item.

```
Next Transaction:  __                           Date: 11/13/91
This Transaction: RQH                           Time: 11:15
                        Request for Quote Header

RFQ Number:  RFQ290399    RFQ Due Date:  12/20/91   Buyer Code: 004

Vendors to Receive RFQ:

Vendor Code        Vendor Name

02930              Cleveland Fastener Corp.
02903              Arbor Screw Company
39092              Quality Screw Products
30290              CSM Company
39029              Bristol Cold Forming

Special Instructions:  Please be sure to provide quote expiration date.
```

Figure 6.10
Request for Quote Header Screen

```
Next Transaction: __                                    Date: 11/13/91
This Transaction: RQD                                   Time: 11:15
                          Request for Quote Detail

RFQ Number:  RFQ290399        RFQ Due Date:  12/20/91       Buyer Code: 004

Part Number: JSL390920        Description: Self Locking Cap Screw

Price Break Quantities Requested:

1
100
1000
5000
10000
20000




More Items?
```

Figure 6.11
Request for Quote Detail Screen

Solution   *Provide tools to automate the request for quotation process.*

Most MRP II Purchasing modules automate the process of soliciting bids from vendors. Requests for quotes are entered on-line, and the system automatically generates a separate RFQ for each vendor.

The buyer initiates the request-for-quote process by entering an RFQ number, the RFQ due date, a list of vendors that are to receive the RFQ, and special instructions that pertain to the RFQ. The buyer enters this information on the Request for Quote Header screen (Figure 6.10).

Then, on the Request for Quote Detail screen (Figure 6.11), the buyer enters pertinent information about the items to be quoted. For example, the buyer may request prices for specific quantities. The system produces a separate RFQ for each vendor, eliminating the need to type the RFQs manually.

Excessive Time Spent Responding to Inquiries from Material Planners and Production Control Personnel

When buyers aren't busy expediting, they're busy being pursued by material planners and production control personnel. These people keep buyers busy with such questions as:

- Has a purchase order been placed from the requisition?

- Has a ship promise date been established?

- Has the purchase order been received?

In companies that have manual or batch purchasing systems, the only way for material planners and production control personnel to obtain accurate answers to these questions is to call the buyer.

Solution   *Provide on-line access requisition, purchase order, and receiving status information.*

```
Next Transaction: ___                                        Date: 11/18/91
This Transaction: RSI                                        Time: 11:15
                           Requisition Status Inquiry

Planner/Requestor Code: 001
```

Requisition Number	Date of Request	Part Number	Due Date	Quantity Requested	Quantity Ordered	PO Number	PO Line
MRP1112021	11/12/91	JSL300394	12/09/91	100	100	1C290129	001
MRP1112020	11/12/91	BJL490304	12/09/91	23	0		
MRP1112131	11/12/91	DG902394	01/07/92	50	50	1C290192	002
MRP1113035	11/13/91	EL302902	02/05/92	1	1	1R293093	001
MRP1113004	11/13/91	TQL200125	03/06/92	6	0		
MRP1114001	11/14/91	MBL490123	12/30/91	12	12	1C320102	004
MRP1114002	11/14/91	MAL102934	02/12/92	1	0		
MRP1115005	11/15/91	ADL303874	02/12/92	4	0		

Figure 6.12
Requisition Status Inquiry Screen

MRP II Purchasing modules provide material planners and production control personnel with on-line access to requisition, purchase order, and receiving status information. This eliminates the need to consume the buyer's time with inquiries of this nature.

The Requisition Status Inquiry screen (Figure 6.12) enables the material planner to find out if the buyer has placed purchase orders from requisitions that were sent to Purchasing.

The Purchase Order Status Inquiry screen (Figure 6.13) provides the material planner with up-to-date information about ship promise dates.

The Receiving History Inquiry screen (Figure 6.14) provides the material planner with a complete history of all receiving activity associated with a purchase order.

```
Next Transaction:  __                                   Date: 11/18/91
This Transaction: PSI                                   Time: 11:16
                        Purchase Order Status Inquiry

Purchase Order Number: 1C290129    Line Item: 001    PO Date: 11/15/91

Buyer: 005    Vendor: 30030    Name: Electric Distributors

Part Number: JSL300394      Quantity:      100     Unit: EA   Price:      6.50 Per: E

Description: Switch

Multiple Ship Schedules? No

Required Ship Date: 12/02/91    Ship Promise Date: 12/02/91

From Requisition: MRP1112021    Requisition Due Date: 12/09/91    Planner: 001
```

Figure 6.13
Purchase Order Status Inquiry Screen

```
Next Transaction:  __                                 Date: 11/18/91
This Transaction: RHI                                 Time: 11:20
                          Receiving History Inquiry

Purchase Order Number: 1C236720   PO Date: 10/02/91

Buyer: 003     Vendor: 23423    Name: RBG Electronics

Receiving History:

Line                 Date of      Receiving     Quantity   Received
Item    Part Number  Receipt      Control No.   Received      by

 001   ADL390293     10/14/91     R290-304          10      DLF
                     11/04/91     R302-102          10      RAL
 003   JSL390294     10/17/91     R292-300          20      DLF
                     10/24/91     R293-102          20      DLF
                     10/31/91     R296-091          20      KOL
 004   MAL302847     11/16/91     R304-190          25      DLF
```

Figure 6.14
Receiving History Inquiry Screen

Poor Productivity in Receiving

Excessive Manual Effort Required to Identify Shipments

When a shipment is received from a vendor, the receiving clerk performs a receiving transaction by entering the following information about the shipment into the purchasing system:

- Purchase order number received

- Purchase order line item number received

- Quantity received

This information is subsequently used for material requirements planning, inventory allocation, and invoice matching, so it is critical that the receiving clerk enter the correct data.

The receiving clerk obtains the information from the packing slip that accompanies the shipment. Unfortunately, packing slips are often incomplete or incorrect. The quantity is usually clearly and correctly indicated on the packing slip, but the purchase order number and/or purchase order line item number may be incorrect or missing. Incomplete and incorrect packing slips often require that the receiving clerk spend a significant amount of time determining the correct purchase order number and purchase order line item number.

The most common packing slip problems are

- Incorrect purchase order line item number specified on the packing slip

- No purchase order number on the packing slip

The following examples illustrate how the receiving clerk detects, investigates, and solves packing slip problems in companies that have outmoded, batch purchasing systems.

Incorrect purchase order line item number specified on the packing slip   An incorrect line item number is often a problem on multiple-item purchase orders. For example, on a four-item purchase order, the vendor may ship purchase order line items 003 and 004, but the packing slip may indicate that the shipment contains line items 001 and 002. Receiving clerks usually know from experience which vendors provide incorrect line item numbers on packing slips. For these vendors, the receiving clerk usually checks the packing slip against a batch report of open purchase orders.

The packing slip usually identifies the part number(s) being shipped. By comparing the part number(s) on the packing slip to the part number(s) on the purchase order, the receiving clerk can usually determine the correct purchase order line item number(s) for receiving. This is called the **part number matching technique**. This technique is illustrated in Table 6.3. The table illustrates that matching the part numbers on the packing slip to the part numbers on the open

Table 6.3
Part Number Matching Technique

Packing Slip		Purchase Order	
Item Number	*Part Number*	*Line Item Number*	*Part Number*
001	ADL100250	001	MBL102960
002	JSL200125	002	MAL400230
		003	ADL100250
		004	JSL200125

purchase order report would show that the vendor had actually shipped line items 003 and 004.

The above example assumes that the correct part number appears on the packing slip. However, packing slips sometimes reference the vendor's part number instead of the internal part number on the purchase order. The part number matching technique cannot be used when the packing slip references the vendor's part number. However, the receiving clerk may still be able to deduce the purchase order line item number by comparing the shipment quantity to the purchase order line item quantity. This is called the **quantity matching technique**. This technique is illustrated in Table 6.4.

In this example, the part number matching technique cannot be used to determine which purchase order line items have been received. However, matching the packing slip quantities to the purchase order line item quantities makes it clear that the vendor has actually shipped line items 003 and 004. The quantity matching technique works only when each purchase order line item has a different order quantity.

If the quantity matching technique cannot be used, the receiving clerk may be able to deduce the correct line item number by comparing the shipment itself to any descriptive information appearing on the open purchase order report or packing slip. This is called the **visual inspection technique**. For example, if purchase order line item 001 is a resistor, line item 002 is a capacitor, and line item 003 is a relay, the receiving clerk can deduce that the vendor has shipped line item 002 if the shipment contains capacitors. The visual inspection technique works only when each purchase order line item is for a different commodity.

If the visual inspection technique cannot be used, the receiving clerk may be able to deduce the correct purchase order line item number by comparing the date received to the purchase order line

Table 6.4
Quantity Matching Technique

Packing Slip			Purchase Order		
Item Number	*Part Number*	*Qty*	*Line Item Number*	*Part Number*	*Qty*
001	VPN346789	36	001	MBL102960	10
002	VPN467678	50	002	MAL400230	10
			003	ADL100250	36
			004	JSL200125	50

Table 6.5
Delivery Date/Due Date Matching Technique

Date Received: 09/07/91
All items on the purchase order are resistors.

	Packing Slip			Purchase Order		
Item Number	*Part Number*	*Qty*	*Line Item Number*	*Part Number*	*Qty*	*Due Date*
001	VPN346789	10	001	MBL102960		
			002	MAL400230	10	09/10/91
			003	ADL100250	10	10/08/91
			004	JSL200125	10	11/12/91

item due date. This is called the **delivery date/due date matching technique**. This technique is illustrated in Table 6.5.

In this example, the part number matching technique, quantity matching technique, and visual inspection technique have all failed to identify the correct purchase order line item number. However, from matching the date received to the purchase order line item due dates, it appears that the vendor has actually shipped line item 002. The delivery date/due date matching technique works only when the shipment contains one item, and when one (and only one) purchase order line item has a due date that is close to the delivery date. This technique is not as reliable as the other techniques because it is possible that the vendor has made an early shipment (or late shipment) of a different purchase order line item.

If none of the above methods work, the receiving clerk must contact the buyer for further assistance. The buyer may have to contact the vendor or come to the receiving dock to help the receiving clerk identify the shipment.

No purchase order number on the packing slip   Occasionally, packing slips fail to reference a purchase order number. If the receiving clerk has access to a report of open orders that is sorted by part number, the clerk may be able to determine the correct purchase order number by comparing the part number and quantity on the packing slip to open purchase orders for that part number. However, if there are several open purchase orders for the part number, or if the packing slip references the vendor's part number, the receiving clerk may be unable to determine the correct purchase order number. In this case, the receiving clerk must contact the buyer for further assistance.

Solution   *Provide receiving clerks with on-line access to purchase order information.*

While no system can correct the problem of incorrect and/or incomplete packing slips, an MRP II Purchasing module can make it easier for the receiving clerk to investigate packing slip problems.

Most MRP II systems provide the ability to cross-reference the internal part number to the vendor part number. This cross-reference is stored on the vendor part record in the database. (See Chapter 4 for an explanation of the differences between the part master record and the vendor part record.)

The Receive Purchase Order screen (Figure 6.15) displays *both* the internal part number and the vendor part number, making it easy for the receiving clerk to determine the correct line item number if the packing slip references the vendor part number. In addition, this screen contains other information that helps the receiving clerk

```
Next Transaction:  __                                   Date: 11/18/91
This Transaction: RPO                                   Time: 11:20
                           Receive Purchase Order

Purchase Order Number: 1C536772    Buyer: Don Gresh       Ext.: 7074
Vendor: 23423          Name: RBG Electronics

Line                                Pur   Balance  Due-On    Quantity
Item   Part Number   Vendor Part Nbr UOM     Due   Dock Date Received
001    ADL394093     RBG902039        EA      50    12/11/91  _____
       Description: Thick Film Resistor

002    JSL579882     RBG346532        EA      50    11/18/91  _____
       Description: Capacitor

003    MBL392343     RBG203069        EA      25    12/30/91  _____
       Description: Potentiometer

004    MAL358064     RBG902346        EA      10    11/29/91  _____
       Description: Thick Film Resistor

Press enter to continue
```

Figure 6.15
Receive Purchase Order Screen

```
Next Transaction:  __                           Date: 11/18/91
This Transaction: PNI                           Time: 11:22
              Open Purchase Orders by Part Number Inquiry

Part Number:  EL29012        Description: Power Interrupt Switch

            Line                       Pur    Order Balance  Due-on-
SEL  PO Number  Item  Vendor Name  Price  UOM  Quantity  Due  Dock Date

     1C239034   003   Electric Distr 12.20  EA      20      10  11/19/91
x    1S339730   001   Ace Electronic 11.90  EA      50      50  12/18/91
     1R249084   001   Barrow Supply  12.30  EA      10      10  01/03/92
     1C237031   002   Electric Distr 12.20  EA      40      40  01/16/92
```

Figure 6.16
Open Purchase Orders by Part Number Inquiry Screen

deduce the correct line item number for receiving. This information includes the order quantity, part description, and due-on-dock date.

If the packing slip fails to reference a purchase order number, the receiving clerk can perform an on-line inquiry to view all open purchase orders for a specified part number (Figure 6.16). Using an "x," the clerk can "tag" the correct purchase order and transfer it to the receiving screen (Figure 6.15). The purchase order number and line item number are automatically "carried forward" to the receiving screen, freeing the receiving clerk from having to write down this information and key it in manually.

JIT proponents feel that implementing JIT purchasing involves selecting vendors (called "trading partners" in JIT language) that provide correct and complete information on packing slips. Certainly this should be the goal of any buyer, but to the extent to which this goal is not realized, MRP II can significantly improve the productivity of receiving clerks.

Poor Productivity in the Stockroom

By definition, stockrooms represent waste because they add cost, not value, to a product. In theory, the implementation of JIT eliminates the need for stockrooms by synchronizing the flow of material so perfectly that material is delivered by the vendor directly to the assembly line precisely when it is needed.

In practice, however, this state of perfection is never attained for two reasons:

The stockroom acts as a necessary buffer for in-transit lead time variances for vendors that are located far away. One of the goals of JIT is to locate sources of supply that are close at hand, but this is not always possible. In fact, many older plants were deliberately built some distance from suppliers in an attempt to keep these plants free from the influence of labor unions. Today, proximity to suppliers plays a more important role in determining the location of a new plant.

The stockroom acts as a buffer for the inability to determine precisely where and when material is needed. Make-to-order and engineer-to-order manufacturers are unable to achieve an assembly-line style of production suited for synchronized material flow. Such companies have long manufacturing cycle times, and they manufacture a large variety of parts in small lot sizes. Therefore, it is not practical for vendors to deliver material directly to the point of use in factories that have thousands of open shop orders. It is more practical to pick the material from a buffer location—the stockroom—and release it to the first operation on a manufacturing routing.

Because stockrooms will continue to exist in most companies, it is important to minimize the cost of operating the stockroom. The indirect labor cost associated with stockrooms is one of the highest manufacturing support costs in some companies. Causes of poor stockroom productivity are explained in the following subsections.

Excessive Material Handling Caused by Staging of Partially Picked Orders

The common practice of staging manufacturing orders to determine material shortages is described in Chapter 2. Staging manufacturing orders results in excessive material handling. The stockkeeper must pick the order and store it in a temporary location until the shortages have been filled. Then the stockkeeper must remove the order from the temporary storage location and release it to the shop floor.

Solution   *Provide a picklist simulation capability.*

The solution to this problem is to provide the ability to simulate the picking function so that material shortages can be determined without having to physically pick and stage manufacturing orders. This solution is described in Chapter 2.

Excessive Manual Effort Required to Locate Materials

In some companies, the stockkeeper is expected to use the shop paperwork as a picklist. The shop paperwork contains a materials list, but it may not include inventory storage location information. The stockkeeper must refer to a Stock Locator Report produced by a batch inventory system to obtain this information. This report is sorted in part-number sequence and identifies the storage locations associated with each part. The stockkeeper must look up each part number on the materials list and write down the inventory location(s) on the shop paperwork. Only when this labor-intensive process is completed can the shop paperwork be used as a picklist.

Some companies try to solve this problem by storing inventory in part-number sequence. In theory, this allows the stockkeeper to find parts easily without a Stock Locator Report. In practice, however, this approach has three drawbacks:

1. It results in wasted space. Space must be reserved for every part to maintain inventory storage by part-number sequence.

2. It is difficult to assign storage locations to new part numbers that "fall between" existing part numbers.

3. The storage requirements for two sequential part numbers may be different. It is impractical to store inventory in part-number sequence if one part requires bin storage and the next part in sequence requires palletized storage.

Solution   *Provide the ability to allocate materials from specific inventory locations.*

Some MRP II packages produce picklists that tell the stockkeeper exactly where to go to pick material. The Inventory Control module automatically allocates material from specific inventory locations when a picklist is requested for a manufacturing or customer order. (A number of different allocation methods are discussed in Chapter 3.) The part number, quantity required, and inventory location are printed on the picklist. This enables the stockkeeper to pick material without first having to look up inventory locations on a Stock Locator Report.

Excessive Manual Effort Required to Report Picking Activity

Many homegrown inventory systems require that the stockkeeper enter an inventory transaction for each item issued to a manufacturing or customer order. If a manufacturing order containing 30 components is picked, the stockkeeper must fill out 30 data entry forms to update inventory balances. Over the course of a week, stockkeepers can fill out thousands of data entry forms to keep inventory records up to date.

Solution   *Provide the ability to perform picklist activity reporting.*

MRP II packages eliminate the need to enter individual inventory transactions for each item that is issued to a manufacturing or customer order. When a picklist is requested, the Inventory Control module stores a permanent electronic copy of the picklist in the database. The purpose of the electronic copy is to facilitate picklist activity reporting.

The Picklist Reporting screen (Figure 6.17) provides the stockkeeper with two efficient ways to report picking activity.

1. *Pick order complete.* The pick order complete feature automatically updates the inventory records for all parts on the picklist. To select this option, the stockkeeper enters Y (yes) in the Pick Order Complete field on the Picklist Reporting screen.

    This option should be used only when there are no exceptions to report, that is, when every item is picked exactly as specified on the picklist. This option should not be used if any part on the picklist is partially picked, overissued, or picked from a location other than that specified on the picklist.

```
Next Transaction:  __                           Date: 11/18/91
This Transaction: PLR                           Time: 11:22
                          Picklist Reporting

Order Number: MO19049   Part Number: BLJ102930   Order Quantity:      5

Pick Order Complete? Y           Pick Page Complete? ___

            Expected   Expected   Expected   Actual     Actual     Actual
SEL  Part Number  Quantity   Location   Lot No.   Quantity   Location   Lot No.
 -   ADL390293        5      SA203        001     _____   _____   ____
 -   BJL255695        5      SB456        002     _____   _____   ____
 -   JSL392345        5      SA234        001     _____   _____   ____
 -   EL230394         5      SD344        003     _____   _____   ____
 -   MBL334232       10      SA345        001     _____   _____   ____
 -   ADL505920        5      SR234        001     _____   _____   ____
 -   MAL680596       20      SA234        002     _____   _____   ____
 -   REL340322        5      SJ346        001     _____   _____   ____
 -   SNG234040        5      SA200        004     _____   _____   ____
 -   LL343654        15      SA435        002     _____   _____   ____

Press enter to display next page
```

Figure 6.17
Picklist Reporting Screen

2. *Pick-by-page.* Most picklists contain more items than can be displayed on one computer screen page. The pick-by-page feature automatically updates the inventory records for all parts on the computer screen. The next screen is automatically displayed for picklist reporting.

This option should be used when there are no exceptions to report on a particular screen.

The Picklist Reporting screen (Figure 6.17) also allows the stockkeeper to report picking activity by individual item. The stockkeeper enters a code next to each item selected for picklist reporting. The stockkeeper can override the expected quantity and location information. The picklist remains open until each item has been picked complete.

Some MRP II packages provide the ability to produce consolidated picklists instead of a separate picklist for each manufacturing or customer order. The consolidated picklist is sorted by inventory location in the stockroom.

Figure 6.18 shows a consolidated picklist for three manufacturing orders. The theory behind the consolidated picklist approach is that it reduces the time required to pick material, because the stockkeeper has to walk through the stockroom only once to pick the requirements for all the orders. However, the picking efficiencies are usually offset by the extra effort required to separate the materials by order after they have been picked.

```
Date: 12/04/91                                              Page: 01
                      Consolidated Picklist Report
                      (Sorted by Inventory Location)


                                    Pick      Order       Order
     Location   Lot   Part Number   Quantity  Number      Part Number

     SA3023     001   ADL390278           10  M029030     ADL239093

     SA3023     001   ADL390278            5  M032010     EL33290

     SA3230     006   JSL302903           10  M029030     ADL239093

     SA3230     006   JSL302903            5  M032010     EL33290

     SA3230     006   JSL302903           10  M034201     SNG309250

     SB2345     001   MAL209394           10  M034201     SNG309250

     SB2501     001   MBL402093            5  M032010     EL33290

     SB2501     001   MBL402093           10  M034201     SNG309250

     SC3023     002   JSL302093           10  M029030     ADL239093

     SC3023     002   JSL390293            5  M032010     EL33290

     SC3023     002   JSL390293           10  M034201     SNG309250

     SC3223     001   BJL302008           10  M034201     SNG309250
```

Figure 6.18
Consolidated Picklist Report

Provide the ability to backflush material from inventory based on actual production.

In companies that have short manufacturing cycle times, it is possible to eliminate picklist reporting altogether. Most MRP II packages provide the ability to automatically update inventory records when production receipts are reported. This technique is called **backflushing**.

Backflushing is generally not recommended for companies that have manufacturing cycle times longer than one day, because too long a delay in updating inventory records will result in inaccurate inventory balances.

Excessive Manual Effort Required to Receive Materials into Stores

In most companies, a minimum of two transactions are required to receive purchased materials. The first transaction updates the purchase order and receives the material at the receiving dock. The second transaction receives the material into an inventory storage location. If the material needs to go through incoming inspection, it makes sense to perform two transactions so that the material can be tracked from dock to stock. However, if the material is moved immediately to a storage location, the second transaction may serve no useful purpose. This is particularly true if a part is always stored in the same location.

Solution   *Provide the ability to define default storage locations.*

Some MRP II systems allow a default storage location to be defined for a part. When the material is received at the receiving dock, it can be received automatically into the default storage location. This eliminates the need to perform a second transaction to receive the material into inventory.

Poor Productivity in Design Engineering

MRP II systems contain productivity features for the Design Engineering and Manufacturing Engineering organizations. In both organizations, poor systems often cause professional engineers to function as high-paid data entry clerks.

Excessive Manual Effort Required to
Add and Maintain Bills of Materials

Design engineers often spend too much time creating and maintaining bills of materials. To create a new bill of materials, the engineer must list all the component information (component part number, quantity per assembly, component lead time offset, effectivity dates, etc.) on a data entry form, even if the new BOM is similar to an existing bill of materials.

Sometimes it is necessary to replace a component with another component on all bills of materials. If part *A* is used on 500 bills of materials, the engineer must perform 500 maintenance transactions to replace part *A* with part *B*.

Solutions   *Provide a copy-same-as-except capability.*

The Bill of Materials module contains a copy-same-as-except feature, which allows an engineer to create a new bill of materials efficiently by copying an existing, similar bill of materials. By adding, modifying, and deleting components on the copied BOM, the engineer can create a new BOM in a fraction of the time that would otherwise be required.

Provide a component global where-used replacement capability.

The component global where-used replacement feature enables an engineer to perform a single transaction that replaces one component with another on all bills of materials. The engineer specifies the old component part number and the new component part number on the Component Global Where-Used Replacement screen (Figure 6.19). The system automatically performs a where-used inquiry to identify all bills of materials that use the old component. The system then automatically updates all the bills of materials, replacing the old component with the new component.

Poor Productivity in Manufacturing Engineering

Excessive Manual Effort Required to
Add and Maintain Shop Routings
(Process Plans)

Manufacturing engineers often spend too much time adding and maintaining shop routings. **Routings,** also referred to as **process**

plans, define the manufacturing operations that must be performed in a particular sequence to produce a parent part from a bill of materials. The following information must be specified for each operation on the routing:

- Operation number (indicates the sequence of the operation within the routing)

- Work center where the operation is performed

- Operation description

- Operation crew size (indicates the number of people required to perform the operation)

- Setup time

- Run time

- Run-time factor (indicates whether the run time reflects the number of pieces that can be produced per unit of time, the

---

```
Next Transaction: ___                                    Date: 11/18/91
This Transaction: CGR                                    Time: 09:13
                    Component Global Where-Used Replacement

Replace:

Old Component Part Number:   ADL390290


With:

New Component Part Number:   ADL290390
```

MSG9033:   150 Product Structure Records will be updated.   Continue? ___

Figure 6.19
Component Global Where-Used Replacement Screen

amount of time required to produce one piece, or the amount of time required to perform the operation regardless of lot size)

- Overlap factor (indicates whether the operation can overlap or be performed concurrently with the previous operation)

To create a new routing, the manufacturing engineer must enter all the above information about each operation on a data entry form, even if the routing is similar or identical to one that has already been established for another part.

Sometimes it is necessary to replace a work center with another work center in the factory. When this happens, every routing that used the old work center must be updated to reflect the new work center. If the old work center was used on 1000 different operations, the manufacturing engineer must perform 1000 maintenance transactions.

Solutions

Provide a copy-same-as-except capability.

MRP II packages provide a copy-same-as-except feature, which allows an engineer to create a new routing efficiently by copying an existing, similar routing. By adding, modifying, and deleting operations on the copied routing, the engineer can create a new routing in a fraction of the time that would otherwise be required.

Provide the ability to define master routings.

It is not unusual for many similar parts to have identical routings. Instead of requiring a unique routing to be created for each part, some MRP II packages allow master routings to be defined. A **master routing** is an independent routing that can be associated with any number of parts. Thus, if 100 parts have the same routing, one master routing eliminates the effort required to create 100 individual part routings.

Master routings also reduce the effort required to maintain routings, because a change to a master routing automatically affects all the parts that are linked to the master routing.

Provide the ability to define master operations.

Many times the same operation is performed on a number of different parts. For example, some parts may require the same plating, heat treating, or inspection operation. To reduce the effort required to add the same operation to a number of individual part routings, some MRP II packages provide the ability to define independent operations called **master operations**. Once a master operation is established, it can be copied into any number of part routings.

Master operations also reduce the effort required to maintain routings. When a master operation is copied into a part routing, the manufacturing engineer can indicate whether future changes to the master operation should automatically update the part routing. This is done by setting an automatic update flag to Y or N (yes or no) on the operation on the part routing.

In Figure 6.20, master operation MO250 has been copied into eight part routings. When a change is made to master operation MO250, the corresponding operations on the routings for parts ADL390489 and EL390894 will be updated automatically because the automatic update flag is set to Y. The corresponding operations on the other six routings will not be updated automatically, because the automatic update flag was set to N when the master operation was copied into the routings.

Provide a work center global where-used replacement capability.

The work center global where used replacement feature enables a manufacturing engineer to perform a single transaction that replaces one work center with another on all operations. The engineer specifies the old work center number and the new work center number on the Work Center Global Where-Used Replacement screen (Figure 6.21). The system automatically performs a where used inquiry to identify all operations that use the old work center. The system then automatically updates each operation, replacing the old work center number with the new work center number.

Limitations of MRP II Systems: Process Planning

MRP II systems help manufacturing engineers create process plans efficiently, but they not help them create efficient process plans (that is, process plans that produce quality parts at the lowest possible cost). For companies that manufacture thousands of complex parts, the most significant manufacturing engineering productivity improvement comes from implementing a computer aided process planning (CAPP) system.

CAPP systems improve productivity by reducing the effort required to develop efficient process plans. The process plans established in the CAPP system database update the MRP II routing file

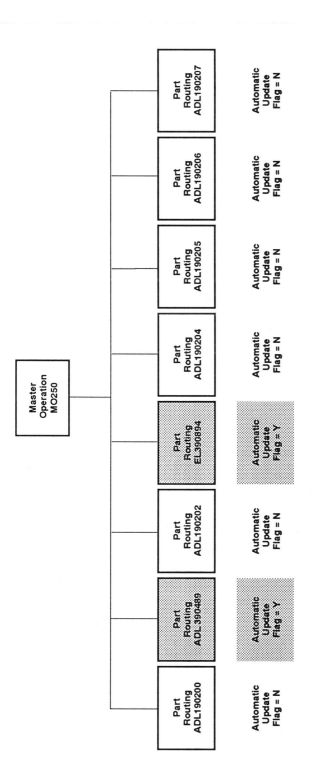

The automatic update flag is used to update part routings when a master operation is updated.

Figure 6.20
Master Operations Diagram

```
Next Transaction: ___                                Date: 11/18/91
This Transaction: WGR                                Time: 10:13
                   Work Center Global Where-Used Replacement

Replace:

Old Work Center:  WC1029


With:

New Work Center:  WC9029






MSG9033    263 Operation Detail Records will be updated.   Continue? _
```

Figure 6.21
Work Center Global Where-Used Replacement Screen

by means of a batch interface. This interface provides the MRP II database with the information required to perform shop scheduling and capacity planning.

There are two types of computer aided process planning systems available today: variant CAPP systems, which account for more than 95 percent of commercially available CAPP systems, and generative CAPP systems.

Variant CAPP Systems   A variant CAPP system extends an MRP II system's copy-same-as-except capability. One major difference between an MRP II system and a variant CAPP system is that the latter helps the engineer find the correct process plan to copy and modify.

Some variant CAPP systems are based on a group technology coding system. The manufacturing engineer assigns a group technology code to each part in the database. This code identifies critical part attributes such as part type, shape, material, finish, and size.

Once a group technology code is assigned, the CAPP system searches the database and retrieves process plans for parts that have the same code. The engineer then copies and modifies one of these process plans to create a process plan for the new part.

The problem with the group technology coding approach is that two engineers might code the same part differently. Modern variant CAPP systems employ an interactive approach in which a "dialog" exists between the CAPP system and the manufacturing engineer. The system queries the engineer about the part's characteristics. Based on the engineer's responses, the CAPP system searches the database and retrieves process plans for similar parts. This question-and-answer session replaces the group technology code and is less prone to problems caused by coding errors.

Generative CAPP Systems   The other approach to computer aided process planning is a generative CAPP system. A generative CAPP system is an expert system that contains the knowledge of an expert manufacturing engineer to develop process plans independent of existing process plans. This knowledge is captured by the system in a set of IF-THEN-ELSE rules that apply the same reasoning that an expert would apply to create a new process plan. For example, IF the finished part is of a certain material AND size, THEN a certain raw stock is selected.

A generative CAPP system also has the "intelligence" to determine which rules to apply based on how previous IF-THEN-ELSE statements have been executed. This process is called **rule chaining**.

A generative CAPP system is more likely to develop an efficient process plan than a variant CAPP system. The reason is that a generative CAPP system uses the knowledge of an expert to create an efficient process plan, whereas a variant CAPP system might result in an engineer copying an inefficient process plan.

By necessity, generative process planning systems are highly specialized; they are used to develop process plans for special classes of parts such as machined cylindrical parts or assembled printed circuit boards. An all-purpose generative process planning system, capable of producing a process plan for any type of part, would be extremely difficult if not impossible to design.

Most generative process planning systems available today are merely semigenerative, because they still require that the engineer respond to IF-THEN-ELSE statements before they can generate a process plan. A truly generative process planning system would be able to scan a drawing produced from a CAD system and develop a process plan without any manual input from a manufacturing engineer. A few, highly specialized, true generative CAPP systems exist today, but these are not commercially available.

Poor Productivity in Material Control

Inability to Manage by Exception

Many homegrown computer systems produce a Part Activity Report (Figure 2.1) for every part on a weekly basis. The planner must review every part on the report and take the appropriate action to balance supply and demand. Studies indicate that only 10 percent to 20 percent of the parts require some type of action. This means that planners spend a significant amount of nonproductive time reviewing parts that require no action.

The format and content of the Part Activity Report are described in Chapter 2.

Solution *Use the Planner Action Report.*

The Planner Action Report (Figure 2.2), which is the primary output of the MRP module, allows the planner to manage supply and demand by exception. Only those parts requiring action are reported on this report. The Planner Action Report alone can more than double the material planner's productivity when an MRP II system replaces a poorly designed homegrown planning system.

The format and content of the Planner Action Report are described in Chapter 2.

Excessive Manual Effort Required to Track Material in Incoming Inspection

Material planners track material from the receiving dock, through incoming inspection, to the stockroom. If a material shortage occurs, knowledge of what is in inspection is extremely important, because it may be possible to fill the shortage by expediting a lot through incoming inspection.

Many homegrown systems only provide material planners with visibility to stores inventory. Therefore, material planners must keep manual records of what is in incoming inspection.

Solution   *Provide on-line visibility to all inventory.*

MRP II systems provide on-line visibility to all inventory. Inventory that is in incoming inspection is clearly identified by an inventory status code. When a material shortage occurs, the material planner can access the Inventory Detail Inquiry screen (Figure 6.22) to determine if there is material in incoming inspection. The planner can also call up the on-line Inspection Work Order Inquiry screen (Figure 6.23) to determine the status and location of the lot in incoming inspection. In a matter of seconds, the planner can determine exactly where to go or who to call to expedite the lot through incoming inspection.

```
Next Transaction: ___                                    Date: 08/01/91
This Transaction: IDI                                    Time: 11:30
                          Inventory Detail Inquiry

Part Number: ADL30543         Qty Available to be Allocated:        140
                              Qty Unavailable for Manufacturing:    280
                              Qty Available for MRP Planning:       310
                              Qty Unavailable for MRP Planning:     180

Lot          Quantity  Quantity  MRP   Inv Reason  Date      Shelf    Order    Lot
Nbr Location On Hand   Allocated Avail? Stat Code   Received  Exp Date Number   Trc

001 RM120      100         0      N     RJ  Reject  04/14/91           1S229328
002 SB127       50         0      Y     AM          05/01/91           1S209348
003 SB132      100        70      Y     AM          05/15/91           1W333842
004 SB132       60         0      Y     AM          06/02/91           1S236493
005 RM120       80         0      N     RJ  Reject  07/15/91           1R334993
006 IN127      100         0      Y     II  Ininsp  08/01/91           1W530402
```

Figure 6.22
Inventory Detail Inquiry Screen

```
Next Transaction: ___                        Date: 08/01/91
This Transaction: IWI                        Time: 11:32
                    Inspection Work Order Inquiry

Part Number: ADL30543     Description: Circuit Breaker Trip Latch
PO Number: 1W530402     Line Item: 001   Vendor: Fine Metal Stamping
Quantity Received:    100       Inspection Sample Size: 5%

Current Inspection Step: 030

       Insp   Labor   Quantity   Quantity   Lot
Seq    Dept   Class   Inspected  Passed     Status

010    I100   R05            5         5    Passed
020    I100   R05            5         5    Passed
030    I100   R05                           In Inspection
040    I110   R10
```

Figure 6.23
Inspection Work Order Inquiry Screen

Poor Productivity in Production Control

High Level of Expediting

Expediting is often the highest support cost in manufacturing. Many companies employ dozens of professional expediters because their systems do little or nothing to help prevent material shortages (see Chapter 2 for a discussion of the material shortages problem).

Expediters may be employed in the guise of several different job titles, but they all perform the same basic job: making shortage lists and expediting. Their contributions are invaluable, but the costs are tremendous. A professional expediter typically costs a company between $50,000 and $75,000 a year in salary and benefits. Since these people add nothing but costs to the product, these costs directly impact the bottom line.

Solution   *Provide the ability to predict and prevent shortages.*

By design, MRP II systems are shortage prevention systems. The Planner Action Report (Figure 2.2) predicts shortages before they actually occur, so that the material planner can take action in time to prevent shortages. By shifting the emphasis from expediting to shortage prevention, an MRP II system makes it possible for a company to eliminate most of its professional expediters. The savings in this area alone is often enough to justify all the investment required to purchase and implement an MRP II system.

Excessive Manual Effort Required to Employ Alternate Routings

Most parts can be produced in more than one way. If a machine is down or if a work center is overloaded, the production control specialist may decide to employ an alternate routing for a manufacturing order. However, a considerable amount of manual effort may be required to modify the routing instructions on the shop paperwork.

Solution   *Provide the ability to define and select alternate routings.*

Some MRP II Shop Floor Control modules provide the ability to define both primary and alternate routing operations on the Part Routing Record. Alternate operations are indicated by an alternate suffix in the operation number. In Table 6.6, operation 0015-01-00 is an alternate for operation 0015-00-00.

Alternate operations that are to be performed together as a group are assigned the same alternate suffix. In Table 6.6, operations 0020-02-00 and 0030-02-00 are always performed together.

Sometimes several alternate operations are required to replace one primary operation. The production control specialist can indicate this on the Part Routing Record by assigning alternate sequence numbers to alternate operations. In Table 6.6, alternate operations 0020-01-01, 0020-01-02, and 0020-01-03 replace primary operation 0020-00-00.

When a manufacturing order is released to the shop floor, the production control specialist can select an alternate routing suffix and the appropriate shop paperwork will be produced. If alternate routing 01 is selected from the routing in Table 6.6, the shop paperwork will contain the following operations:

Table 6.6
Primary and Alternate Operation Numbers on a Part
Routing Record

Operation Number	(Primary Number - Alternate Suffix - Alternate Sequence)
0010-00-00	
0015-00-00	
0015-01-00	(Alternate to primary operation 0015-00-00)
0020-00-00	
0020-01-01	(Alternate to primary operation 0020-00-00, first in the sequence)
0020-01-02	(Alternate to primary operation 0020-00-00, second in the sequence)
0020-01-03	(Alternate to primary operation 0020-00-00, third in the sequence)
0020-02-00	(Second alternate to primary operation 0020-00-00)
0030-00-00	
0030-01-00	(Alternate to primary operation 0030-00-00)
0030-02-00	(Second alternate to primary operation 0030-00-00)

0010-00-00

0015-01-00

0020-01-01

0020-01-02

0020-01-03

0030-01-00

Note that primary operations are selected if there is no alternate associated with the chosen suffix.

If alternate routing 02 is selected from the routing in Table 6.6, the shop paperwork will contain the following operations:

0010-00-00

0015-00-00

0020-02-00

0030-02-00

Caveat   Some MRP II packages only allow alternate routings to be created by adding and deleting operations to individual shop orders "on the fly." These software packages do not allow alternate routing operations to be *permanently* stored in the routing file. This approach requires more effort because production control must enter the alternate routing each time it is used.

Poor Productivity in Master Scheduling

Excessive Manual Effort Required to Develop a Feasible Production Plan

A major part of a master scheduler's job is to ensure that the Master Production Schedule represents a statement of what a company is truly capable of producing. Many companies lack the tools to help the master scheduler develop a feasible production plan. This forces the master scheduler to spend many hours evaluating production plans to determine if there is enough capacity in critical (bottleneck) work centers to meet the plan.

Solution *Provide for rough cut capacity planning.*

MRP II software packages provide a rough cut capacity planning (RCCP) feature within the Master Production Schedule (MPS) module. This feature helps the master scheduler evaluate a proposed production plan to determine whether there is enough capacity (labor and equipment) to meet the schedule. RCCP eliminates the hours of manual effort that would otherwise be required to evaluate production plans.

The operation of the rough cut capacity planning feature is discussed in Chapter 5.

Excessive Manual Effort Required to Maintain the Master Schedule

Make-to-stock manufacturers may produce many different items within a product family. For example, a television manufacturer may produce ten different models of 19-inch TV sets. Scheduling each product individually can be an onerous task. For example, if a company has ten product families and each family has an average of twenty items, the master scheduler must schedule a total of 200 different end-items. If the planning horizon is 26 weeks, the master scheduler must schedule a total of 5200 time periods (200 × 26). Because of the amount of effort required to schedule so many items over the planning horizon, some companies must have several master schedulers. Each master scheduler is responsible for certain product families.

Assemble-to-order manufacturers face a similar scheduling problem. Here, the number of product options makes for an almost infinite number of end-items. Because it is impossible to schedule every possible end-item, the master scheduler must schedule hundreds of make-to-stock options independently.

Solution

Provide the ability to schedule by product family.

MRP II systems provide the ability to define special kinds of bills of materials known as **planning bills of materials**. Chapter 5 discusses how one type of planning BOM, the configuration BOM, can be used to help order entry clerks configure customer orders in assemble-to-order environments.

Planning bills of materials also play an important role in master scheduling. In make-to-stock environments, a planning BOM can be established for each product family. Production schedules are loaded at the family level and are automatically distributed across the individual products in the family in accordance with predefined percentages.

In Figure 6.24, a family of 19-inch TV sets is produced at a rate of 3000 units per week. This quantity is automatically distributed among ten different models of 19-inch TV sets using the percentages specified on the planning bill of materials. This eliminates the need to schedule each item individually.

In assemble-to-order environments, the configuration bill of materials is used to determine production schedules for make-to-stock options by distributing production quantities across options in accordance with predefined percentages (Figure 6.25).

Caveat

Planning BOMs work best when the production mix remains relatively stable. If the mix varies significantly from week to week, it may be necessary to schedule each item individually.

Poor Productivity in Management Information Systems (MIS)

Excessive Effort Required to Maintain Old Systems

Surprisingly, some of the biggest productivity gains from implementing MRP II come from the MIS organization. In companies that have homegrown systems, MIS departments typically spend about 80 percent of their available resources maintaining these systems. Homegrown systems are expensive to maintain for a number of reasons.

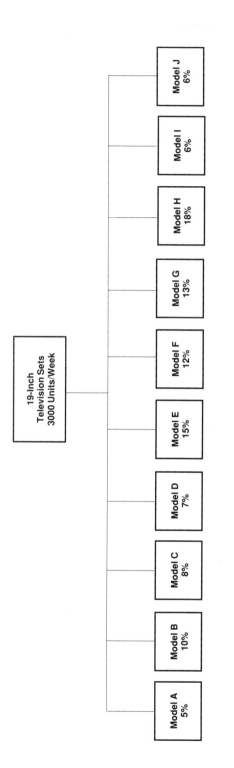

Figure 6.24
Family Planning Bill of Materials (Make-to-Stock Manufacturer)

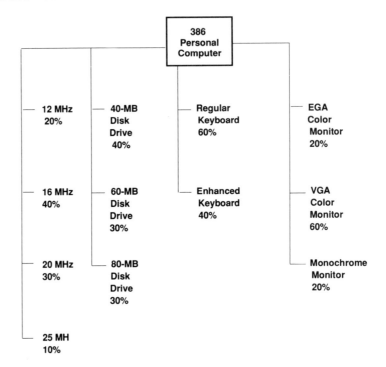

Figure 6.25
Configuration Planning Bill of Materials
(Assemble-to-Order Manufacturer)

Many homegrown systems are not well documented. Home-grown systems are often poorly documented. The documentation may be limited to comments embedded in the program code, and these comments may not have been kept up to date as changes were made over several years. This causes serious problems when the original system developers leave the company. Simple changes may take weeks to complete, because the new programmers are not familiar with the system and have no documentation to guide them. To change one line of code in a program, a programmer may have to search through thousands of lines of poorly documented code.

Due to the poor documentation, the effect of a program change cannot always be predicted. Sometimes program changes can cause other system problems that go undetected for weeks, resulting in massive recovery efforts.

Many homegrown systems are not parameter driven. Many of the parameters that control system logic in homegrown systems are "buried" within the actual computer programs. Simple changes that users could otherwise make have to be made by programmers, because the users do not have access to these management parameters.

Many homegrown systems are not well integrated. Few companies have sufficient programming resources to develop a complete, integrated manufacturing planning and control system in a reasonable period of time. Because of this, homegrown systems are often developed over a number of years. The resulting system is often a hodgepodge of modules that run on several different hardware platforms, operating systems, and databases. Because the systems do not share a common database, data is stored redundantly. For example, each module usually has its own Part Master Record. If the Accounts Payable and Purchasing modules are on different computers, there may be two vendor files and two purchase order files. The data in these redundant files must be synchronized through a series of complex system interfaces. Writing and maintaining these interfaces is a full-time job for several programmers.

Solution   *Replace homegrown systems with well-documented, parameter-driven, integrated MRP II systems.*

MRP II software packages are thoroughly documented, and the software vendor updates the documentation with each new release of the package. Moreover, MRP II packages require less maintenance than homegrown systems. With each new release, the software vendor provides a number of enhancements that add value to the system and keep it up to date. Because maintenance costs are spread across a large customer base, MRP II software vendors can maintain the system for a fraction of what it costs a company to maintain its own homegrown system.

MRP II packages are designed to be parameter-driven. Users can maintain the parameters that control system logic by means of on-line transactions. Changes that previously required days or weeks for an expert programmer to complete can be done in seconds by end-users.

MRP II software vendors have the resources to develop integrated systems that operate in a homogeneous computing environment. This eliminates redundant data files and complex interfaces that are a major cause of high maintenance costs in homegrown systems.

Excessive Effort Required to Process End-User Requests for Reports

In homegrown systems, requests for new reports typically comprise about 75 percent of the maintenance backlog. MIS departments apply several person-years of effort each year to work on this maintenance backlog. Even a simple request, such as a request to change the sort sequence on an existing report, may require MIS involvement.

Solution   *Provide a management reporting system.*

All MRP II packages include a management reporting system that allows end-users to query the database and produce reports. These systems are designed for people who have no programming experience and no knowledge of the database. Management reporting systems are user-friendly, menu-driven systems that guide the user through a series of steps to produce a report. These steps allow the user to define the report selection criteria, select the data to be included in the report, define the report title and headings, and specify the report sort sequence. Some systems also allow the user to perform calculations on data and to calculate report totals.

Management reporting systems eliminate about 80 percent of the requests that would otherwise go through the MIS department.

Poor Productivity in Order Entry

Excessive Manual Effort Required to Enter Customer Orders

Chapter 5 discusses the following six order-entry features from a customer service perspective:

1. Automatic customer identification

2. Customer profile feature

3. Automatic order pricing

4. Realtime order promising

5. Automatic credit checking

6. Electronic data interchange (automatic order entry)

These features have another important benefit: They produce significant gains in productivity by reducing or eliminating the effort required to enter customer orders manually. Chapter 5 contains a comprehensive discussion of these features.

Summary

Table 6.7 summarizes the causes of poor salaried and indirect labor productivity that were discussed in this chapter, and the solutions found in MRP II systems.

Table 6.7
Summary of Causes of and Solutions to Poor Salaried
and Indirect Labor Productivity

Cause	MRP II Solutions
Accounts Payable	
Excessive manual effort required:	
1. To perform invoice matching	1. Provide electronic three-way matching.
2. To obtain invoice approval signatures	2. Provide electronic signature approval.
3. To approve large payments	3. Provide the ability to print checks in sequence by dollar amount.
4. To reconcile payments	4. Provide for automatic payment reconciliation.
5. To respond to vendor inquiries	5. Provide on-line access to invoice status information.
Purchasing	
Excessive manual effort required:	
1. To place purchase orders	1. Provide for: - Automatic purchase order generation. - The ability to define purchasing defaults. - The ability to define standard messages. - The ability to define unit of measure conversion factors. - Electronic exchange of purchase orders.
2. To perform file maintenance	2. Provide: - On-line, realtime file maintenance. - Mass maintenance productivity tools. - The ability to automatically close purchase orders that are received short. - Default values for data fields. - The ability to calculate actual prices from discounts off a base price. - System logic to ensure data integrity. - On-line file maintenance audit trails.
3. To expedite purchase orders	3. Provide expediting exception reports.
4. To solicit bids from vendors	4. Provide on-line RFQ processing.
5. To respond to inquiries from material planners and production control personnel.	5. Provide on-line access to requisition, purchase order, and receiving status information.

Table 6.7
Summary of Causes of and Solutions to Poor Salaried
and Indirect Labor Productivity (continued)

Cause	MRP II Solutions
Receiving Excessive manual effort required to identify shipments	Provide on-line access to purchase order information.
Stockroom 1. Excessive material handling caused by staging of partially picked orders	1. Provide a picklist simulation capability.
2. Excessive manual effort required to locate materials	2. Provide the ability to allocate materials from specific inventory locations.
3. Excessive manual effort required to report picking activity	3. Provide for: - Picklist activity reporting - Automatic backflushing of inventory balances
4. Excessive manual effort required to receive materials into stores	4. Provide the ability to define default storage locations.
Design Engineering Excessive manual effort required to add and maintain bills of materials	Provide: - A copy-same-as-except capability - A component global where-used replacement feature
Manufacturing Engineering Excessive manual effort required to add and maintain shop routings	Provide: - A copy-same-as-except capability - The ability to define master routings - The ability to define master operations - A work center global where used replacement capability
Material Control 1. Inability to manage by exception	1. The Planner Action Report allows the material planner to manage by exception.
2. Excessive manual effort required to track material in incoming inspection	2. Provide on-line visibility to all inventory.
Production Control 1. High level of expediting	1. Provide the ability to predict and prevent shortages using the Planner Action Report.
2. Excessive manual effort required to employ alternate routings	2. Provide the ability to define and select alternate routings.
Master Scheduling Excessive manual effort required: 1. To develop a feasible production plan	1. Provide for rough cut capacity planning.
2. To maintain the master schedule	2. Provide the ability to schedule by product family using planning bills of materials.
Management Information Systems Excessive effort required: 1. To maintain old systems	1. Replace homegrown systems with a well-documented, parameter-driven, integrated MRP II system.
2. To process end-user requests for reports	2. Provide a management reporting system that allows end-users to generate their own reports.

Table 6.7
Summary of Causes of and Solutions to Poor Salaried
and Indirect Labor Productivity (continued)

Cause	MRP II Solutions
Order Entry	
Excessive manual effort required to enter customer orders	Provide the following features: 1. Automatic customer identification 2. Customer profile feature 3. Automatic order pricing 4. Realtime order promising 5. Automatic credit checking 6. Electronic data interchange

The Cash Management Problem

T*he Manager of Finance was in deep trouble. The corporate auditors had just completed an audit of the division, and they had uncovered a very serious problem: The company had paid for a number of invoices before the materials were actually received. In some cases, vendors had billed the company months prior to shipment and had still been paid immediately. Although there was no proof that any vendors had defrauded the company, the auditors had concluded that, at the very least, the finance organization had done a poor job of cash management. The Audit Report prompted a meeting between the Manager of Finance and the Manager of Accounts Payable.*

"How did this happen?" the Manager of Finance asked. "How could we possibly have paid a $5000 invoice three months before the shipment was actually received?"

"Well, as you know, many of our suppliers offer a cash discount for prompt payment," said the Manager of Accounts Payable. "Our accounts payable system was designed to ensure that we would never lose a prompt payment discount. Therefore we pay all invoices immediately, and we randomly audit purchase orders to ensure that material has actually been received. It was only a matter of time before some vendors realized that we weren't routinely matching invoices with receipts. A few vendors may have been taking advantage of our policy of paying invoices immediately."

"We've been given 90 days to correct the problem," the Manager of Finance said, "and we need to implement a solution that prevents this from happening again. Do you have any suggestions?"

"Well, the short-term solution is to hire three clerks. This will give us the ability to match every invoice with a purchase order and receipt. The long-term solution is to modify our system to automate the invoice-matching process."

"How long will that take?" asked the Manager of Finance. "The General Manager is going to read me the riot act when I tell her we need to hire three new clerks."

"Well, it depends on what approach we take. If we try to modify our existing system, I'm told that we'll need to expend about eight person-years of programming effort to provide electronic invoice matching. Our purchasing and accounts payable systems aren't integrated. In fact, they don't even run on the same computer! Major modifications are required to integrate the two systems to achieve electronic invoice matching.

"However, there may be a simpler, better solution," added the Manager of Accounts Payable. "I understand that there is a project underway to purchase and implement an MRP II manufacturing system. From what I've read, many of these systems include integrated financial modules. We can probably implement new, integrated systems in less time than we can modify our homegrown systems. Also, a packaged solution will be far more reliable than any solution resulting from an attempt to integrate our old, homegrown systems."

"It sounds like the right approach to me," the Manager of Finance nodded. "Let's get involved in the software evaluation process to make certain that the MRP II system solves our business problem."

Introduction

Chapter 6 addresses a serious productivity problem: the productivity of salaried and indirect labor. This chapter addresses another serious productivity problem: the productivity of money.

The basic difference between Material Requirements Planning (MRP) and Manufacturing Resource Planning (MRP II) is that an MRP II system includes financial modules that help a company manage all its resources, including material, labor, capacity, and capital. The Purchasing, Accounts Payable, Accounts Receivable, and Order Processing modules of an MRP II system contain a number of features designed to help companies control one of their most valuable resources: cash.

The biggest cause of poor cash management is high inventory. The inventory problem is addressed in Chapter 3. This chapter addresses the causes of poor cash management related to payments to suppliers and payments from customers.

Some of the major causes of poor cash management are listed below. These causes, and the solutions offered by MRP II systems, are discussed in the sections that follow.

Causes related to payments to suppliers

1. Inability to manage payment cycles to optimize cash flow
2. Inability to predict cash requirements
3. Paying for material before it is received
4. Inability to prevent payments for duplicate invoices
5. Lost discounts caused by delays in processing invoices

Causes related to payments from customers

1. Inaccurate pricing of customer orders
2. Delays in producing customer invoices
3. Ineffective credit management, caused by an inability:
   a. To analyze customer payment statistics to determine trends
   b. To establish credit limits and perform credit checks
   c. To review past-due accounts that meet certain delinquency criteria
   d. To expedite overdue payments
   e. To charge interest on overdue payments
   f. To charge back customers that take unearned discounts on payments

Inability to Manage Payment Cycles to Optimize Cash Flow

Many vendors offer a discount ranging from 1/2 to 2 percent of the purchase price if the invoice is paid within a specified number of days. Typical invoice terms are 2 percent in ten, net 30. This means that a company may take a 2-percent discount if payment is made within ten days, or it may pay the net amount within 30 days.

The benefit of paying an invoice early should be balanced against the cost of money. Sometimes a company is better off paying the net amount in 30 days instead of taking a cash discount for early payment. Many companies are unable to evaluate every invoice to determine the optimal payment date. Often, companies pay early and take the offered discount even if it is not the best decision.

Solution

Provide the ability to calculate optimal payment dates.

Most MRP II Accounts Payable modules calculate the optimal payment date for each invoice by comparing the cash discount savings to the interest that is lost by paying the invoice early. This is illustrated in the following example:

Invoice date: 11/04/91

Payment terms: Discount of 1/2 percent if invoice is
    paid within 10 days, or net 30 days

Invoice amount: $5000

Annual cost of money: 12 percent

The company has the choice of either paying the invoice by 11/14/91 and taking the 1/2 percent discount or paying the total invoice amount by 12/04/91. The cash discount for prompt payment is:

$$0.005 \times \$5000 = \$25.00$$

If the invoice is paid within 10 days, 20 days of interest will be lost on $4975. This amounts to:

$$(0.12/365 \text{ days}) \times 20 \text{ days} \times \$4975 = \$32.71$$

Since the lost interest amount is greater than the cash discount amount, the optimum payment date is the net 30 days date of 12/04/91. This becomes the scheduled payment date.

While the difference of $7.71 may not seem significant, the total annual savings obtained from calculating the optimum payment date on thousands of invoices can be very significant indeed.

It is interesting to note that some MRP II Accounts Payable modules provide the ability to delay payment beyond the discount date and still take advantage of the cash discount. Some companies may want to use this feature to squeeze every last dollar out of their suppliers. I strongly advise companies *not* to use this feature because of the negative impact on vendor relations. Using this feature to take advantage of suppliers is totally contrary to the principles of JIT purchasing.

Inability to Predict Cash Requirements

Many companies are unable to predict accurately the amount of cash that is required to meet future payments to suppliers. The inability to accurately forecast cash requirements causes companies to plan conservatively and have more cash on hand than they may actually need. This causes companies to miss out on opportunities to apply cash more productively, such as long-term investments, capital equipment purchases, new hires, or research and development.

Solution   *Use the Cash Forecast Requirements Report.*

Some MRP II packages provide a Cash Forecast Requirements Report, also known as a Purchasing Commitment Report (Figure 7.1). This report provides both a summarized and a detailed time-phased analysis of a company's future cash requirements. The cash requirement is calculated by multiplying the purchase order line item balance due by the purchase order price. The cash requirement is time-phased; that is, it is placed in a weekly time bucket based on the scheduled or estimated payment date.[1] If the invoice has already been received, the scheduled payment date is used to time-phase the cash requirement. Otherwise the payment date is estimated from the scheduled delivery date. The scheduled delivery date should be calculated in the following manner:

If a ship promise date has been entered:
Scheduled Delivery Date = Ship Promise Date + Transit Time

If no ship promise date has been entered:
Scheduled Delivery Date = Due-on-Dock Date

Caveat   Some MRP II systems only provide an Invoice Aging Report to predict cash requirements. Such a report is only good for predicting short-term cash requirements. The Purchasing Commitment Report should include *all* open purchase orders, not just those that have outstanding invoices.

Paying for Material Before It Is Received

The opening scenario to this chapter describes how a company pays first and audits later to avoid losing cash discounts for prompt payment. In a perfect world where all vendors are trustworthy JIT trading partners, this approach works. In the real world, however, it is usually desirable to verify receipt prior to payment.

Solution   *Provide for electronic, three-way invoice matching.*

---

1. If a purchase order line item contains multiple ship schedules, the cash requirement is calculated and time-phased for each ship schedule.

••

Date: 06/03/91   Page: 01
                    Cash Forecast Requirements Report

Summary of Cash Requirements by Week ($M) for Week Ending:

06/07	06/14	06/21	06/28	07/05	07/12	07/19	07/26
8.2	11.2	9.4	8.7	7.2	11.2	3.6	4.5

08/02	08/09	08/16	08/23	08/30	09/06	09/13	09/20
11.2	23.1	10.3	9.2	7.2	6.5	6.8	8.5

09/27	10/04	10/11	10/18	10/25	11/01	11/08	11/15
6.3	5.3	5.3	2.3	4.3	4.2	3.2	2.2

11/22	11/29	12/06	12/13	12/27
2.1	1.3	.5	2.4	2.3

Cash Forecast Requirements Detail by Week

Week Ending: 06/07/91

Scheduled Pay Date	Invoice Number	PO Number	Vendor Code	Payment Amount
06/03/91	4030490	1S390293	38992	125.00
06/03/91	3892839	1C398023	23094	2034.00
06/03/91	3920391	1R390203	20303	1100.00
06/04/91	2901029	1C392032	19309	250.00
06/04/91	03203	1W390940	39039	52.00
06/04/91	392093	1S290305	20404	125.50
06/05/91	23423	1C346732	13669	2150.30
06/05/91	46573	1W460948	34656	49.95
06/05/91	323553	1S298905	23784	325.00
06/05/91	390434	1C346732	13669	150.00
06/06/91	2342	1W462245	45556	27.00
06/06/91	313456	1R345655	23784	1300.00
06/07/91	290434	1C346732	13669	150.00
06/07/91	323452	1S445255	24656	125.00
06/07/91	23342	1R342435	23253	200.35

Week Ending: 06/14/91

06/10/91	324442	1R345255	45656	123.00
06/10/91	None	1R335433	23454	230.30

••

Figure 7.1
*Cash Forecast Requirements
Report*

MRP II systems solve this problem by providing the ability to perform electronic three-way matching of invoices, packing slips, and purchase orders. This feature is discussed in Chapter 6.

Inability to Prevent Payments for Duplicate Invoices

If a vendor has not received payment within 30 days, the vendor often presumes that the original invoice was lost and submits a second invoice. Companies that do not have electronic invoice matching often end up paying both invoices. The problem is usually discovered (by the vendor) after the fact, and a credit is applied toward future purchases. Until the credit is used, the vendor enjoys the use of the company's cash.

Solution   *Provide the ability to detect duplicate invoices automatically.*

MRP II systems detect duplicate invoices at the time of on-line invoice data entry. If the invoice clerk attempts to enter an invoice number that is already in the system, the system will display an error message indicating that the invoice is a duplicate. The invoice clerk can then check the payment status of the original invoice and contact the vendor.

Lost Discounts Caused by Delays in Processing Invoices

For many companies, invoice matching is a manual task that is fraught with delays. Such delays can cause a company to lose discounts that would have been taken if invoices had been processed in a timely fashion.

Solutions   *Provide electronic invoice matching and electronic invoice signature approval.*

MRP II systems eliminate the delays associated with manual invoice matching by providing electronic invoice matching and the ability to perform electronic invoice signature approval. These features are discussed in Chapter 6.

Provide the ability to track lost discounts.

Some Accounts Payable modules capture information about cash discounts that were lost due to delays in invoice processing. The Lost Discounts Report (Figure 7.2) can help the Manager of Accounts Payable determine whether the lost discounts problem is costing the company enough money to justify some corrective action, such as hiring an additional invoice clerk.

Inaccurate Pricing of Customer Orders

Accurate pricing of customer orders is an important element of cash management. The Order Entry module provides seven features that help to ensure accurate pricing of customer orders:

••

```
Date: 06/17/91                                         Page: 01
                          Lost Discounts Report

Summary of Lost Discounts, Year to Date:

January                      102.23
February                     120.23
March                        193.11
April                        210.22
May                          203.22
June                          87.44

Year to Date Total:          916.45


Lost Discounts Detail for current month:

Payment    Invoice     PO      Vendor   Payment  Discount  Discount
Date       Number    Number     Code    Amount   Percent     Lost

06/03/91   329203   1C390232   20390    2340.00     1.0      23.40
06/05/91    30493   1R390293   23044     304.00      .5       1.52
06/06/91   230392   1C902094   10394    1580.00     2.0      31.60
06/11/91    21023   1R102934   20129     892.25     1.0       8.92
06/12/91   201293   1S329389   29048    1100.00     2.0      22.00
```

••

Figure 7.2
Lost Discounts Report

1. Automatic order pricing

2. Base pricing

3. Pricing by effectivity date

4. Pricing based on order date or ship date

5. Automatic repricing

6. Customer group pricing

7. Price tolerance parameters

These features are explained in detail in Chapter 5.

From a customer service perspective, these features are important because they help prevent customers from being charged too high a price. From a cash management perspective, these features are equally important because they help prevent customers from being charged too low a price, as illustrated in the following examples.

Example 1   A customer places an order for 100 pieces of a product that has the following price breaks:

Order Quantity	Unit Price
1	$150.00
25	$135.00
50	$120.00
100	$100.00

The order is priced at the $100.00 unit price by the automatic order pricing feature. A few weeks later, the customer reduces the order quantity to 50. The automatic repricing feature reprices the order at the $120.00 unit price. This prevents the customer from being charged too low a price when it is no longer entitled to the quantity discount.

Example 2   A new labor contract is scheduled to go into effect at a company on September 1. The company decides that all products shipped after September 15 should reflect the higher cost of direct labor. Accordingly, new pricing is entered in the product pricing file with an effectivity date of September 16. New customer orders with a shipment date later than September 15 will be automatically priced at the higher level. Existing customer orders with a shipment date later than September 15 will be automatically repriced.

Delays in Producing Customer Invoices

Delays in invoicing can have a serious impact on a company's cash position. Some companies produce invoices manually, and several days or weeks may elapse from the time an order is shipped until the time the invoice is generated.

Solution *Provide for automatic invoicing.*

The MRP II Order Entry module automatically produces an invoice when the shipment is reported to the system. Pricing is automatically verified at the time the invoice is created to ensure that price increases are included on the invoice (if pricing is based on date of shipment). Payment discount policies are automatically printed on the invoice to encourage early payment.

Ineffective Credit Management

Effective credit management is key to managing accounts receivables and reducing bad debts. To manage credit effectively, credit analysts need to have access to data about outstanding customer invoices and customer payment trends. Using this data, the credit analyst can set and adjust customer credit limits and do a more effective job of collecting payments.

The most common causes of ineffective credit management are as follows:

- Inability to establish credit limits and perform credit checks
- Inability to analyze customer payment statistics to determine trends
- Inability to review past-due accounts that meet certain delinquency criteria
- Inability to expedite overdue payments
- Inability to charge interest on overdue payments
- Inability to charge back customers that take unearned discounts on payments

The Accounts Receivable and Order Entry modules provide solutions to ineffective credit management. These solutions are explained below.

Solutions

Provide the ability to establish credit limits and perform credit checks.

The Accounts Receivable module allows the credit analyst to assign a credit limit to each customer. The Order Entry module in most MRP II systems is integrated with the Accounts Receivable module to perform automatic credit checking. When a customer order is entered, the system automatically calculates the total value of the customer order and adds it to the unbilled totals amount and accounts receivable amount to calculate the total credit exposure. This total is then compared to the credit limit that has been established for the customer. If the limit is exceeded, the order is automatically placed on credit hold. Otherwise the order is automatically approved and processed.

Some MRP II systems also allow the credit analyst to assign an order limit. If a customer order exceeds this limit, the order is automatically placed on hold for review by the credit analyst.

Changes to the accounts receivable balance, unbilled orders balance, order limit, and/or credit limit may require some open customer orders either to be placed on hold status or to be removed from hold status. This is done automatically by a daily batch update program that examines all open orders. This program automatically places orders on hold or removes orders from hold status, depending on how the customer's credit exposure has changed. For example, if a customer has made payments on account, it may be possible to remove an order from hold status.

Provide the ability to analyze customer payment data.

One of the primary goals of the credit analyst is to predict and prevent credit problems. Armed with the proper data, a professional credit analyst can determine unfavorable payment trends, which provide early warning signals about customers with financial problems. This gives the credit analyst time to take preventive action to minimize bad debts, such as lowering customer credit limits or putting shipments on hold.

As payments are applied to customer invoices, the Accounts Receivable module automatically captures data to help the credit analyst determine unfavorable payment trends. Payment statistics are shown by time period so that unfavorable trends can be detected easily.

Figure 7.3 is a Payment History Inquiry for the Clifton Supply Company. Payment statistics are displayed for the current quarter and the previous three quarters. From this inquiry, the credit analyst can make the following observations about the Clifton Supply Company's payment habits:

- The incidence of late payments has steadily increased during the last four quarters from 7 to 52 percent.

- The average number of days overdue has increased from 4 to 36 days.

- The discount amounts that have been charged back to the customer have increased from $125.00 in the first quarter to $620.00 in the last quarter.

- The highest credit amount occurring during a period increased from $25,234 to $67,290.

Clearly, an unfavorable payment trend has developed. Sensing possible impending financial troubles for the Clifton Supply Company,

```
Next Transaction: ___                                Date: 12/04/91
This Transaction: PHI                                Time: 11:15
                         Payment History Inquiry

Customer Code: 19039   Name: Clifton Supply Company
Credit Analyst: 002

                          Current    07/01/91-   04/01/91-   01/01/91-
                          Quarter    09/30/91    06/30/91    03/31/91

Sales                    133,245.20  152,356.34  142,353.23  133,454.55
Avg Days Early (Late)       (36.0)      (21.5)       (7.3)       (4.0)
Percent Late Payments         52.0        28.6        14.3         7.0
Discounts Taken            1,234.34    1,423.24    1,324.23    1,245.30
Discounts Charged Back       620.00      334.20      233.49      125.00
Highest Credit Amount     67,290.34   48,203.23   37,234.90   25,234.65
```

Figure 7.3
Payment History Inquiry Screen

● ●

```
Date: 06/17/91                                              Page: 01
                    Late Payments Exception Report
                     (Sorted by Customer Name)

Credit    Avg Days   Customer
Analyst   Overdue      Code     Customer Name

 003       32.3       29402     Albertson Equipment Corp.
 003       28.3       23909     General Drives Company
 003       31.2       49092     LBX Manufacturing
 003       23.4       24365     Modern Craft Machines
 003       39.0       29094     Peterson Industrial Supply
 003       28.4       29892     Standard Electric Motors
```

● ●

Figure 7.4
Late Payments Exception Report

the credit analyst may reduce the credit limit and place future shipments on hold until Clifton's financial situation stabilizes and all outstanding invoices have been paid. Without this data, the company may continue to extend credit to the Clifton Supply Company, and an enormous outstanding balance would exist if Clifton declares bankruptcy.

The MRP II Management Reporting System is often used to generate reports that help the credit analyst manage by exception. Figure 7.4 shows a report of all companies for credit analyst 003 that have an average number of days overdue greater than 20 days. Using this report as a starting point, the credit analyst can call up the Payment History Inquiry screen for each company on the report to access more detailed data about payment trends.

Provide the ability to review past-due accounts that meet certain delinquency criteria.

The Accounts Receivable module provides several ways for a credit analyst to review past-due accounts.

Aged Receivables Report
(Sorted by Customer Name)
Break on Credit Analyst

Credit Analyst: 001

Customer Code	Customer Name	Current	001-030 Past Due	031-060 Past Due	061-090 Past Due	091-120 Past Due	Over 120 Past Due	Total
12031	Action Manufacturing	3,043.00	324.25	230.50			50.00	3,647.75
13020	Bryerson Corp.	920.00	250.25		150.00			1,320.25
15029	Carpman Company	2,040.25	200.00	250.00		230.50		2,720.75
17902	Draper Industries		932.50	190.20	450.00		200.50	1,773.20
18920	Everest Mfg Corp	3,029.00	2,033.75	1,003.50	950.00			7,016.25
	Totals for Credit Analyst 001:	9,032.25	3,740.75	1,674.20	1,550.00	230.50	250.50	16,478.20

Figure 7.5
Aged Receivables Report

The Aged Receivables Report (Figure 7.5) shows accounts receivable amounts by aging category for every customer assigned to a credit analyst. This information can also be viewed on-line for a particular customer on the Customer Account Status Inquiry screen (Figure 7.6). The Customer Account Detail Inquiry screen (Figure 7.7) provides a detailed list of outstanding invoices within each aging category.

The MRP II Management Reporting System can be used to produce a report (Figure 7.8) that lists all outstanding invoices for an account, sorted in descending order by dollar-days (that is, by the product of the invoice amount times the number of days overdue). By prioritizing (sorting) overdue invoices in this manner, a $10,000 invoice that is 30 days overdue will be given a higher expediting priority than a $3,000 invoice that is 90 days overdue:

$$\$10,000 \times 30 \text{ Days} = 300,000 \text{ Dollar-Days}$$

$$\$\ 3,000 \times 90 \text{ Days} = 270,000 \text{ Dollar-Days}$$

```
Next Transaction: ___                              Date: 12/04/91
This Transaction: CAS                              Time: 11:15
  ⁏               Customer Account Status Inquiry

Customer Code: 18920              Name: Everest Mfg Corp

Credit Analyst: 001

Account Receivable Status:

            001-030    031-060    061-090    091-120   Over 120      Total
Current     Past Due   Past Due   Past Due   Past Due  Past Due     Amt Due

3,029.00    2,033.75   1,003.50    950.00                          7,016.25


Credit Limit:     $20,000         Order Limit:     $2,000
Unbilled Orders:   5,250.00
Total Exposure:   12,266.25
Available Credit:  7,733.75
```

Figure 7.6
Customer Account Status Inquiry Screen

```
Next Transaction: ___                            Date: 12/04/91
This Transaction: CAD                            Time: 11:17
                     Customer Account Detail Inquiry

Customer Code: 18920          Name: Everest Mfg Corp

Credit Analyst: 001           Aging Category Selected: 001-030 Days Past Due

Total Amount Due in Aging Category: 2,033.75

Invoice    Customer                          Item    Invoice    Days
Number     PO Number    Part Number          Amount  Date       Past Due

192032     302930       ADL390293            239.00  10/09/91   25
192134     302930       MBL234292            144.50  10/14/91   20
192234     304902       JSL390343            223.25  10/16/91   18
193220     312340       MAL392340            250.00  10/19/91   15
193468     323560       EL335694             200.00  10/22/91   12
194782     303532       ADL324397            385.00  10/26/91   8
195700     323650       SNG389594            289.00  10/29/91   5
196056     324575       ADL234653            303.00  10/30/91   4
```

Figure 7.7
Customer Account Detail Inquiry Screen

The credit analyst can use all the above reports and inquiries to expedite payment of delinquent accounts.

Provide the ability to automatically produce dunning letters.

The Accounts Receivable module helps to automate the collection of past-due payments by producing dunning letters to customers. The dunning letter includes a message requesting payment and a list of overdue invoices. The following information is listed for each overdue invoice:

- Invoice number

- Invoice date

- Customer's purchase order number

- Amount due

- Number of days past due

Most MRP II systems allow credit analysts to establish their own dunning policies for the accounts they manage. The dunning policy defines when a customer will receive a dunning letter and what message will be printed at the top of the letter. Most systems allow each credit analyst to define at least five different dunning categories. Accounts are automatically classified into dunning categories based on the age of the oldest past-due invoice.

The credit analyst can define a customized dunning letter message for each dunning category. For example, if the oldest past-due invoice is between 15 and 30 days overdue, the message on the dunning letter may be a polite reminder (Category 1):

"Your account is more than 15 days past due. Please remit payment promptly."

If the oldest past-due invoice is between 30 and 60 days overdue, the dunning message may read (Category 2):

"You have not responded to our previous letter regarding your account, which is now more than 30 days past due. Please remit payment immediately."

• •

```
Date: 06/03/91                                             Page: 01
                  Overdue Invoices Exception Report
          (Sorted in Descending Order by Dollar-Days Past Due)
                     Account: Major Electronics
```

Invoice Number	Customer PO	Part Number	Item Amount	Days Past Due	Dollar-Days Past Due
234432	345430	ADL390293	259.00	25	6475.00
345434	234543	BJL239090	120.00	50	6000.00
239409	230490	EL290394	150.00	35	5250.00
234090	204905	JSL390209	38.00	120	4560.00
229090	208938	MBL239045	269.00	15	4035.00
234893	204590	ADL234045	113.00	25	2825.00
230590	304038	MBL394050	83.00	28	2324.00
204859	345234	ADL302340	150.00	10	1500.03
109840	209409	REL390293	10.00	93	930.00
809820	345093	EL048945	13.50	39	526.50
349800	345039	ADL453897	3.50	103	360.50

• •

Figure 7.8
Overdue Invoices Exception Report

If the oldest past-due invoice is more than 60 days overdue, the dunning message may read (Category 3):

"You have not responded to our previous two letters regarding your account, which is more than 60 days past due. We are withholding further shipments until your account is settled. Please settle your account immediately."

If the oldest past-due invoice is more than 90 days overdue, the dunning message may read (Category 4):

"Fourth and final notice! Your account is more than 90 days past due. Unless full payment is received within 10 days, we will take appropriate legal action to collect payment."

Dunning policies are defined on-line by the credit analyst. In Figure 7.9, the credit analyst has defined a dunning policy for the

---

```
Next Transaction: ___                                    Date: 12/19/91
This Transaction: CDP                                    Time: 02:35
                          Create Dunning Policy

Credit Analyst: 001    Dunning Category: 01

Range for Oldest Past-Due Invoice:

Minimum Days Past Due:  15 Days   Maximum Days Past Due:  30 Days


Dunning Message:

Your account is more than 15 days past due.  Please remit payment promptly.
```

Figure 7.9
Create Dunning Policy Screen

first dunning category. A Category 1 dunning letter will be automatically printed when the oldest past-due invoice is more than 15 days overdue but less than 30 days overdue.

Provide the ability to charge interest on overdue payments automatically.

Some Accounts Receivable modules provide the option to automatically charge interest to customers on past-due payments. The credit manager establishes an annual interest rate. Each month, the system calculates a finance charge for each invoice as follows:

Finance Charge =
(Annual Interest Rate ÷ 365) × Number of Days Past Due

The system adds together all the individual invoice finance charges to calculate the total finance charge, which will appear on a monthly account statement.

Provide the ability to charge back unearned discounts automatically.

Even though it is not ethical, some customers remit payment after the discount date and still take the discount for prompt payment. However, the Accounts Receivable module detects unearned discounts. When payments are entered into the system, the discount amount is entered, and the system automatically determines whether the discount was earned by comparing the payment date to the discount date. Unearned discounts are automatically charged back to the customer as a line item on the next invoice that is produced.

Summary

Table 7.1 summarizes the causes of and solutions to the poor cash management problems that were discussed in this chapter.

Table 7.1
Summary of Causes of and Solutions to Poor Cash
Management

Cause	MRP II Solution
1. Inability to manage payment cycles to optimize cash flow	Provide the ability to calculate optimum payment dates.
2. Inability to predict cash requirements	Use the Cash Requirements Forecast Report.
3. Paying for material before it is received	Provide for electronic, three-way invoice matching.
4. Inability to prevent payments for duplicate invoices	Provide the ability to detect duplicate invoices automatically.
5. Lost discounts caused by delays in processing invoices	Provide for: - Electronic, three-way invoice matching - Electronic invoice signature approval - The ability to track lost discounts
6. Inaccurate pricing of customer orders	Provide for: - Automatic order pricing - Base pricing - Pricing by effectivity date - Pricing based on order date or ship date - Automatic repricing - Customer group pricing - Price tolerance parameters
7. Delays in producing customer invoices	Provide for automatic invoice generation at the time the shipment is reported.
8. Ineffective credit management, caused by an inability: - To establish credit limits and perform credit checks - To analyze customer payment statistics to determine trends - To review past-due accounts that meet certain delinquency criteria - To expedite overdue payments - To charge interest on overdue payments - To charge back customers that take unearned discounts on payments	Provide: - The ability to establish credit limits and perform credit checks - The ability to analyze customer payment data by time period - The Aged Receivables Report, Customer Account Status Inquiry, Customer Account Detail Inquiry, and the Management Reporting System help the credit analyst review past-due accounts - The ability to produce dunning letters - The ability to charge interest to customers on overdue payments automatically - The ability to verify discounts and charge back unearned discounts automatically

The Software Vendor: Ally or Adversary?

The Software Vendor's Agenda

In your battle to solve your business problems, are software vendors your allies or your adversaries?

When you are in the evaluation phase of an MRP II project, your goal is to select the best solution for your business problems. However, software vendors have a different agenda: They want to sell you *their* solutions, whether or not they are the best solutions. This complicates the evaluation process, because no software vendor is going to volunteer information that will hurt the chance of winning your business. It's up to you to determine whether or not a particular package meets your business needs. No software vendor is going to grab your arm as you are about to sign the contract and say, "Before you sign that, let me tell you about several things that you didn't ask about that make our system a poor fit for your business environment."

It's easy to be misled into treating software vendors as allies, because they are "so helpful." MRP II software vendors will always be eager to help you develop your request for proposal (RFP) and to conduct a survey of your business needs. This gives vendors an ideal opportunity to slant the RFP toward the strengths of their products (and toward the weaknesses of the competitors' products). In the three years that I worked for an MRP II software company, we never lost an evaluation in which we "helped" write the RFP for the customer. In fact, we won many evaluations in which we did *not* have the best solution for the customer. Conversely, we never won an evaluation in which the RFP had been prepared by our competition, even when we *did* have the best solution for the customer. *The more help you accept from a software vendor, the less likely you are to select the best solution to your business problems.*

This is not to say that software vendors don't care about your success. Software vendors want you to have a successful implementation. Every vendor needs a certain number of good references, but most vendors will happily sell you a product that you either do not need or cannot use if you are willing to spend the money.

The Art of Passive Misrepresentation

My experiences both as a user of packaged software and as a consultant for a software company have taught me that, as long as software vendors do not actively misrepresent their products, they run very little risk of being sued or having to refund money to dissatisfied customers. This is because most companies that spend $200,000 to $500,000 on software are extremely reluctant to admit to *anyone* that they made a mistake.

Because software vendors know that they will avoid trouble unless they make a false statement about their products, some vendors use **passive misrepresentation** (lies of omission) to sell their products.

Passive misrepresentation is the art of leading a prospect to believe something that isn't true without actually making a false statement about the product. Software vendors consider this to be "showing the product in the best possible light." Others might call it deception or white-lying.

Passive misrepresentation can be as simple as answering a question with a factually correct but incomplete answer, such as:

Customer: "Does your system have a cycle counting feature?"
Vendor: "Yes."

The more complete answer—the one you don't hear—is:

Vendor: "Yes, we have cycle counting, but none of our customers has been able to use this feature because it is not designed properly."

Some forms of passive misrepresentation are more subtle (and more deceptive). Sometimes software vendors tell two truths that add up to one lie. For example, one software vendor often uses two consultants to present its MRP II system. One consultant presents the Manufacturing system and the other presents the Purchasing system. Both consultants truthfully describe the capabilities of each system. However, the Purchasing consultant fails to mention that, because of the way the two products were integrated, some important features in the Purchasing system cannot be used when the two products are used together. Both consultants tell the truth about the individual capabilities of the products, but neither consultant addresses the integration issues.

The four most common types of passive misrepresentation used by software vendors are as follows:

- Marketing materials (brochures, slide presentations, etc.)
- Vendor responses to questions about their products
- Naming conventions (the use of misleading names to describe certain data fields or product features)
- Software vendor product demonstrations

Each of these types of passive misrepresentation is examined in more detail in the following subsections.

Marketing Materials

Marketing materials are prime examples of passive misrepresentation. Software vendors know that the best way to sell an intangible product is to give customers something tangible that describes the product. Slick sales brochures, printed on glossy paper that feels and smells good, can work wonders for an old, batch-oriented software package. Computer-based presentations, with animation and carefully crafted scenarios, can obscure the deficiencies of a bad product.

Product Brochures

You should read product brochures primarily to determine what *isn't* in the system, not what *is* in the system. This requires the skill and experience to read between the lines.

For example, one vendor's MRP II product brochure discusses many of the system's on-line inquiry capabilities, with no mention about the system's realtime update capabilities. The vendor wants you to infer that the system has full realtime update capability when, in fact, it does not.

Another vendor's brochure devotes seven pages to a detailed discussion the capabilities of the Material Requirements Planning module, with no mention of whether the system is a bucketed or a bucketless planning system. The vendor wants you to infer that the system is bucketless when, in fact, the system plans in weekly time buckets.

Product brochures rarely address integration issues. The brochures describe the capabilities of the individual software modules, but they do not mention any features that cannot be used when the modules are integrated.

Carefully read any brochures given to you by software vendors, but read them as a detective would and don't assume anything. Make a list of important features that are *not* mentioned, and verify whether or not these features are present.

Vaporware

A consultant for one software vendor describes selling software as "the art of talking about what you don't have and may never have in order to sell what you do have." Software companies are infamous for presenting **vaporware**, which is the industry term for software that is not currently deliverable. During the sales cycle, the vendor may present both current and future deliverables, and the distinction between the two is often (deliberately) vague.

Vendors spend many thousands of dollars developing marketing materials, and they cannot afford to develop new materials every year. Therefore, in the promotional literature, some vendors include *all* the capabilities that they hope to add to their products over the next few years. These capabilities are presented as if they are currently available when, in fact, they are not. This distinction is often lost during the sales cycle, especially if a future deliverable is one of your critical requirements. If development plans change, as they often do, some features described in the marketing materials may never be delivered.

Before you make a purchase decision, you should develop a list of your critical requirements and review it with the vendor to make certain that the features you need are currently available. If a critical feature is not available, ask the vendor to guarantee a delivery date in the contract. If the vendor is unwilling to do so, it is unlikely that the feature will ever be available.

Personal-Computer-Based Presentations

In the last few years, software vendors have incorporated personal-computer-based presentation software into their product demonstrations. These software packages enable software vendors to develop presentations with graphics, animation, and sound, adding glitz and sizzle but little substance to the presentations. As one software consultant wryly observed, "The software that we use to talk about our software is better than our software." Customers are so impressed with these "Star Wars" presentations that they often fail to evaluate the software package thoroughly.

Vendors Responses to Questions

Software vendors hire and train system consultants to demonstrate their software. Many of these consultants are highly skilled in the art of passive misrepresentation. An experienced consultant can respond affirmatively to most questions without making a false statement about the product. Unless your questions are *extremely* specific, the consultant will usually be able to give you the answer you want to hear. When you discover the truth later on, the consultant can say that he misunderstood the intent of your question.

You can avoid this problem by asking specific, carefully worded questions. Never begin a question with the word "can." (Software vendors *love* questions that begin with this word. Can the system generate this type of report? Can the system do this? Can the system do that?) A consultant can think of a creative way that a system *can* do just about anything. One consultant jokingly says that he would answer "Yes" if a prospect asked, "Can your Accounts Payable system solve world hunger?" His reasoning: If you used the Accounts Payable system to cut enough checks, you could indeed solve world hunger. After all, he reasons, the prospect didn't ask, "*Does* your Accounts Payable system solve world hunger?"

To reduce the chances of the system consultant misinterpreting your questions, either intentionally or unintentionally, I offer the following advice:

- Tell the vendor's consultant up front that you plan to eliminate the vendor *immediately* if you have any reason to believe that his answers to your questions are misleading. A division of Northern Rockwell uses a very effective approach. Before they allow a software vendor to begin a presentation, they hold up a picture of a bull with a line through it. Most vendors heed the message; those that don't are never asked to make a second presentation.

- Ask detailed, specific questions. Never begin a question with the word "can." Where possible, ask questions that require quantitative answers. Instead of asking, "Does your system have realtime update capabilities?," tell the vendor, "Please provide us with a list of all on-line transactions that *do not* perform realtime updating."

- Ask the same question several different ways and listen for discrepancies in the answers.

- Probe any vague answers with specific follow-up questions. If you still don't understand the answer, ask the vendor to demonstrate the feature.

- Turn off your "happy ears" when the vendor arrives. Don't be so eager to believe that the vendor has a solution to your business problems that you fail to listen carefully and probe for details.

Naming Conventions

Software vendors sometimes give an inappropriate name to a data field or product feature to show their product in the best possible light. This is illustrated in the following examples:

Inappropriate name for a data field. One software vendor describes its inventory system as being able to support a multiwarehouse environment. Indeed, the inventory detail record has a data field called WAREHOUSE, and the system does allow a part to be stored in a location within a warehouse. In that sense, the system supports a multiwarehouse environment.

However, the system is not designed for a true multiwarehouse environment. For example, the system will allocate materials automatically *from more than one warehouse* to satisfy the requirements of a manufacturing order. This may not be a problem if the warehouses are physically next to each other, but if one warehouse is in Pittsburgh and another is in Atlanta, it is not practical to issue six pieces from the Pittsburgh warehouse and four pieces from the Atlanta warehouse to satisfy a requirement for ten pieces. In reality, the system supports having *multiple stockrooms within a single warehouse.* A more appropriate name for the data field would have been STOCKROOM, because people generally understand the term "stockroom" to be an entity within a warehouse. Unfortunately, some customers that have multiple warehouses have purchased the system believing that it was designed to operate in a multiwarehouse environment.

In the strictest sense, the software company is not misrepresenting the system as a multiwarehouse system. Rather it has chosen to define the term "warehouse" to suit its marketing purposes.

Inappropriate name for a feature. All MRP II software packages provide an engineering change control feature in the Bill of Materials module. To most people, the term "engineering change control" implies a system that is capable of electronic entry, notification, tracking, approval, and implementation of engineering changes. In reality, most MRP II systems only support the implementation of engineering changes that have already been approved outside the system. What MRP II software vendors refer to as "engineering change control" is the ability to enter engineering change numbers and effectivity dates on bills of materials. This capability is extremely important, but it is not what most people would consider to be an engineering change control subsystem.

Product Demonstrations

The software vendor has the buyer at an immediate disadvantage during the sales cycle because the consultant knows the product better than the customer does. A system consultant will spend thousands of hours learning the product; you will spend a few dozen hours at most evaluating it. Consultants can use their knowledge to manipulate the prospect. They can skillfully lead you away from the product's weaknesses and toward its strengths.

Software vendors try to keep product demonstrations as short as possible to minimize the possibility of something going wrong. Some vendors use high-caliber consultants to compensate for mediocre products. The most effective consultant I know rarely gives a demonstration. He shows the customer a screen from each module and talks about the capabilities of each module for about ten minutes. His presentation skills are so good that, at the end of an hour and a half, the prospect is convinced he has seen a demonstration, when all he has actually seen was about ten screens. The customer walks away impressed with the system when, in reality, he was impressed with the consultant. Unfortunately, software companies deliver source code, not consultants.

Product demonstrations conducted by software vendors reveal very little about the weaknesses of a product. If the software lacks realtime functionality, for example, the consultant will demonstrate the flow of the system up to point A, where a batch run is required, and pick up the demonstration at point B, where the batch run is completed, without missing a beat. The demonstration data may be designed to make it appear as if there was no batch run between point A and point B. Unless you are very observant or unless you ask, you will never know that a batch run is required during normal system operation.

All systems have bugs, but you will rarely see one in a demonstration conducted by a vendor. The consultant knows what works and what doesn't, as well as how to avoid any transactions that would expose any system problems.

Product demonstrations are an important part of the evaluation process, but they should not be performed by the software vendor. You should insist that the vendor allow *you* to perform a hands-on benchmark test that simulates the system's operation in your environment. Software vendors don't like customers to perform benchmarks, because they are expensive to support and they expose the weaknesses of a system. Some vendors have lost business due to problems that came to light during such a test. However, only this type of demonstration will give you a true idea of what the system can and cannot do.

Controlling the Sales/Evaluation Cycle

Your evaluation cycle is the software vendor's sales cycle. If you are in control, you will buy the best solution to your business problems. If the vendor is in control, you will buy the best marketed solution.

How the Vendor Seeks to Gain Control

The software vendor will try to gain control of the sales cycle by doing the following things:

- Eliminate the competition early in the evaluation cycle
- Sell high
- Develop an inside sponsor
- Control the evaluation schedule
- Define the evaluation criteria
- Avoid a detailed evaluation

Eliminate the Competition

The last thing a software vendor wants is a competitive evaluation. Software vendors will use a variety of tactics to try to eliminate the competition early in the evaluation cycle.

One approach that software vendors use to eliminate competition is to influence the choice of the database management system. When I worked for Management Science America (MSA), one of our strongest competitors was Cullinet (now a division of Computer Associates). Cullinet has an excellent MRP II system, but it only operates under Cullinet's own database management system, IDMS. MSA's MRP II system operated under IDMS, but it also ran under other database management systems, such as IBM's IMS and Applied Data Research's DATACOM/DB product. MSA's ability to run under these other database management systems gave MSA a competitive edge over Cullinet. If the customer did not already have a database management system, MSA would try to influence the customer's technical people to select either IMS or DATACOM/DB. Where MSA was successful in doing this, Cullinet was eliminated before the evaluation for application software even began!

Another tactic used by software vendors is to influence the choice of the hardware platform. One MRP II software vendor supports two different hardware platforms but has far less competition on one platform than the other. This vendor tries to eliminate the competition by influencing customers to select the platform on which there is less competition.

A third tactic that software vendors use to eliminate the competition is to position a unique product feature as a critical requirement. This is called "creating an issue." One of MSA's competitors (Cullinet), was very skilled at creating an issue out of multiplant. **Multiplant** is a term used to describe those features in an MRP II system that are designed to help manufacturers control multiplant operations. Cullinet had some unique capabilities in this area. When Cullinet was in control of the sales cycle, it was able to convince the customer that multiplant was a critical requirement. It didn't matter if the customer had only one physical plant—Cullinet would sell the customer on the advantages of using the multiplant feature to set up several logical plants within one physical plant. Cullinet's ability to create an issue out of multiplant put MSA on the defensive throughout the sales cycle. Instead of selling the strong points of its system, MSA had to concentrate on selling around the multiplant issue. Unfortunately, once multiplant became a critical requirement in the customer's eyes, MSA was unable to overcome the advantage that Cullinet had established.

If all else fails, a software vendor may try to use fear and uncertainty to eliminate a competitor. This is often done by providing the customer with negative publicity about a competitor, such as reports of financial losses or lawsuits that have been filed against a competitor. Sometimes a vendor will offer to show you a list of "competitive knockoffs." However, it is unwise to buy software from a company that uses negative selling techniques. Vendors who say negative things about their competitors generally do so because they don't have a good product to say positive things about.

Sell High

Another technique that software vendors use to control the sales cycle is to sell high within the customer's organization. Software vendors want to sell to upper management for two reasons:

1. Software vendors want to deal directly with decision makers. Only upper management can authorize the expenditure of funds.

2. Upper management does a superficial job of evaluating software, because they don't have the time, inclination, or knowledge to perform an in-depth software evaluation. Superficial evaluations are to the vendor's advantage because they reveal none of the product's deficiencies.

Develop an Inside Sponsor

Early in the sales cycle, the software vendor will try to identify a sponsor within your organization. The sponsor is usually a decision maker or a person who wields considerable influence over a decision maker. This contact is carefully cultivated as an inside source of information. The sponsor provides the vendor with information about the competition, along with other information that will help the vendor win the business.

Control the Evaluation Schedule

The software vendor will try to develop and coax you to agree on an evaluation schedule. The schedule of evaluation activities will seem fair and thorough, but it will not permit enough time for you to evaluate other solutions. If the vendor can talk you into an evaluation schedule, his chances of winning the business are extremely good.

Define the Evaluation Criteria

Software vendors do not like to respond to requests for proposals (RFPs). However, if you insist on writing an RFP, software vendors will offer to survey your business requirements and help you write the RFP. This enables vendors to bias the RFP toward their solution.

Avoid a Detailed Evaluation

Software vendors want to avoid in-depth evaluations because such evaluations prolong the sales cycle and are likely to expose weaknesses in the product. If a software vendor is controlling the sales cycle, the customer will see only a very high-level demonstration of the software. Such demonstrations do little more than confirm that the software exists. A more detailed evaluation is necessary to determine if the system is designed properly and has the features you need to solve your business problems.

How You Can Maintain Control

Here is how your company can remain in control of the evaluation phase:

Do not allow a software vendor to help you select a database management system or hardware platform, or to help define your requirements. The vendor will have an ulterior motive in providing any assistance. If you accept the vendor's assistance, you will probably end up buying that package.

Determine what features you need to solve your business problems, and make certain that they are designed properly and described truthfully. Use this book to help you identify your critical requirements.

Educate your MRP project team before you begin the evaluation phase. Some companies allow software vendors to educate the project team as part of the evaluation process. However, a software vendor is less likely to be able to position a unique feature as a critical requirement if your project team understands the requirements *before* they begin evaluating software.

Do not allow a vendor to gain an undue amount of influence within your organization. There is an old saying in the software industry: "People buy from people they like." Software vendors are not really in the software business; they are in the people business. They will try to win your business by establishing personal relationships with key decision makers and people of influence in your organization. Force vendors to compete on the merits of their software and not on the quality of their contacts.

Develop a detailed evaluation schedule that gives you ample time to evaluate at least three MRP II packages. Drive vendors to adhere to *your* schedule. Vendors may deliberately try to prolong the sales cycle if they feel that they are losing in the evaluation and need time to gain lost ground. This is seldom in the best interest of the buyer.

Perform a detailed evaluation. Don't base your decision on a product demonstration conducted by the software vendor. Conduct your own exhaustive, hands-on benchmark test.

Summary

Software vendors want their customers to be successful, but they are not your allies during the evaluation phase of an MRP II product. If you need any further convincing, ask a software vendor to provide you with a copy of its standard contract. Most software vendors insist on payment terms of 90 percent at contract signing, 10 percent on delivery of tapes. Software vendors will negotiate price and support, but they will almost never negotiate payment terms. They want their money up front, because your *real* education begins *after* you take delivery of the software!

Software vendors will not deliberately misrepresent their products, but they will do everything possible to show their products in the best possible light. A healthy degree of skepticism will help you to select the best solution for your business problems.

Multiplant: Solution in Search of a Problem?

By the early 1980s, the MRP II software market had become extremely competitive. One of the ways that MRP II software vendors responded to increased competition was by adding differentiating features to their products. One MRP II vendor led all others in one particular area of functionality. This vendor was the first to offer a multiplant MRP II system, that is, a system designed specifically for companies that have multiple manufacturing sites. This MRP II software vendor exploited its competitive advantage in this area so skillfully that it was often successful in creating a demand for a solution when there was no problem. Overnight, multiplant became a critical requirement for any company evaluating MRP II software packages. Even companies that had only one plant wanted a multiplant MRP II system, in case they ever decided to become a multiplant operation.

Multiplant: A Carefully Chosen Misnomer

Much of the confusion surrounding multiplant MRP II has been caused by the use of the term "multiplant." The collection of features commonly referred to as multiplant should really be referred to as **interplant control**. Interplant control is a more appropriate name because these features are designed to help manufacturers control multiplant environments in which there is a significant amount of interplant activity. The fact is, there are many companies that have multiple plants that really don't need a multiplant MRP II system.

For example, consider a large corporation comprised of several independent, unrelated divisions that happen to share a common, regional data processing center. The key words here are *independent* and *unrelated*. These divisions share a corporate logo and data processing center, but they have nothing else in common. Each division has its own manufacturing facility, makes a different product, and operates as a separate company. However, because the divisions share a corporate logo and data center, they decide to standardize operations on one MRP II system.

This is where the confusion begins, aided and abetted by software vendors that sell multiplant MRP II. This corporation does *not* require multiplant (interplant control) because there is no interaction between the plants. However, confusion over the term "multiplant," fostered by MRP II software vendors that use multiplant as a product differentiator, has led such companies to believe that they need a multiplant MRP II system.

Some multiplant manufacturers have a significant level of interplant activity, but they still do not require a multiplant MRP II system. Consider a company that has four manufacturing facilities all located in the same city. The company manufactures one product line. Three of the plants produce subassemblies and ship them to the fourth plant, where all final assembly takes place. All interplant shipments are handled by company trucks, and the in-transit time between plants is less than a day. Material control and planning for all four plants is performed centrally at the final assembly plant.

Clearly, the plants in this example are dependent and related. There is a tremendous amount of interplant activity in this company. However, the company does not require multiplant software, because all four plants function *logically* as a single plant. All four plants are managed by one centralized organization. The three subassembly plants are treated logically as work centers within a single facility. The in-transit time between plants is treated as move time after the final operation on a routing.

The True Multiplant Manufacturer

Multiplant MRP II systems are designed to help true multiplant manufacturers manage interplant activity. A true multiplant manufacturer is one that meets the following criteria:

- The plants are too far apart to be managed logically as one plant (i.e., work centers within a single facility).

- There is a significant amount of interplant activity. Interplant relationships may be simple, with several feeder plants producing subassemblies for one final assembly plant. Or, they may be more complex, with each plant doing some subassembly and final assembly work.

- Each plant has a high degree of autonomy. As a minimum, each plant is responsible for planning and controlling material that is used locally. Each plant may have its own Master Production Schedule, but this is not a requirement.

- In-transit times for interplant shipments are several weeks. This is common in companies that produce subassemblies overseas and do final assembly domestically.

- Parts and assemblies may be manufactured concurrently in more than one plant.

- A part or assembly that is produced in more than one plant may have a different bill of materials and routing in each plant. This is because different plants may have different process capabilities.

- There is a strong desire on the part of management *not* to manage each plant as a separate business entity (i.e., profit/loss center). If each plant sells a significant percentage of its output to external customers, it may be desirable to treat each plant as a separate business entity.

The last criterion is extremely important. If each plant operates as a separate profit/loss center, the most appropriate way to handle interplant transactions is to establish a buyer/vendor relationship between plants. In other words, the best solution for some multiplant manufacturers is to use the tried and proven Purchasing/Order Entry approach to manage interplant transactions. With this approach, plant A places a purchase order on plant B. Plant B treats the purchase order as a customer order and enters it into their order entry system. Plant B acts as a vendor to plant A. This approach allows plant B to operate as a separate profit/loss center.

Many large companies have operated in this manner for decades. GE purchasing departments place purchase orders on external vendors and allied vendors (other GE product departments). In fact, GE has a formal policy that allows buyers to purchase a competitor's product if the external vendor quotes a lower price than the allied vendor. This rarely happens, but it is possible, for example, to purchase a General Electric appliance that has a Westinghouse motor.

A company that meets the criteria for a true multiplant manufacturing environment can still use the tried and proven buyer/vendor approach to manage interplant transactions. However, some companies believe that the buyer/vendor approach is philosophically counter to establishing close relationships between plants. Such companies may want to consider a multiplant MRP II package.

Interplant Control

There is no standard approach to designing a multiplant MRP II system. The most popular design approach to multiplant MRP II is to provide a separate database for each plant and to link the plant databases by means of an Interplant Control module (Figure B.1). The Interplant Control module manages all interplant transactions. The two basic components of this module are interplant demand planning and interplant shipment control.

Interplant Demand Planning

Conventional MRP II systems recognize two types of supply orders: manufacturing orders and purchase orders. True multiplant manufacturers require a third type of supply order: the **interplant order**. An interplant order is an order placed by one plant, known as the **using plant** or **receiving plant**, to another plant, known as the **supply plant** or **shipping plant**. An interplant order is similar to a purchase order, except that it is processed by the Interplant Control module instead of the Purchasing module.

Figure B.2 shows a typical multiplant environment, with three supply (shipping) plants producing subassemblies for one using (receiving) plant. All final assembly is done at the using plant.

Viewed from the perspective of the using plant, an interplant order is a supply order. Viewed from the perspective of the supply

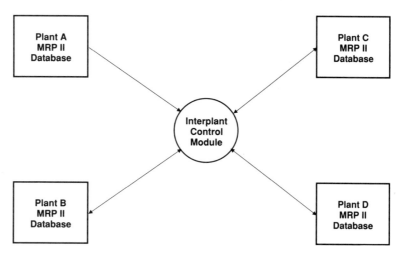

Figure B.1
Multiplant MRP II Database Design

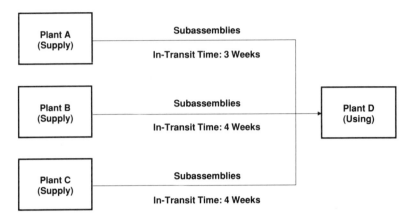

Figure B.2
Typical Multiplant Environment

plant, an interplant order is a requirement. The Interplant Control module functions as an Electronic Data Interchange module that passes interplant demand from the using plant's MRP II database to the supply plant's MRP II database. Interplant demand can be treated either as independent demand or as dependent demand by the supply plant. If the supply plant has its own Master Production Schedule, the requirement is entered into the supply plant's MPS module as independent demand. Otherwise the requirement is entered into the supply plant's Material Requirements Planning module as dependent demand.

Figure B.3 shows interplant demand being passed to supply plants B and C. Plant B has its own Master Production Schedule. Plant C is driven from plant A's Master Production Schedule.

There is no right or wrong way to process interplant demand. The decision to treat interplant demand as independent or dependent demand is a management philosophy decision. Strong arguments can be made for and against both approaches.

The interplant demand planning function should be designed to allow the using and supply plants to assign different part numbers to the same item. This situation often occurs when a company acquires one of its suppliers. The interplant demand planning function should provide the ability to cross-reference part numbers automatically between the using and supply plants. Thus, the interplant order transaction should carry both the using plant and the supply plant part numbers.

Companies that have capacity constraints may produce the same subassembly concurrently in more than one plant. Such companies

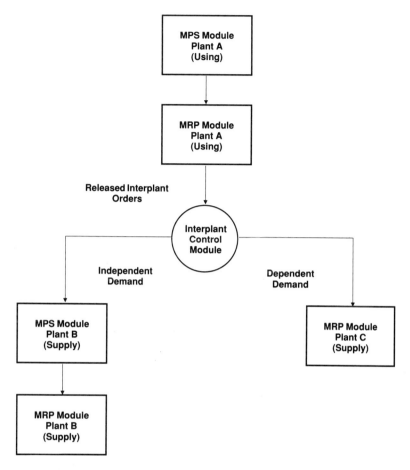

Figure B.3
Interplant Demand Planning

may require an interplant demand planning system that is capable of splitting demand quantities between plants automatically in accordance with predefined percentages. (This feature is similar to the feature in a Purchasing module that would split a requisition quantity among multiple vendors.)

Some companies may need the ability to perform interplant demand planning based on effectivity dates. If the primary supply plant is shut down for a period of time, this feature can be used to plan demand on an alternate supply plant during that period.

Interplant Shipment Control

Because of the large number of interplant shipments and long in-transit times, true multiplant manufacturers may need to perform interplant shipment planning and in-transit inventory tracking. Interplant shipment planning allows the shipping plant to consolidate many interplant orders into one economical shipment that meets specified volume and weight constraints. In-transit inventory tracking provides the receiving plant with visibility to detailed information about each shipment, including the date of shipment and expected arrival date.

Do You Really Need Multiplant?

Before you decide to implement a multiplant MRP II system, evaluate your company against the criteria for a true multiplant manufacturer. Even if your company meets all these criteria, consider using the buyer/vendor approach to managing multiplant operations. Ask yourself the following questions:

- *Do you really need interplant demand planning?* An interplant order is, after all, a purchase order in disguise. Maybe you really don't need another type of supply order.

- *Do you really need interplant shipment control?* Maybe you really don't need more information about interplant shipments than you have about shipments from external vendors.

If you decide to implement multiplant MRP II, examine the multiplant solutions closely. Some multiplant designs have serious limitations. For example, some multiplant MRP II packages are designed to work only in centralized computing environments, in which all plants operate off one huge mainframe computer. This approach usually is not feasible in true multiplant environments, because the plants are located too far from one another to share computing resources economically and reliably.

The time zone difference between two or more plants may also make it impossible to share computing resources, because some MRP II systems do not allow on-line and batch processing to be performed concurrently. This means that the on-line system must be powered down overnight to allow nightly batch processing. If there is a 12-hour time difference between plants, batch processing is not feasible. The on-line system must be up 24 hours a day, because one plant's night is another plant's day.

Also, bear in mind that multiplant MRP II packages are difficult to develop and support. One MRP II vendor tried for five years to develop a multiplant version of its MRP II system before it abandoned the project all together.

Look for simple, proven solutions before you decide that a complex, multiplant MRP II system is necessary. For most companies, multiplant MRP II is a complex solution in search of a problem that has already been solved with the Purchasing, Order Entry, and Electronic Data Interchange modules of an MRP II system. Prior to EDI, two objections to using the buyer/vendor approach were the administrative cost of placing purchase orders and the time required to mail purchase orders from one plant to another. EDI has solved both problems neatly by making it possible to place interplant purchase orders without ever producing a piece of paper.

In the 1990s, multiplant mania may subside as companies recognize that a purchase order by any other name is still a purchase order.

MRP II Systems: Integrated versus Interfaced Solutions

Earlier chapters of this book contain several examples of business problems caused by poorly integrated homegrown manufacturing planning and control systems. Chapter 2 explains how poor integration between the Planning and Execution modules causes material shortage problems. Chapters 3 and 5 describe how poor integration between the Order Processing and Master Production Schedule modules causes inventory and customer service problems. Chapter 6 discusses how poor integration causes productivity problems in the Order Entry, Purchasing, Accounts Payable, and MIS organizations.

The solutions presented may lead you to assume that all MRP II packages provide integrated software solutions. Unfortunately, this is not the case. Some MRP II packages on the market today are no better integrated than the homegrown systems they seek to replace, as illustrated in the following case histories.

Case 1

A manufacturer of rider lawn mowers and garden tractors purchased and implemented a well-known mainframe MRP II system. The company was successful in applying the features described in this book to increase their customer service level from 93 to 99 percent, and their inventory turns from 11.5 to 14 turns per year.

In spite of these improvements, the company was not satisfied with the MRP II package they had selected. While they were pleased with the way the individual modules of the package performed, they had numerous complaints about the way the modules were "integrated." These integration problems are described below.

The integration between the Material Requirements Planning module and the Purchasing module was cumbersome and inflexible. When the integration between these modules was "turned on," purchase orders could not be entered directly into the Purchasing module. A purchase order could not be placed until a requisition was released from the MRP module to the Purchasing module. This approach worked well in companies that had material planners and buyers, but in this company, the buyer performed both the planning and purchasing functions. This inflexible approach to integration required that the buyers perform on-line transactions to release requisitions from the MRP module to the Purchasing module before they could place purchase orders. These extra transactions caused a 30 percent increase in the buyers' workload.

The receiving transactions in the Purchasing module were not integrated with the Inventory Control module. Because of this, the receiving clerk had to perform two transactions for every receipt, one to receive against the purchase order and one to receive material into inventory.

Each module had a different look and feel in the on-line screens. This caused considerable confusion and consternation among the users. In one incident, the company lost two days of data entry effort while loading data into the Purchasing module. The data entry clerk incorrectly assumed that the Purchasing screens operated in the same manner as the on-line transactions in other modules. Without realizing it, the clerk aborted every transaction before completing the update. At the end of two days, the company discovered that no data had been loaded into the database!

The integration between the Order Processing module and the Inventory Control module required several batch runs (and several days) to enter, pick, and ship a customer order. Because of this, the company was unable to provide same-day shipment on orders for spare parts.

The systems did not share a common database. There was far too much data redundancy, including several part master files, and it was difficult to keep the redundant files synchronized. For example, when a part master record was added to the Bill of Materials module, a batch run was required to create a part master record in the Order Processing module. If the batch run was not performed, the Bill of Materials part master file did not agree with the Order Processing part master file. In effect, the part could be manufactured but it could not be sold!

The software vendor was unable to provide adequate customer support for the integration problems. The company complained that they "got the runaround" whenever they called the customer support hotline with an integration problem. For example, when the company experienced problems in transferring requisitions from the MRP module to the Purchasing module, the MRP customer support specialist claimed that the problem resided in the Purchasing module and the Purchasing customer support specialist blamed the MRP module. No one took responsibility for customer support of the MRP/Purchasing integration issues!

Case 2

Another company purchased an MRP II system from a different MRP II software vendor. When they installed the package, they discovered that the system was, in fact, four separate systems that were developed and maintained by four different divisions of the software company. Each system had its own independent database, and they were linked together by means of several complex, batch-oriented interfaces.

The project team had based their software decision on the latest releases of each system. Unfortunately, the latest releases had not yet been "integrated" and wouldn't be for at least two years. The company had no choice but to take delivery of earlier releases—releases that were integrated but lacked many of the features that had influenced the project team's software decision. It had never occurred to the team that the software vendor would have separate, unintegrated releases of modules of an integrated system.

Both these companies thought that they had purchased an integrated MRP II software package, only to discover later that they had purchased a collection of modules linked together by interfaces. The purpose of this appendix is to help you prevent your company from making the same mistake.

Integration Defined

The word "integration" is one of the most overused, abused, and misunderstood buzzwords in the lexicon of applications software. All software vendors claim to have integrated software solutions, but few would dare to measure their claims against the following yardstick definition of integration.

An integrated software solution is one that has *all* the following characteristics:

The individual application modules share a common database, eliminating the need for redundant data files. For example, an Accounts Receivable module is not integrated with an Order Processing module if they each have their own customer files. Similarly, a Purchasing module is not integrated with an Accounts Payable module if they each have their own vendor files.

The individual modules have a common look and feel, that is, a common user interface. The modules are not integrated if the on-line screens, batch reports, and documentation for each module don't have the same format.

The system is borderless; namely, it is not necessary to perform an intermediate step (such as returning to a main menu screen) to go from one module to another.

It is not surprising that the word "integration" is so misunderstood. The most popular buzzword of all in manufacturing today—"computer integrated manufacturing"—is a misnomer. In most cases, the term computer *interfaced* manufacturing more accurately describes projects that link islands of automation to create an enterprise-wide computing environment. Each island of automation is an application with its own independent database and unique user interface.

A Time and Place for Interfaces

To some extent, interfaces are necessary and unavoidable. No software vendor offers a complete computer *integrated* manufacturing solution that includes MRP II, computer aided design, computer aided process planning, quality management, and all the other manufacturing applications. If one software vendor ever did develop a comprehensive, integrated solution, probably no one would purchase the entire package—someone would always find a reason to buy one or more applications from another company. For instance, the Manager of Engineering might have a bias for a particular CAD package, or the Manager of Industrial Engineering might have a bias for a particular computer aided process planning (CAPP) system.

In some cases, an interfaced solution is even *desirable*. When linking packages purchased from different software vendors, the interface approach is often the low-cost, low-risk solution, as illustrated in the following example.

Consider a company that purchases a computer aided process planning system from one vendor and an MRP II package from another vendor. Both packages have a routing file. However, the routing file in the CAPP system is viewed as being the master routing file, because it is the one used by Industrial Engineering to create new routings.

An integrated solution would eliminate the MRP II routing file and would have the other modules of the MRP II system access the CAPP routing file directly. However, this would require significant modifications to the MRP II package and very little would be gained in return. In fact, a lot would be lost, because it would be virtually impossible to install the next release of the MRP II system. Modifications to the CAPP system might also be required if the CAPP routing file does not have all the data elements that the MRP II system requires. An interface between the two systems (to pass routing information from the CAPP routing file to the MRP II routing file) would eliminate the need to modify the source code of either system.

Within the boundaries of an MRP II system, however, interfaces are inexcusable. MRP II systems are marketed and sold as a single product. Representing a loose collection of modules as an integrated system is, at best, misleading. MRP II, by definition, is an integrated approach to manufacturing planning and control. As noted throughout this book, interfaced manufacturing planning and control systems don't *solve* problems—they *cause* problems.

The Trouble with Interfaced MRP II Systems

Interfaced MRP II systems typically have the following problems:

Interfaced MRP II systems are not as reliable (bug-free) as integrated solutions. An interfaced MRP II package is far more complex than an integrated system. An interface between two modules is actually a third software module (Figure C.1). The user may not be aware of its presence, but the Interface module has to be maintained just as any other application software module does. This means that with each new release of the product, the customer must cope with software bugs in three modules, instead of two modules, for each interface that exists.

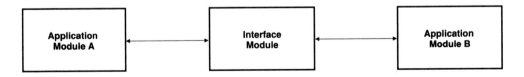

Figure C.1
Interface Module between Two Application Modules

Software packaging problems are also common in interfaced MRP II systems. These are problems in which one module fails to recognize the output from another module because each module is using a different name to refer to the data that is being passed through an interface. Software packaging problems usually cause the system to abort during batch processing.

Interfaced MRP II systems lack realtime functionality. The existence of several independent databases makes it difficult to perform realtime updating of information. Often, several batch runs are required to perform a business function that should be completed within one day.

Interfaced MRP II systems often compromise the functionality of the individual modules. One company purchased a particular MRP II package because the Purchasing module had a specific feature that was very important to its method of operation. The company later discovered that this feature was disabled when the MRP module was integrated (interfaced) with the Purchasing module, because the MRP module was unable to support this feature. Viewed from the software vendor's perspective, the customer asked the wrong question during the software evaluation phase. Instead of only asking, "Does your Purchasing module have this feature?," the project team should have asked, "Does your Purchasing module have this feature, and does the feature work when the MRP and Purchasing modules are used together?"[1] The project team can hardly be blamed for asking the wrong question, because it would never occur to most people that the sum of the parts (modules) was less than the whole (integrated solution).

Interfaced MRP II systems frequently suffer from data-integrity problems. Case 1 at the beginning of this appendix pointed out this problem. Experience has proven that whenever human intervention (to execute batch programs) is required to keep databases synchronized, errors will occur, and the databases will diverge over a period of time.

Size differences in data fields can also contribute to data-integrity problems. For example, in one MRP II system, the Order Processing module has a 20-digit part number field and the other modules have 15-digit part number fields. Any part number in the Order Processing module that is longer than 15 digits cannot be recognized by the other modules.

---

1. See Appendix A for a discussion of how some software vendors use passive misrepresentation (lies of omission) to sell their products.

Interfaced MRP II systems are more difficult to use than are integrated systems. One major problem in interfaced MRP II systems is the lack of a consistent user interface. The on-line transactions may be difficult to use because the screen layouts, navigational techniques (the way in which users move from screen to screen), and data entry techniques may be different in each module. For example, one MRP II software package uses function keys to navigate among the screens in one module, but it requires the user to input transaction codes in other modules. In some modules the transaction codes are numeric; in other modules they are alphabetic.

Also, the interfaces are often very difficult to use and understand, and they are not well documented. Because the software vendor does not like to advertise the fact that there is an Interface module sitting between the two application modules, any user documentation about the interface is scant or nonexistent. In fact, the documentation for the individual modules may instruct the user about features *that cannot be used when the modules are integrated.*

Identifying Interfaced MRP II Systems

There are several ways to determine whether an MRP II system is integrated or is a collection of independent modules linked together by interfaces.

Technical Evaluation

An MIS professional can easily determine if a system is integrated by reviewing the system's Bachman diagram. The **Bachman diagram** is a blueprint of the database that shows the relationship between sets and records. Most software vendors will allow their prospective customers to review this diagram during the sales cycle. However, you will have to ask for the diagram, as it is not part of the normal sales and marketing literature distributed by the vendor. Redundant files and independent databases will be readily apparent on the diagram. Not incidentally, if the vendor produces three or four separate diagrams, you don't even have to look at the diagrams to know that the system is built on interfaces.

User Evaluation

Most users lack the expertise to analyze a Bachman diagram. So here are some questions you can ask and tests you can apply to determine if an MRP II system is integrated or interfaced.

Ask the vendor if any of the modules were acquired from other software vendors. If the vendor developed some modules and acquired others, the system probably contains some interfaces.

Ask the vendor for the release numbers of the software products you are evaluating. If each product has a different release number, the modules are not truly integrated. In a truly integrated system, the vendor never has separate releases of individual modules. Instead, the vendor provides new releases of the entire system.

A note of caution: Some software vendors are beginning to use common numbering systems for interfaced solutions, giving the *appearance* of true integration.

Ask the vendor what programming language, screen generation technology, and reporting system was used for each module. If the vendor replies, "COBOL," ask what version of COBOL. If the modules were written in different languages or different versions of the same language, or if different tools were used to produce screens and reports, the modules were probably developed at different times or by different divisions of the software company. The net result is that the system probably contains interfaces.

Notice how the vendor refers to the individual modules. If the vendor refers to some modules as modules and other modules as systems, it is an indication that the package is comprised of several independent systems linked together by interfaces.

Observe how many people the vendor uses to present and demonstrate the solutions. It is extremely difficult for one consultant to master the idiosyncrasies of many independent products. If the vendor brings in a different consultant to demonstrate each product, the modules are probably not truly integrated. In cases where the interface is extremely complex, the vendor may use three consultants to demonstrate two modules, one for each module and a third to demonstrate the "integration" of the modules.

Ask the vendor how many part master records exist. If each module has its own part master record, the system is not truly integrated. The vendor may try to defend the existence of several part master records, claiming that each record contains unique data needed for a specific module. This may be partially true, but the very existence of several part master records is usually a strong indication that the package is built on interfaces.

Observe the sizes of the fields in different modules. If key fields (such as part number, order number, and vendor number) are different sizes in different modules, the modules were developed independently and are linked together by interfaces.

Observe the screen layouts, navigational techniques, batch reports, and system documentation. Some key questions to ask are as follows:

- Do some modules use numbers to identify screens while other modules use alphabetic characters?

- Are the key fields located in the same area of the screen in every module?

- Do some modules allow the user to press a function key to change screens while other modules require the user to enter a transaction code?

- Do some modules combine inquiry, add, modify, and delete capability into one screen while other modules have separate screens for each function?

- Does the same field have different names in different modules? For example, is the part number field called "part number" in one module, "item number" in another module, and "catalog number" in a third module?

- Do all the batch reports have the same format?

- Does the documentation for each module look the same?

Another note of caution: Some vendors are beginning to modify their screens, reports, and documentation so that the modules have a common look and feel, giving the *appearance* of integration. Remember, there are three criteria for integration: (1) a common data base, (2) a common look and feel, and (3) a borderless system. It is much easier to provide a common look and feel than it is to design an integrated database or borderless system.

Observe whether the system is borderless. Can the user go directly from screen A in module X to screen B in module Y? If the user has to proceed to a menu as an intermediate step, the modules are probably separate systems.

Ask the vendor how long the package has been on the market. Older packages are less likely to be integrated than the newer MRP II systems.

Ask the vendor if it complies with the definition of integration presented in this appendix. Ask the vendor to demonstrate how it complies with this definition.

Observe how much realtime functionality the system has. Interfaced solutions often require batch runs to process data between modules.

Conduct a hands-on benchmark test of the system. Don't base your decision on a demonstration conducted by the software vendor. Vendors are skilled at demonstrating their products in a manner to make them appear integrated. By performing your own benchmark test, you will expose any situations that require the user to enter redundant data, as well as any batch runs necessitated by interfaces.

The key indicators of interfaced MRP II systems are summarized below.

- The existence of more than one Bachman diagram
- The fact that the vendor acquired some modules and developed others
- Different release numbers for modules
- Modules that are written in different languages or different versions of the same language
- Multiple tools used to produce screens and reports
- The fact that the vendor refers to some modules as modules and other modules as systems
- The fact that the vendor uses several consultants to demonstrate the system
- Multiple part master records
- Key fields that are different sizes in different modules
- Different screen layouts and navigational techniques in different modules
- Documentation that does not look the same for all modules
- The same field having different names in different modules
- Batch reports that do not look the same for all modules
- The need to proceed to a menu as an intermediate step in going from one module to another
- The package is more than ten years old
- Lack of realtime functionality

The Indefensible Defense: Interfaces Are Necessary in MRP II Systems

Some vendors defend their approach to integration by claiming that interfaces are necessary to allow companies to do a phased implementation of MRP II. They claim that the interfaces are necessary to make it easy for a company to link the MRP II modules to the customer's old system for a phased implementation.

This is a marketing ploy. The most integrated MRP II package available solves this problem neatly with **skeleton transactions**. These are transactions that are used temporarily during a phased implementation of MRP II.

For example, the Purchasing module allows a user to enter hundreds of items of information about a purchase order. However, the MRP module only requires four items of information for each order: the part number, order number, quantity, and scheduled receipt date. This MRP II package provides a skeleton transaction that allows the user to enter (either on-line or in batch mode) these four items of information for every purchase order. This transaction can be used until the Purchasing module is implemented. A similar transaction is provided to enter skeleton information about customer orders into the system until the Order Processing module is implemented. Thus, true integration is achieved without impacting the ability to do a phased implementation.

Why Do Interfaced MRP II Packages Exist?

Software vendors rarely set out to develop interfaced solutions on purpose. To understand why some packages contain interfaces, it is necessary to understand how the MRP II software industry and software packages evolved.

Industry Evolution: Interfaces Caused by Acquisitions

One MRP II software vendor started out as a financial software vendor. It developed its financial applications in-house, and the financial modules constituted a well-integrated system.

In the early 1980s, the vendor decided to expand its product line. It acquired a software company that sold an order processing system and another software company that had a manufacturing system (minus the financial and order processing modules).

The software company was then faced with an important strategic decision. They had three separate systems. Should they start over and design one integrated system, or should they link the three existing systems together with interfaces, providing the appearance of integration where it was easy to do so? They chose the latter approach, because they believed that it would be easier and faster to develop interfaces than to design and build an integrated system. (Also, the management of the company did not understand the difference between integration and interfaces.) Even if the company had wanted to develop an integrated system, it would have been difficult to do so, because the development organizations for the three systems were in three different locations. (It's difficult to build integrated systems without an integrated development organization.)

As it turned out, the interfaces took far longer to develop than the company had originally estimated, and the resulting system had many of the problems discussed earlier in this appendix. Even after the interfaces were developed, they were never synchronized with the latest releases of the individual modules. If a customer wanted an "integrated" solution, it had to take delivery of an older, less functional release of one or more modules. The interfaces were so complex that few of the vendor's consultants in the field were capable of demonstrating the "integrated" product set.

Package Evolution: Interfaces Caused by Product Enhancements

Interfaces are sometimes the result of product enhancements. One MRP II software vendor had an Inventory Control module that lacked many important features, among them being the ability to produce picklists, to perform lot tracing, and to assign shelf life expiration dates to inventory lots. The vendor could not add these features to the existing Inventory Control module without performing a major rewrite of the software. Instead, the software vendor decided to develop a new Inventory Control module and interface it to the old one. This meant that customers had to buy two Inventory Control modules to obtain a fully functional system.

The software vendor's marketing organization skillfully made it appear as if this had been the master plan all along. They developed marketing materials that positioned the old Inventory Control module as one that tracked material in a staging area while it was being received into the stockroom or issued out of the stockroom. The new Inventory Control module was marketed as one that provided a more

Original System Configuration

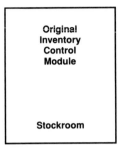

Original
Inventory
Control
Module

Stockroom

Repackaged System Configuration

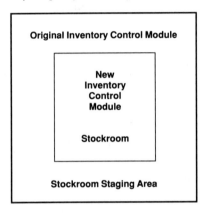

Original Inventory Control Module

New
Inventory
Control
Module

Stockroom

Stockroom Staging Area

The border between the stockroom and the stockroom staging area represents the interface between the old Inventory Control module and the new Inventory Control module.

Figure C.2
Interface between Two Inventory Control Modules

detailed level of material control in the stockroom. Figure C.2 illustrates this clever repackaging of an interfaced solution.

When it became apparent that neither of the two inventory modules had certain features that were required to manage finished-goods inventory, the company decided to develop a third Inventory Control module and interface it to the first two modules.

Interestingly enough, the company that has one of the most integrated MRP II packages didn't even start out as an applications software vendor. This company was originally a database management system vendor. When they moved into the applications business, they already understood the importance of a common, integrated

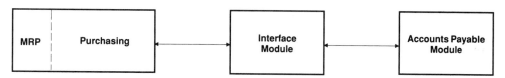

Figure C.3
*MRP II System with the Interface Module between the Purchasing and
Accounts Payable Modules*

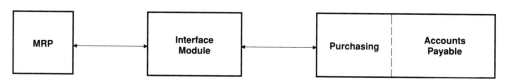

Figure C.4
*MRP II System with the Interface Module between the MRP and
Purchasing Modules*

database, and they took the time to develop an integrated database
design before they developed any applications.

The Marketplace Today

In today's marketplace, you should expect to find anything and
everything. One software vendor may provide true integration between the MRP and Purchasing modules, but then have an interface
between Purchasing and Accounts Payable (Figure C.3). Another
vendor may have true integration between Purchasing and Accounts
Payable, but then have an interface between MRP and Purchasing
(Figure C.4). It all depends on how the software package evolved.

When a software vendor uses the word "integration," my advice
is to let it go in one ear and out the other. Many vendors meet only
one or two of the criteria for true integration. You will be wise to
apply the real tests of integration to make sure you are buying a
package that will solve, not create, business problems.

The Ergonomics of MRP II Software Packages

Most companies use the following criteria to evaluate and select an MRP II software package:

- Software functionality
- Financial stability of the software vendor
- Quality of vendor implementation support
- Quality of technical and user documentation
- Technology used to develop the system

These are important criteria, but a company can select a package that scores high in every one of these categories and still make the wrong choice. This happens because companies often overlook one of the most important software evaluation criteria: **ergonomics**, or human engineering.

An on-line MRP II software package *must* be easier to use than the system it is intended to replace or the users will not accept it. The fact is, if it is significantly easier to use, a system that meets only 80 percent of a company's functional requirements may be a better choice than a system that meets 95 percent of these requirements.

Consider the following example of a company that failed to consider ergonomics when selecting a software package.

A manufacturer of consumer electronics products purchased an MRP II system to replace a homegrown, batch manufacturing planning and control system. The company selected a well-known mainframe MRP II system using the evaluation criteria listed above. The first module to be implemented was the Bill of Materials module. At first, the engineers were enthusiastic about the idea of replacing their batch system with an on-line Bill of Materials module. Support quickly turned to resistance when it became apparent that the new on-line system was far more difficult to use than the old batch system. With the new system, an engineer had to perform a total of seven on-line transactions to create a bill of materials. This process took about 15 minutes to complete. With the old system, the engineer could create a bill of materials by completing a single batch data entry form. The engineer could complete the data entry form in less than half the time required to create a bill of materials using the new system.

The company encountered a similar situation when it attempted to implement the Purchasing module. A buyer had to perform a minimum of five on-line transactions to enter a purchase order. With the old system, the buyer could place a purchase order by completing one batch data entry form. The Accounts Payable and Inventory Control modules suffered similar problems.

To overcome these problems, the company spent a great deal of time and money to develop new on-line transactions that made the new system as easy to use as the old one. This time and expense might have been avoided if the company had included ergonomics as one of their evaluation criteria.

Ergonomics Evaluation Criteria

A company should include an industrial engineer on the MRP II software evaluation team to lead the ergonomics evaluation. Some important things to consider in such an evaluation are discussed in the following subsections.

Consistent User Interface

Each module should employ the same screen formats and navigational techniques (techniques used to move from one screen to another). If the MRP II software vendor is not designing to a strict set of standards, each module may end up having a different look and feel. Users will become frustrated if they must learn a different user interface for each module.

Design for Normal Working Conditions

To appeal to a broad customer base, MRP II software packages are designed to accommodate complex environments. The result is that packages are designed around a worst-case scenario, even though most users operate in a simpler environment most of the time. For example, a Purchasing module may provide three separate data entry screens for purchase order header, purchase order line item, and line item scheduling information. This design allows buyers to enter a lot of detailed information about a purchase order. While it is important to provide this kind of flexibility, a well-designed MRP II package should also provide shortcuts that allow users to work at peak efficiency. For example, the system should provide a single screen that allows the buyer to place a single-item purchase order with up to five ship schedules. In some companies, this screen may be used 90 percent of the time.

Sometimes there is a tradeoff to consider between high technology and user productivity. Some MRP II packages were developed using fourth-generation programming languages. These languages improve programmer productivity, but they may impact user productivity adversely. Some fourth-generation languages require a great deal of system overhead, which limits the amount of processing that can be done in a single transaction. This leads to a proliferation of on-line transactions. Programmer productivity is important, but user productivity is more important because users have to work with the resulting product for years.

All-Function Screens

Some MRP II packages provide four separate on-line transactions to add, modify, delete, and inquire against a record. This forces the user to remember four different transaction codes. A better approach is to provide a single screen that allows the user to perform all four functions at once. The user can select the desired function by entering an action code at the top of the screen. The user enters an action code of A to add a record, M to modify a record, D to delete a record, or I to perform an inquiry. The system checks the action code against the user's ID to verify that the user has the authority to perform the transaction. Thus, all users have access to a transaction, whereas only certain users are allowed to add, modify, or delete a record.

Chained Screens

Some transactions are always performed in sequence. For example, a buyer may have to perform certain transactions in sequence to enter a purchase order, or an order entry clerk may have to execute a series of transactions to enter a customer order. Transactions that are always performed in sequence should be chained together so that the system automatically displays the next transaction in sequence. Thus, after the buyer enters the purchase order header data, the Add Purchase Order Line Item screen should be displayed automatically. This eliminates the need for the buyer to enter the transaction code manually for the next transaction.

The screen-chaining feature is often overlooked by MRP II software vendors. One MRP II system has four transactions that are always performed in sequence by the material planner. These transactions allow the planner to review and release MRP-planned orders. Amazingly, these transactions are *not* chained together. The user must enter a transaction code to go from one screen to the next.

Automatic Carry Forward of Key Fields

Often it is necessary to perform several transactions pertaining to the same part number or order number. For example, a user may create a part master record and then create a bill of materials for the new part. The system should automatically carry the key information (part number or order number) forward from one screen to the next so that the user does not have to reenter this data.

Field Grouping and Highlighting

On-line transactions have four types of data fields:

1. Key fields, which are used to retrieve data

2. Display fields, which cannot be changed

3. Data fields, which can be modified

4. Required or "must-enter" data entry fields

For example, the make/buy code on the part master record is a must-enter field, because important system processing logic keys off this code.

In a well-designed system, all modifiable data fields should be highlighted so that the user can see where the fields begin and end. This can be done by filling the fields with question marks (?????) or by using a reverse video "mask." Must-enter fields should be highlighted differently from optional data entry fields. Different levels of reverse video shading intensity can be used to highlight must-enter fields. Optional data entry fields can be highlighted in white inverse video, and must-enter fields can be gray-shaded.

Must-enter fields should be grouped together near the top of the screen so that the user doesn't have to tab through the optional data entry fields to reach the must-enter fields.

Key fields should be located prominently at the top of the screen and should be set apart from all other fields. Some MRP II packages place a horizontal line on the screen to separate the key fields from all other data fields.

On-Line Help Facilities

The system should include on-line help text for all transactions. Most MRP II systems require the user to press a "help" key to display a Help screen. The problem with this approach is that the user must memorize the instructions before returning to the transaction. A better approach is to display help text in a pop-up window, so that the user can view the help text while entering data.

Error Messages

Error messages should be meaningful and nonthreatening. One MRP II system displays the following message whenever an unusual error condition is detected:

FATAL SYSTEM ERROR—CALL BUSINESS SYSTEMS

Upon receiving such a message, few users would be inspired to "call business systems." Who wants to admit responsibility for causing a "fatal system error"?

Expert and Novice Modes

The system should operate in both expert and novice modes. In the expert mode, the system should allow the user to process the current transaction and go to the next transaction in the same step. In the novice mode, the system should respond with a confirmation message after each transaction. Users should be able to set their own mode of operation.

Performing an Ergonomics Evaluation

The only way to perform an ergonomics evaluation is to perform a benchmark test of the MRP II package. A **benchmark** is a hands-on test that simulates the way the system will operate in your environment.

As a rule, MRP II vendors dislike the idea of benchmark tests because they expose the weaknesses of a system. MRP II vendors prefer to use their own consultants to demonstrate their software. If the system is difficult to use, a trained consultant can make it appear less so because the consultant has spent many hours working with the system. Certainly a consultant should be present to assist you and answer your questions during the benchmark test, but the consultant should not be sitting at the keyboard.

The best way to perform an ergonomics evaluation is to enter real data from your company into the system. This will quickly give you an idea of how easy (or difficult) it is to use the system. For example, you may find that you need to perform several transactions to enter all the data from one data entry form. Entering your own data has two important benefits that are indirectly related to the ergonomics evaluation:

1. It will point out any data fields that you need which are not in the package.

2. It will point out any field-length problems. If your company uses a ten-digit vendor number and the MRP II package only provides an eight-digit field, this problem will become obvious during the ergonomics evaluation.

It is recommended that you bring actual users from each department to perform the data entry tasks, under the supervision of an industrial engineer. An engineer should test the Bill of Materials module; a buyer should test the Purchasing module; an order entry clerk should test the Order Entry module; etc. User involvement in the benchmark is the surest way to gain user support during implementation.

The ergonomics evaluation should not be limited to the on-line transactions. The users should evaluate the documentation and batch reports to determine if they are easy to understand and use. Poorly designed reports may require users to look in several places to access all the information needed to solve business problems.

The Current State of Affairs

You would expect that MRP II software vendors pay a great deal of attention to ergonomics in their system designs. Sadly this is not the case, because software vendors generally don't employ industrial engineers to help them design their systems. Most MRP II software vendors pay more attention to features and functions than they do to human engineering. Features are important, but an MRP II project will only succeed if the system makes life easier for the users. A thorough ergonomics evaluation is critical to making the right choice for your company.

MRP II: The Next Generation

Most of the MRP II packages available today were developed during the 1970s and early 1980s. These packages are rapidly approaching the end of their product life cycles. During the next few years, these products will be replaced by a new generation of MRP II software packages. Some software companies have promised delivery of the first modules of these new products during 1990. These new packages will address a number of technical and functional deficiencies found in the current generation of MRP II software systems.

Technical Issues

User Interface

A common complaint about the current MRP II software systems is that users have to spend too much time entering data into the system. This is because today's MRP packages rely on the Tab and arrow keys as the mechanisms for moving the cursor to the desired data entry fields. Studies show that more than 50 percent of the keystrokes performed by users are nonproductive, that is, keystrokes that move the cursor around the screen.

The next generation of MRP II software packages will solve this problem by providing a mouse-driven interface, allowing users to point directly to a field without using the keyboard. The point-and-click capability of the mouse will also eliminate the need to use the keyboard to select menu options.

Integration

Many "integrated" MRP II packages are, in reality, a collection of individual systems linked together by interfaces. The many problems associated with these interfaces are discussed in Appendix C. These problems should diminish as software vendors develop new packages with modules that share a common database.

Realtime Updating

Most of today's MRP II systems were originally developed as batch processing systems. Over the years, software vendors have replaced many of the batch transactions with transactions that perform realtime updates to the database. Unfortunately, the conversion process was never completed in most systems. In fact, some software vendors still seem to adhere to a philosophy of "Let's do a batch update unless it positively, absolutely has to be done in real time." This philosophy was valid years ago when computers were expensive and processing capabilities were limited. The next generation of MRP II software packages will be developed under the opposite philosophy.

Concurrent Batch and On-Line Processing

Most of the current MRP II packages were not designed to allow on-line processing to be performed concurrently with batch processing. This means that the systems are not available for on-line updates while large batch programs, such as the Material Requirements Planning explosion program, are being run. In businesses that operate three shifts, it is not practical to take the system down for several hours a day to perform batch processing. The next generation of MRP II software systems will be designed to allow concurrent on-line and batch processing.

Functional Issues

Process Industry Functionality

Most of today's MRP II software packages were developed for the discrete manufacturing industry. A few MRP II software vendors have tried to "bend" their packages to fit the process industry by adding features such as lot tracing and allocation of inventory by earliest expiration date. However, most attempts to fit discrete MRP II packages into process environments have been unsuccessful due to the fundamental differences between discrete and process manufacturing environments.

Discrete versus Process Manufacturing

Generally speaking, discrete manufacturers make products in discrete units from components that are purchased in discrete units. Both the components and the end-product have their own distinct shapes. In contrast, process manufacturers make products from ingredients that take the shape of their containers, that is, liquids, gases, and powders. The finished products may also take the shape of their containers, but this is not always true.

Discrete and process manufacturing environments differ in a number of ways, including:

- The way in which value is added during the manufacturing process

- The flexibility to add manufacturing capacity

- The quality and consistency of materials used in the manufacturing process

These differences are covered in more detail below.

The way in which value is added during the manufacturing process

Discrete manufacturers add value by machining, fabricating, and assembling parts. All material is usually input at the beginning of the manufacturing process. This process produces one output unit (i.e., a completed subassembly or finished product). This type of manufacturing process can be modeled using the bill of materials and routing files in a discrete MRP II software package.

Process manufacturers add value by using energy, equipment, and other resources to blend or separate ingredients and cause chemical reactions. The manufacturing process consists of multiple steps or stages. Each stage may require ingredients and resources to be input, and each stage may yield multiple outputs such as coproducts, by-products, waste, energy, and recyclable materials (Figure E.1).

Coproducts are two or more products of approximately equal value that are produced together. Usually one of the coproducts is identified as the target product of the manufacturing process. The choice is often arbitrary. **By-products** are products that are incidental to the manufacturing process that have some residual value. Chicken legs and breasts are coproducts in a plant that processes chickens; feathers are a by-product.

Complex, multistage processes that produce coproducts, by-products, and other outputs cannot be modeled using the bill of materials and routing files in a discrete MRP II software package. An entirely different data structure is required to model such pro-

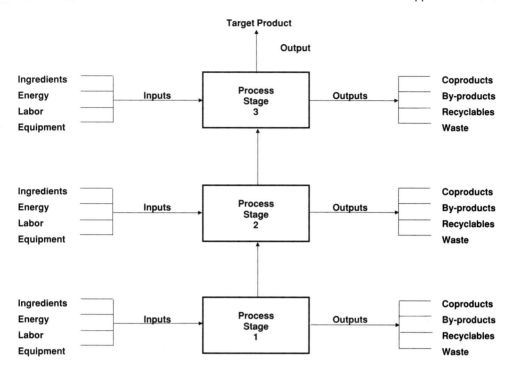

Figure E.1
Process Model of Multistage Manufacturing

cesses. This data structure must integrate the bill of materials (known as a **formula** or **recipe** in process industries) with a multistage process. The data structure must be capable of representing the inputs and outputs associated with each stage of the process.

The flexibility to add manufacturing capacity   Discrete manufacturers usually have a number of options for adding capacity. A discrete manufacturer can often increase capacity by hiring additional workers, buying or leasing more machines, or subcontracting work to external suppliers. Because of this flexibility, the infinite capacity planning capability provided in discrete MRP II software packages may be adequate for discrete manufacturers.

In contrast, process manufacturers generally must work within the constraints of fixed capacity. Short of building an additional plant, there is often little that a process manufacturer can do to increase capacity. In a very real sense, discrete manufacturers sell products, whereas process manufacturers sell capacity. Therefore, process manufacturers require finite planning and scheduling features to optimize the use of fixed capacity. For example, a process MRP II software package should be capable of calculating the optimum scheduling sequence for a group of products produced on the same line.

The quality and consistency of materials used in the manufacturing process Discrete manufacturers use raw materials and components purchased to very exact and consistent specifications. Because of this, the Inventory Control module in a discrete MRP II package needs only to store information about the number of physical units of material in inventory.

Process manufacturers often use natural resources for raw materials. Therefore, they have less control over the consistency of ingredients and may have to accept materials that cover a broad range of specifications. This is especially true in the food and beverage industry. Because of this, the Inventory Control module in a process MRP II package must store information about both physical units and potent units, as illustrated below:

	Potency (%)	Physical Units (kg)	Potent Units (kg)
Lot A	20	1000	200
Lot B	25	1000	250

In the above example, lots A and B contain the same number of physical units, but lot B has 50 more kilograms of potent units. (The number of potent units is the product of the lot potency and the number of physical units.) If a formula calls for 100 potent units of material, the stockkeeper can dispense 500 physical units of lot A or 400 physical units of lot B. The inventory allocation logic must take into account the potency of each lot and instruct the stockkeeper regarding how many physical units to issue.

Process Industry Solutions

The next generation of MRP II software modules will include a number of packages that are designed specifically for the process industry. The key features that will be provided in process MRP II packages are listed below.

Formula- and Process-Related Features

1. The ability to specify a multistage manufacturing process, and to link multiple inputs and outputs to each stage of the process

2. The ability to define ingredient quantities either as percentages of a formula or as quantities required to produce a standard batch quantity

3. The ability to define different formulas and process versions to produce the same product

4. The ability to define compatibility codes that determine what products can be stored in the same containers or manufactured on the same lines without cleaning the storage tanks or process vessels

5. The ability to define multiple unit of measure conversion factors for each item

Inventory-Related Features

1. The ability to perform lot tracing

2. The ability to store lot potency information in the inventory detail record

3. The ability to allocate quantities of material based on the potency of the lot from which the material is issued

4. The ability to allocate material that has the earliest shelf life expiration date

5. The ability to associate quality assurance test results with each stored lot

6. The ability to specify a maturity date to prevent a lot from being used before a particular date

7. The ability to define inventory storage requirements (temperature, relative humidity, etc.) for each item

8. The ability to define capacities for each material storage location

9. The ability to define fill height tables associated with a storage tank to facilitate cycle counting

10. The ability to assign a grade code to each inventory lot

Product-Costing-Related Features

1. The ability to take into account the value of by-products, coproducts, and recyclable materials produced by the manufacturing process

2. The ability to take into account the cost of disposing the waste produced by the manufacturing process

Scheduling- and Capacity-Planning-Related Features

1. The ability to calculate the optimum scheduling sequence (the sequence that minimizes changeover costs) for a group of products produced on the same line

2. The ability to specify coshipments (products that should always be scheduled and shipped together)

3. The ability to do finite scheduling around bottleneck resources

4. The ability to take vessel constraints into consideration to determine the number batches required

Sales-Order-Processing-Related Features

1. The ability to check both available-to-promise inventory and capacity for order promising

2. The ability to ship an alternative, acceptable grade of inventory

Production-Reporting- and Monitoring-Related Features

1. The ability to "forward flush" receipts into inventory, that is, automatically receive coproducts and by-products into inventory based on the completion of each process stage

2. The ability to track all outputs at each stage of the process

3. The ability to analyze process yields (i.e., compare actual yields to planned yields at each stage of the process)

Repair and Remanufacturing Industry Functionality

Many businesses repair or remanufacture parts to "like new" condition. MRP II is a good solution for the repair/remanufacturing industry because the components that are used to repair or remanufacture products have a time-phased demand. However, there are important differences between the manufacturing and the repair/remanufacturing environments, and some features must be added to an MRP II system before it can be implemented in a repair/remanufacturing environment.

Manufacturing versus Repair/Remanufacturing

The Need for Usage Factors When a product is manufactured, the bill of materials is exploded to create time-phased material requirements. Every component on the bill of materials is used. However, when an item is repaired or remanufactured, only those components that are worn out or missing are required. If the MRP II system explodes the entire bill of materials, components that are not needed will be ordered.

The solution is to provide the ability to establish a usage factor for each component on the bill of materials. For example, if past history indicates that a component is replaced 20 percent of the time when a certain type of repair is performed, a usage factor of 0.2 would be established on the bill of materials. If 100 repairs are forecasted on the Master Production Schedule and if the quantity per assembly is three, the result will be a gross requirement of 60 $(100 \times 3 \times 0.2)$ when the bill of materials is exploded.

Usage factors must be updated periodically based on the actual frequency of component usage. The system should capture this information from actual repair/remanufacturing orders and periodically suggest changes to the usage factor.

The Need for Occurrence Factors   When a product is manufactured, the routing is used to determine time-phased capacity requirements. Every operation on the routing is used to calculate capacity requirements. However, when an item is repaired or remanufactured, only certain operations are performed, depending on the necessary repairs. If the MRP II system uses the entire routing for capacity planning, capacity requirements will be overstated. This may cause a company to acquire additional capacity when it isn't needed.

The solution is to provide the ability to establish an occurrence factor for each operation on the routing. The occurrence factor functions in a manner similar to the usage factor on the bill of materials. Thus, if an operation is performed 25 percent of the time, an occurrence factor of 0.25 is established on the routing. If 100 repairs are forecast and it takes 0.30 hour to perform the operation, then 7.5 hours of capacity are needed $(100 \times 0.25 \times 0.3)$.

Occurrence factors must be updated periodically based on the actual frequency an operation is performed. The system should capture this information from actual repair/remanufacturing orders and periodically suggest changes to the occurrence factor.

The Need to Support Different Types of Repairs   The first step in the repair/remanufacturing process is to inspect and evaluate the product being repaired. This involves disassembling the product to determine what parts and operations are required. Depending on the results of the evaluation, a specific type of repair/remanufacturing order will be placed.

MRP II systems must be modified to provide an easy way for the inspector to place a repair order that will cause the right components to be picked and issued and route the order through the required operations. Most MRP II systems allow the BOMs and operation details to be modified on a specific order, but these features are designed to be used on an exception basis *after* the manufacturing order has been generated. For repair/remanufacturing environments, the system should allow the inspector to indicate easily the required components and operations as part of the process of creating the repair order.

An alternative approach is to preestablish several bills of materials and routings that correspond to different types of repairs. For example, a major overhaul would require more components and operations than would routine maintenance. This approach will work provided that each type of repair is forecast independently, so that the appropriate BOM and routing are used to determine material and capacity requirements. If this approach is used, the MRP II package should include a front-end repair order menu that allows the user to select the type of repair required. The system should then create a repair order using the BOM and routing associated with the specific type of repair.

Repair/Remanufacturing Solutions   Most of the current MRP II packages do not have the features required to support repair/remanufacturing environments. The next generation of MRP II software will support repair/remanufacturing environments as well as traditional manufacturing environments.

Shop Floor Management Functionality

Current MRP II packages focus on the foundation and planning modules (Bill of Materials, Inventory Control, Master Production Scheduling, and Material Requirements Planning). The execution modules, and especially the Shop Floor Control module, are very weak in comparison to the foundation and planning modules. Because of this, several software companies have developed independent, comprehensive shop floor management systems. These systems are so comprehensive that a detailed discussion of their capabilities is beyond the scope of this appendix. However, Chapter 4 discusses some of the differences between an MRP II Shop Floor Control module and a comprehensive shop floor management system.

The only problem with these independent systems is that they *are* independent. Complex interfaces between the MRP II system and the shop floor management system must be developed for both systems to function properly. A software vendor that provides a more complete shop floor control solution that is an integrated module of an MRP II package will have a significant competitive advantage over MRP II vendors that must interface to an independent shop floor control system. This may inspire some MRP II software vendors to provide more shop floor control functionality in the next generation of MRP II software packages.

Summary

MRP II packages will continue to evolve in the 1990s to keep pace with technology advances and to provide solutions for different types of manufacturing environments. The next generation of MRP II software will be better integrated, will be easier to use, and will provide more balanced planning and execution solutions.

MRP II Bibliography

Fogarty, Donald W., and Hoffman, Thomas R. *Production and Inventory Management*. Cincinnati, OH: South-Western Publishing Company, 1983.

Gray, Christopher. *The Right Choice: A Complete Guide to Evaluating and Installing MRP II Software*. Essex Junction, VT: Oliver Wight Ltd. Publications, 1987.

Lubben, Richard T. *Just-In-Time Manufacturing*. New York, NY: McGraw-Hill Book Company, 1988.

Luber, Alan. "Does Homegrown Really Taste Better?" *Production and Inventory Management Review*, February 1988.

Tulkoff, Joseph (ed.). *CAPP: From Design to Production*. Dearborn, MI: Society of Manufacturing Engineers, 1988.

Vollman, Thomas E., Berry, William L., and Whybark, D. Clay. *Manufacturing Planning and Control Systems*. Homewood, IL: Dow Jones-Irwin, 1984. (This is the most complete and readable MRP II textbook available today.)

Wight, Oliver W. *Production and Inventory Management in the Computer Age*. Boston, MA: CBI Publishing Co., 1974.

Index